Church
Related
Higher
Education

Church Related Higher Education

Perceptions and Perspectives

Robert Rue Parsonage, Editor

Contributors:

Merrimon Cuninggim
James H. Smylie
Robert Rue Parsonage
Martin E. Marty

Judson Press® Valley Forge

CHURCH RELATED HIGHER EDUCATION

Copyright © 1978
Judson Press, Valley Forge, PA 19481

Second Printing, 1979

Library of Congress Cataloging in Publication Data

Main entry under title:

Church related higher education.

   Includes bibliographical references.
   1. Church colleges—United States.   2. Higher education and state—United States.
   I. Parsonage, Robert Rue.
LC427.C48   377   78-10823
ISBN 0-8170-0831-4

The name JUDSON PRESS is registered as a trademark in the U.S. Patent Office. Printed in the U.S.A. ✣

Contents

Editor's Preface

The production of this volume truly has been a cooperative and ecumenical venture.

In his Introduction to the book, Harry E. Smith, chairperson of the Study/Action Committee which has guided the project through its various stages, acknowledges the contributions which have been made by the many persons who conceived the study, shepherded its development and progress, conducted the campus visits, wrote, and responded to the major papers contained herein. There are others whose contributions deserve a word of recognition as well.

Bobby Alexander and Susan Roth provided valuable research assistance. Adelaide Hartpence, Iris Palmer, and Ellen Lovell gave careful attention to the preparation of the manuscript. Their good work is gratefully acknowledged.

Frank T. Hoadley, publisher, and Harold Twiss, managing editor of Judson Press, have been extraordinarily cooperative and helpful in bringing this publication project to completion. The interest they have shown in the study and the care they and their colleagues have taken in the editorial and production processes are very much appreciated.

We are grateful to the Association of American Colleges, which is demonstrating its continuing commitment to church-related colleges by distributing copies of this study to the presidents of all its member institutions, public as well as private.

Finally, a special word of appreciation is offered to William N. Lovell, a most valued colleague and friend. At every stage in the preparation of this volume, he has provided encouragement, perceptive counsel, and patient good humor. Simply put, this book would not have been completed without Bill Lovell's assistance.

Though the work of many hands, final responsibility for the content of this book rests with the authors and with the editor and does not represent the official position of the National Council of Churches or its agencies.

Robert Rue Parsonage

Introduction

In a time when agreement on the worth of education no longer exists, crucial issues and challenges face the institutions of higher education in the United States. The crisis is particularly pressing for the church-related colleges. These colleges share the general problems confronting all independent institutions in a time of retrenchment, but they also face some special problems and questions of their own—problems of purpose, self-doubt, support, even survival. Do the church-related colleges have a distinctive contribution to make to the churches? To the enrichment of higher education? To the quality of life in America? If so, how can these contributions best be made?

Questions such as these prompted the E. Fay Campbell Lecture Committee of the National Council of Churches early in 1975 to alter its usual practice of sponsoring an annual lecture on some phase of higher education and to bring together a group of persons to design a multiyear project on "Pluralism and Church-Related Higher Education." Working with the staff of the unit on Education in the Society of the National Council of Churches, that group designed a four-stage project to assist church-related colleges to clarify their self-understanding and to help denominations assess alternative models of church-relatedness. Funding for the project was secured from the E. Fay Campbell Lecture Committee, participating denominations, and the Ford Foundation; and a Study/Action Committee was established to direct the four-stage project.

During the first phase, the study stage, this committee spent many hours examining the central historical and theoretical issues, revising the project design, and seeking to determine the best way to secure data on the various ways church-relatedness is perceived and practiced. It soon learned to appreciate the different philosophies of higher education in the various denominational traditions, shaped in large part by the understanding of the mission of the church in relation to its membership and society at large. The committee reviewed the Danforth Commission's study, *Church-Sponsored Higher Education in the United States* by Manning M. Pattillo, Jr., and Donald M. MacKenzie (American Council on Education, 1966), and C. Robert Pace's study for the Carnegie Commission, *Education and Evangelism: A Profile of Protestant Colleges* (McGraw-Hill Book Company, 1972), and the progress reports of the denominational studies then in progress. The committee also commissioned the writing of three papers, one on the history of the churches' involvement in higher education by James H. Smylie, one surveying current denominational policies and studies by Robert Rue Parsonage, and one examining future church-culture relations and their impact on church-related higher education by Martin E. Marty.

The original focus on the importance of church-related colleges in maintaining a viable pluralism in American higher education through a variety of forms of sponsorship in the independent sector shifted in the course of the committee's study to interest in the pluralism which exists within the independent, church-related sector with its various perceptions of church-relatedness.

In its deliberations the committee addressed the following issues, many of which were identified by Charles R. Bruning in his review of the literature, *Relationships Between Church-Related Colleges and Their Constituencies* (Lutheran Church in America, 1975):

1. Both churches and church-related institutions of higher education are questioning the meaning of church-relatedness and the educational purposes and distinctiveness of church-related

colleges and universities. What makes the church-related college distinctive? What prevents it from being distinctive?

2. There is a need to identify viable models of church-related colleges which embody sound historical perspectives and clear self-understandings of purpose and which may contribute in the future to both Christian purpose and societal values. What is the purpose of the church-related college? How does the college relate to the mission of the church? How does the church relate to the purpose of the college?

3. Differences of opinion about the meaning of pluralism and diversity and their importance within American higher education make it difficult to assess the rightful contributions of church-related colleges and universities. What should be the priority goals of church-related institutions in light of the rapidly changing order of things?

4. In a time of widespread suspicion of all of higher education and when all private higher education is confronted by rising costs and diminishing resources, survival is at stake. What is there about the church college that is worth preserving? What are the alternatives for the church-related college in view of the pressures upon it?

In order not to duplicate the massive studies of church-related higher education under way in several denominations, the committee decided to mount a sample study rather than an inclusive one, drawing from as many denominations as possible for illustrative models. At this point, the committee was fortunate to be able to engage the services of Merrimon Cuninggim, former president of the Danforth Foundation and currently president of Salem College, a church-related institution in North Carolina, to serve as project consultant and to organize and interpret the data collected in the second stage of the project.

Drawing upon the suggestions of denominational executives in higher education and the project consultant, the committee then selected fourteen colleges representing thirteen different Christian traditions for visitation. Consciously excluding large universities and nondenominational Christian colleges, the committee chose institutions which represented a geographical diversity and different points on a spectrum of strong to weak identification with a religious tradition. The Society for Values in Higher Education, a national network of faculty and administrators, was asked to provide campus visitors in this second stage. Fourteen persons in teams of two spent two days at each of the participating institutions. Brought together before and after their campus visits, these faculty and administrators sought to assess the intentionality of each college's relationship to the church and the intentionality of the denomination in relation to the college as perceived by faculty, students, administrators, and, in some cases, trustees, alumni, and others. They looked closely at how the program, personnel, and climate of the college reflected these intentionalities as well as at the external determinants on the college's church-relatedness, asking the following questions:

—What distinctive marks are there, if any, that might pertain to a college that is related to a body of the Christian church? What authentic marks are there that pertain particularly to the religious heritage or present denominational relationship of the institution?
—What will be lost either to church or to education if a number of the institutions continue as liberal arts colleges (or whatever) but not as church-related institutions, if they no longer evidence with integrity some distinguishing marks of church relationship in their purposes and practices?
—What alternative styles, models, or options can be envisioned for the future that seem viable and represent integrity and quality with regard to both the educational mission and the purpose of the church?

Their written and verbal reports became a primary resource for the analysis undertaken by the project consultant, Merrimon Cuninggim, and were presented at the Wingspread Consultation on "Perceptions of Church-Relatedness in Higher Education" at Racine, Wisconsin, November 18-20, 1977.

This consultation, held in cooperation with the Johnson Foundation, brought together representatives of the fourteen participating colleges, denominational executives of higher education, the members of the Study/Action Committee, the project consultant, and other resource persons for the initial presentation of the papers contained in this volume. Lively discussion and an enthusiastic commitment to comparing perceptions and experiences characterized the weekend, the third stage of the project. Although this volume makes no attempt to report fully the discussions at Wingspread, each of the chapters was altered by that event as it provided an occasion for official representatives of denominations and colleges to talk candidly about expectations. Efforts to justify present practices or to argue uniqueness or even distinctiveness as sufficient reasons for survival—themes which so often dominate such gatherings—seemed refreshingly absent as participants assessed Merrimon Cuninggim's categories of church-relatedness, debated the essentials of church-relatedness he proposed, and questioned one another about different policies and procedures. At no point did the consultation revert to playing the "more church related than thou" game so endemic to church-college administrators and church bureaucrats.

This volume represents the fourth and final stage of this three-year project, an effort to begin the dissemination of some of the findings to the churches and the educational community. Much has been learned in this process by the committee, campus visitors, and institutional representatives, and it is hoped that this collection of papers will widen the circle of those who have benefited from this effort to clarify how various denominations and colleges perceive what it means to be college-related churches and church-related colleges.

Special thanks are due the members of the original project design group, including Frederick Blumer, Margaret Claydon, Edward Lindell, Charles McCoy, William Miller, Frank Wuest, and Harry E. Smith. The project is indebted to the following campus visitors who contributed so generously of their time and insights: George Allan, Louis Brakeman, Donald Costello, Thomas Davis, Ralph Dunlop, Patricia P. Kendall, Mary Metz, Anne A. Murphy, William Nelsen, Edgar C. Reckard, Glen Stassen, Haywood Strickland, Herndon Wagers, and Prince Wilson. Thanks are also due the presidents, deans, faculty, and students of the following fourteen colleges who cooperated so wholeheartedly in this process of self-reflection about their relation to the church: Austin, College of St. Thomas, Concordia Teachers College in Nebraska, Drury, Furman, Goshen, Kalamazoo, Manchester, Morris Brown, Seattle University, St. Augustine's, West Virginia Wesleyan, Wittenberg, and Whitworth. To the authors of the study papers, James H. Smylie, Martin E.

Marty, and Robert R. Parsonage, and especially to Merrimon Cuninggim, the project owes its thanks. Appreciation is also extended to those persons who responded to the papers at the Wingspread Consultation: Ben C. Fisher, Wesley A. Hotchkiss, William R. Johnson, Jr., Shirley M. Jones, William A. Kinnison, Mary C. Kraetzer, Edward B. Lindaman, Albert J. Meyer, John D. Moseley, John F. Murphy, Douglas Sloan, and William J. Sullivan. And most of all, to the members of the Study/Action Committee, who spent long hours trying to pose the right questions and provide a formulation of issues which would be helpful to others, the project owes the greatest thanks: Mary C. Kraetzer, Joseph T. McMillan, Jr., Dorothy M. Schneider, Douglas Sloan, and Harry E. Smith, plus William N. Lovell and Robert R. Parsonage of the NCC staff.

It is the hope of those who planned and directed this project that the discussion begun here will contribute to a clearer understanding in church-related colleges and college-related churches of what it means to be faithful to God in American higher education in the crucial years ahead.

Harry E. Smith
Chairperson
Study/Action Committee

SECTION I

Varieties of Church-Relatedness in Higher Education

Merrimon Cuninggim

CHAPTER 1

Myths of
Church-Relatedness

The aim of this exercise is to find some examples of church-relatedness that are credible not merely to church men and women of the concerned denominations but also to other church men and women and to secular educators. What is it that makes an institution really church related? What does the college have to be—and do—in order to qualify for the descriptive?

Once we have tried to put our finger on some of these essentials, we shall have to ask: Is that good? Does being genuinely church related make any difference? What difference does it make?

But those questions are well ahead of us. We must begin by being clear about the entity under review. The adjectival phrases are numerous, imprecise, and vaguely synonymous—"church-sponsored," "church-related," "church-supported," "church-connected," "church-affiliated," "denominational," and just plain "church." "Church-controlled" appears to be tighter than any of the others; "Christian" perhaps looser. Vague, tight, or loose, they are merely the modifiers. "College" or "university" is the noun.

Which is to say that we are not talking about a specific function of the church; we are talking, instead, about a specific kind of college. The former approach is quite sound for any who wish to make it—

and denominational leaders may indeed need to look occasionally at the question of whether their conception of the church allows or requires them to maintain colleges.

Our point of beginning, however, is different from that question. We start with the college; and as a preliminary to inquiring about the essentials of church-relatedness, we must first take note of those numerous nonessentials with which discussions of this subject are often cluttered. If we can cut through some of the mythology surrounding church-sponsored higher education, we may then be ready to look at the real thing.

Myths or misunderstandings about church-related colleges are of at least two main types: those that are supposed marks of the church-related college, held largely by partisan insiders, and those that are mistaken opinions about such institutions, held largely by critical outsiders. Is any other type of institution so thoroughly misunderstood by both its friends and its critics, its supporters, and its detractors? The list of such myths is long and depressing, so much so that we don't need to spend extra time exposing the gross non sequiturs of the tub-thumpers. One college boasted: "Anything distinctively concerned with the individual is Baptist; this College is deeply concerned with the individual, therefore it is strongly Baptist." Let that kind of comment fall of its own dead weight.

The first alleged mark of church-relatedness is ownership. To be sure, some colleges are owned by their parent churches or by some church agency or board, but the number today is probably very small. The normal pattern is that ownership is vested in the college's own governing body, and its being so does not necessarily decrease or affect in any way the institution's church-relatedness. Ownership is no touchstone.

Even historic ties or the founding agency are not universal benchmarks. After all, when the Mormons take over an old Presbyterian college or when the Methodists adopt a formerly independent one, we are reminded that the first sponsorship may not be the last. Yet as the various popular tests of churchiness go, this is more reliable than any other—that is, if the institution has stayed hitched at all. If it were founded by, say, Lutherans and is still admitting a church connection, then it's almost certainly Lutheran. This tells almost nothing about the college, however.

It is widely believed that a church college is marked by having members of that church on its board, but this, too, is an unreliable indicator. Sometimes all, or at least a majority, of the trustees are required to be of one denomination; sometimes no such requirement is present—in which case they may or may not be of one denomination, as custom or accident provides. Sometimes a church body—synod, conference, or whatnot—may confirm names of board members nominated by the college; but even here there is variation as to whether names submitted for a church agency's approval must all be adherents of that, or possibly any, faith. In short, habits in this regard are so varied, so unsystematic, so contradictory that any general conclusion is bound to be shaky.

Much the same has to be said about clergy on boards. It was once thought that their presence was a dead giveaway, and this probably is as true as ever; but their absence doesn't necessarily mean the separation of the college from the denomination. For church-related institutions as well as all others, ministers aren't as attractive candidates for board membership as was once the case. And certainly there is no general agreement as to how many, if any, should be on the board.

One further mark having to do with governing structure is sometimes thought determinative: the chief executive officer, at the least, is expected to be a practicing believer of that college's religious brand. Like these other supposed tests we've noted, this one is still observed in a number of institutions and a few denominations. Sometimes it is still observed in practice although no longer professed—for the college or denomination may want to put a more liberal face on its public mien than it manages to live up to. But on many a campus this criterion of supposed church-relatedness has ceased to be either professed or practiced; and the president's belonging to some other denomination may or may not be a detriment to that college's church tie. In other words, this, too, has come to be irrelevant.

Let us take note, now, of a few illusory tests having to do with a college's program. It is widely trumpeted that a church-related college is one that takes religion seriously; and as we shall develop later, this essay gives full support to the proposition that such colleges *ought* to. But it is an entirely different set of propositions that maintains that such colleges do support religion, that they are the only kind that do, and that their doing so is sufficiently strong and characteristic to justify the conclusion that taking religion seriously is a distinctive mark of the church-related institution.

Such propositions don't stand up, for the facts don't support them. Church-connected colleges don't always support religion, whatever the word may include, and those that do are joined by a fair number of independent institutions and by even a few tax-supported ones. It is good to know that a college takes religion seriously, but knowing as much is no guarantee that the institution is church related.

Take, for example, required courses in religion—or for that matter, take any kind of courses in religion; all types of colleges provide such courses these days, offered in the regular curriculum, paid for out of regular institutional funds. It is true that some church-related colleges (and a few others) require students to take work in religion, alone or in transdepartmental courses; and it is also true that many do not make such a requirement. Some church-related colleges have very strong departments of religion, and—you've guessed it—some do not. It would be extremely difficult to prove that the strongest religion departments around the country are in church affiliates. All in all, nothing about either the incidence or the quality of course work in religion could legitimately be used as a mark of church-relatedness.

The same holds true for chapel, voluntary or required, and for other services of worship, lecture series, religious activities. You can find church colleges (and some others) that make such provisions, and you can find others that don't.

Creedal conformity, or its less rigorous manifestation, member-ship, is a somewhat tricky item of identification, and every now and then some determinedly church-oriented institution will be caught short in not having thought through carefully the demands of this sort it places on its various personnel. Requirements can sometimes stay on the books long past the time anyone has thought to enforce them, and when somebody remembers and wants compliance, considerable embarrassment can ensue. Little wonder that, when institutions even within the same denomination differ as greatly in their practice as they do, no blanket qualification can be formulated.

Look at a few of the variables:

—Membership of faculty and staff: On the rolls, or sympathetic association? All faculty, or some proportion? All departments, or selected ones? All ranks, or just higher ranks? Promotions and tenure reserved for the related denomination? Is membership enough, or must attendance also be considered? How much?

—Creedal conformity for faculty and staff: Whose creed? How worded, applied, enforced? All personnel subject to the same creedal test, or just major administrative officers, or trustees, or department heads? A percent of the faculty? How much?

—Membership and/or creedal conformity for students: Does a nucleus of the student body need to be attracted to, or at least sympathetic with, the sponsoring denomination? Any ineligibilities or special dispensations for dissenters? Desirable proportion of believers? How much?

It is important to be clear. The point is not that membership and creedal tests are often ill defined and silly, or maybe even well defined and silly; nor am I prepared to argue with someone who thinks they aren't silly. The point is, rather, that, however defined, they do not serve as a persuasive touchstone for determining either the fact or the degree of a college's church-relatedness. Various church schools have their various restrictions, and in any one instance a college, and maybe even its parent denomination, can be identified by a particular pattern of conformity. But there is no such pattern that fits all church-affiliated institutions.

Not long ago Davidson College got some undeserved notoriety for a local dustup in respect to creedal conformity. The news stories, mistaken on several counts, gave the impression that denominational influence in the college was at stake. But Davidson was not more church related back when some folks thought that a Jew was ineligible for tenure. And it didn't become less church related when it freely changed its outmoded rules and clarified the situation. Davidson was proudly affiliated with the Presbyterian Church in the United States all along.

Related to this is the question of whether a church-connected college has a certain, unmistakable air, a sanctified odor about it that pretty well separates it from its independent and tax-supported fellows. This notion may come from a dyed-in-the-wool believer who wishes it were so or from a naive secularist who shares the same wish—in his or her case, because he or she could then dismiss the institution more readily. Two such "good ole church college" stereotypes have sometimes been said to exist: the college that strives to protect and fortify the inside faithful, and the college that acts as missionary to the outside and heathen world. A few may fit this rough picture. Moreover, such an oversimplification may describe fairly well some nondenominational, self-termed "Christian" institutions that try to out-pietize the denominational colleges. But the "good ole church college," like the "good ole boy" who supposedly goes to it, is more fictional than real; and however else the church-related college has to be described today, it is almost never a nineteenth-century throwback, a camp-meeting-ground stereotype.

As for various sociological factors that might be and sometimes are used to identify church-connected institutions, such colleges are not always small, or poor, or academically weak, or homogeneous. In fact, they are often enough just the opposite and still oftener somewhere in between, to make us wary of all such sweeping descriptions. We shall say a bit more about some of these when we come to the errors more likely to be perpetrated by outsiders.

Two of these factors deserve at least brief comment here. First is the proposition that a church-related college is one that receives substantial financial support from its denomination. At an earlier time, it might have been assumed that the college had benefited from sacrificial efforts, but this could now be claimed by only a very few, probably no more than (and not the same ones as) those which self-righteously refuse all support from outside contaminating sources, such as government. The safe thing to say about finances is that church-related colleges are as needy as all other types these days, perhaps more so; and that what they get from their churches swings all the way from generous to penurious and worse. Some colleges get immense amounts, and some others get the back of the hand from their denominations. Things are so diverse that it is not the amount of the church's subvention, or the proportion of the college's budget it represents, that determines whether or not the college is church related.

The other sociological item to be noted is the disposition to define church-relatedness in terms of the rules governing student social behavior. Now and again it is supposed that if a college is related to a denomination, it will produce conservative regulations on one or all of the sinful quartet—dancing, drinking, drugs, and sex. To be sure, many church-related colleges are indeed concerned about such mischief, but many others, by comparison, look like dens of laxity. Colleges follow closely or dimly the lead of their churches on such matters, and needless to say, their students are of all sorts and habits. There is no party line of moral attitude or behavior that serves to characterize the church-related college.

Before leaving this list of alleged marks, perhaps we should inquire whether, though none of these by itself is sufficient, all together these do add up to something close to a reliable description. This is, in fact, the way many of the items we have noted have been treated by commentators and students in the field ever since the Pattillo–Mackenzie volume.[1] For example, confessing his dependence on Pattillo–Mackenzie, Richard E. Anderson of Teachers College, Columbia, has developed what he calls a "religiosity index" using "eight variables":

> . . . percentage of full-time equivalent students of the same religion, percent of total church support, religious requirements for members of the governing board, required chapel attendance, compulsory religious courses, strict moral demands placed upon students (e g , no smoking or dancing or required missionary service) [sic!], statement of religious purpose in catalog, and specification of denominational ties in the catalog.[2]

Anderson explains: "Institutions which scored below three on the index were considered secular."[3] In other words, although a college doesn't have to have all eight in order to be "religious," it does have to have at least three, presumably any three, apples and oranges together.

But if as few as three, then how reliable are these factors? The fact is, they aren't reliable at all in measuring the degree of church affiliation; for it is possible, if highly unlikely, that some institution with a score of, say, two is more genuinely related to its church than some other with a score of eight or nine. The fault, of course, is the reliance upon particularities. We need to renounce the absurdity of defining church affiliation by the fiction, "It may consist in this, this, this, and this; and you can take your pick."

Another current inquiry, by Thomas R. Giddens, associate dean of Rockford College, falls into a similiar trap. Intending to "replicate in part" the Pattillo-Mackenzie study, he developed a questionnaire that presumably will get at the present condition of many of the supposed marks that we've already noted; the questionnaire includes this summary proposition:

> The current status of your institution's affiliation with a religious organization may best be summarized as (check one of the following):
>
> _____very religiously related
> _____moderately religiously related
> _____slightly religiously related
> _____not at all religiously related[4]

Ignoring the "moderately" loose language, what are we to make of this kind of determination? "Religiously related" is not defined except by implication from the preceding questions having to do with the composition of boards, the amount of financial support, preference in the selection of faculty, etc. Again, the respondent is invited to add one plus one plus one, and if the total is high enough, then surely the level attained is "very." But we have it on good authority that if I give all my goods to feed the poor and have not love, it profiteth me nothing.

In what has now come to be an annual "Directory of Christian Colleges and Bible Schools," the *Christian Herald* in its October, 1977,[5] issue makes distinctions among 450 institutions on the basis of such characteristics as whether chapel is required, how much course work in religion must be taken, and where prohibitions exist against smoking, drinking, dancing, firearms, gambling, card playing, and movie attendance. Presumably, drugs and sex are so unthinkable as not to need proscription. The implication, of course, is that these things say something determinative about whether or to what degree an institution is "Christian"; but all they really tell us is what the compiler thinks.

A final footnote to the argumentation of mark-conscious insiders: One can occasionally hear the plaint, if the marks themselves seem to be few in number and inconclusive, "Why would X College want to be considered church related if it weren't?" (Uncomplimentary answers are beside the point.) In other words, the supposedly reliable benchmark hereby being suggested is that a college's desire to be so considered is proof aplenty. Later on in this essay we shall have much to say about the importance of intentionality, which when valid produces supportive behavior. Now, however, let it simply be said that if those in the church can take some comfort on listing alone, they are too easily satisfied.

We must now turn to other myths about church-related colleges that consist in mistaken opinions held largely by highly critical, yet often poorly informed, outsiders. The first is perhaps the most pervasive: church-relatedness and academic excellence are inconsistent and, thus, can hardly be expected to exist in the same institution.

What is the actual situation? First, we deal here with two uncertainties, not just one. The foregoing discussion shows that church-relatedness is a slippery concept, but now we need to note that academic excellence is also, shifting from time to time, school to school, department to department. No longer, if ever, can one identify precisely all that makes for high scholastic quality, nor is it possible to name a guaranteed list of permanently achieving institutions. Even Phi Beta Kappa hasn't succeeded in doing so.

This much of an answer, however, is to dodge the issue. As we shall note later in respect to church-relatedness, so let it be recognized now in regard to academic excellence: though precision and finality of determination may be lacking, enough valid indicators are present to enable us to speak in terms of reliable approximation. There *are* such things as church-related colleges, and such things as colleges of high quality. And one simply has to say that the notion that these two can't and don't go together is false, for on occasion they can and do. The myth is put to rest not by partisan shouts of church men and women who would have us think better of St. Podunk or Siwash Wesleyan than it deserves. All we need to do is look at the unquestioned lists for each category, and note on both lists the presence of such institutions as Haverford, Kenyon, Notre Dame, Occidental, the two Randolph-Macons, both Lake and Wake Forest, Agnes Scott, Austin, St. Olaf—the list could go on for quite a while. But not all church-related colleges appear on both lists, for most such colleges simply can't pretend to have arrived at academic distinction. But enough of them can to give the lie to the smug notion that the two factors never go together.

Somewhat similar, and similarly mistaken, opinions need correction: that church-relatedness is inconsistent with diversity, or with academic freedom, or with "liberalism," usually meaning political liberalism, or, even in one remarkable misconception, with political conservatism. These notions crop up from time to time in treatments by educators who simply are ignorant of the church-related sector and jump to or perpetuate half-truths or no-truths that reveal their ignorance. Take diversity, for instance—and let ride the question as to whether it's always a good thing: some church-related colleges, it is true, can be oppressively homogeneous, with nobody in here 'cept us chickens; but others, like their nonchurch counterparts, are intentionally heterogeneous in personnel, diverse in program, and kaleidoscopic in point of view. No sweeping generalization fits.

A special word is in order concerning what might be called the political tendencies of church-related and other colleges. Who are "liberals" and "conservatives"? And why are eggheads the way they are, whatever their type of institution? Perhaps it needs to be said that there *are* lots of eggheads in church-related institutions, even as, perversely, there are a few Republicans in Harvard—which is not meant to speak ill of either Republicans or Harvard. Most denominations, of course, don't get captured by some one political point of view, and their colleges are, if anything, more independent. Incidentally, the charge about conservatism comes from a right-wing pseudo-Christian college that would have its constituency believe that the main-line church-related colleges have bowed their knee to Washington as well as to Baal. We can make a quick end to this business by saying that political generalizations are nearly all nonsense.

But the assumption about academic freedom deserves a more explicit answer. "Some of my best friends" in prestigious state universities or in parochial Ivy League schools have been misled into thinking that, whereas they are protected against anti-intellectualism and the pressures of superpatriots, their colleagues in church-related institutions are highly vulnerable. The sorry fact of our academic enterprise today is that anybody, anywhere, might be vulnerable, but the happy fact is that belief in and a rousing defense of academic freedom might also take place anywhere. The famous Bassett case was a long time ago, in little Methodist Trinity, now Duke, and the institution has remained both church affiliated and free. It is not any college's church-relatedness, or lack of it, that can serve as a dependable touchstone for its academic freedom.

This puts us in mind of the indispensable element, that is, the key individual, in bringing to pass any good thing such as academic freedom in our colleges and universities. Sometimes it is said that whether or not a college is truly church related turns on the influence of some special person in the institution's life. Usually that crucial individual is the president, but he or she might be, on occasion, the chaplain, or the chairman of the board, or some revered faculty member. In any event, the identification can be made so forcefully as to say that So-and-so College is church related because President and/or Mrs. Guiding Hand have made it so. We must demur. Though such a position may be a lovely, and justified, tribute to some charismatic individual, it is not an acceptable definition of a church-related college.

Nonessential characteristics, then, are legion. Any church-related college may have them in small or large degree, sparingly or voluminously. But we don't correctly determine church-relatedness on the basis of how many, or for that matter how few, such marks are present. We need to free ourselves of the easy grounds of definition often used in the past and try to examine church-related colleges as they really are.

NOTES—Chapter 1

[1] Manning M. Pattillo, Jr., and Donald M. Mackenzie, *Church-Sponsored Higher Education in the United States* (Washington, D.C.: American Council on Education, 1966). This is the most extensive study of the subject yet undertaken.

[2] Richard E. Anderson, "A Financial and Environmental Analysis of Strategic Policy Changes at Small Private Colleges" (manuscript, May 8, 1977), p. 21. For a fuller treatment, see Richard E. Anderson, *Strategic Policy Changes at Private Colleges* (New York: Teachers College Press, 1977), pp. 6-7 and passim.

[3] Anderson, *Strategic Policy Changes*, p. 3.

[4] Thomas R. Giddens, "Questionnaire on Church-Related Institutions" (manuscript, June, 1977).

[5] "Directory of Christian Colleges and Bible Schools," *Christian Herald*, vol. 100, no. 9 (October, 1977), pp. 55-78.

CHAPTER 2

Categories of Church-Relatedness

Let us assume, then, that we will overcome the temptation to make church-relatedness a matter of benchmarks and touchstones, whether firm and univeroal or merely tentative and occasional. Furthermore, let us reject the mistaken opinions of unobservant observers. We still can't escape the fact that colleges differ one from another in, among other ways, the degrees of intimacy and congruence they feel for their ecclesiastical sponsors.

To speak of degrees is to suggest that categories or types of colleges are not watertight compartments, distinct from each other in describable, mutually exclusive ways. And to speak of intimacy and congruence is to suggest that, although supposed marks of church-relatedness are inconclusive, a college can feel close to and harmonious with its parent denomination in numerous and widely diverse ways.

The categories of church-relatedness seem to spread across a considerable spectrum, the ends of which can perhaps be determined by the pseudo- or crypto-church colleges we do not mean to include. Let us assume that, whatever else qualifies a college for a place on the spectrum, it needs to be an institution that, first, puts forth some sort of claim to being connected with a church and, second, supports that claim with some sort of observable action that makes the claim credible. One or another degree of claim and action together is requisite for inclusion. Outside the two ends of the spectrum would be, in one direction, those colleges that make no claim (and, of course, produce no supporting action) and, in the other, those whose claims turn out on examination to be hollow.

Let us take a quick glance at each noneligible type in turn before we dismiss them from the discussion. The no-claim/no-action schools get mistaken for church-related colleges only when some misconception of history or present condition enters the picture. The break with the churchly past may have been sharp, even acrimonious, or slow and amicable, but in either case some of the constituency may not yet have gotten the word. On rare occasions you can hear Vanderbilt referred to as a Methodist institution, but that somewhat messy divorce was back in 1915. More often you can find somebody who thinks Western Maryland is still in the Methodist fold, for its litigious disaffection was as recent as 1974. Northwestern, Southern California, and Wesleyan of Connecticut, to name a few, slipped away from the Methodists more quietly. Other denominations also furnish examples early and late of loud or silent losses, to such an extent that one can safely say that the great majority of today's independent colleges and universities started out as church related. Even a few tax-supported institutions once had a church tie. But whatever the historical account shows, we are dealing in this discussion with only the present company of claim-and-action colleges.

Those that make a claim but have nothing to back it up are only a handful, and there may soon be none. After all, it's hard to figure how a college could profit from pretending to be church related if the church disavows the claim. Sometimes the denomination itself gets fooled, for colleges have been known to say one thing to Washington and something else to church headquarters; and the church may want to hang on to some connection as long as it can. But we don't have time in this limited treatment to bother with either two-faced claimants or outright impostors; our concern has to do with claim-and-action colleges that show both some willingness to be considered and some evidence of being church related.

Let us, then, turn to our spectrum. The first thing to notice is that it is long and multihued. The question rises naturally: Is there any way to divide the whole into more manageable parts, to observe and describe gradations, to set up categories based on identifiable similarities and differences?

The answer, I think, is "yes." In fact, others have done so in a variety of ways. The Pattillo-Mackenzie study divides the universe of authentic church-related colleges into three types: the "defender of the faith college," the "non-affirming college," and the "free Christian (or Jewish) college."[1] C. Robert Pace's study for the Carnegie Commission, *Education and Evangelism,* begins by identifying "four major types" of Protestant colleges:

1. Institutions that had Protestant roots but are no longer Protestant in any legal sense
2. Colleges that remain nominally related to Protestantism but are probably on the verge of disengagement
3. Colleges established by major Protestant denominations and which retain a connection with the church
4. Colleges associated with the evangelical, fundamentalist, and interdenominational Christian churches.[2]

Before he finishes, he cuts the pie differently:

[1] a group . . . originally Protestant . . . now largely if not totally independent. . . . Their present reputation is owing . . . to the character and quality of their educational programs.
[2] . . . the strongly evangelical and fundamentalist colleges.
[3] a third group . . . that have neither a national reputation based on educational programs nor any strong support from the churches . . . tepid environments—neither warmly spiritual nor coolly intellectual.[3]

None of these, I think, does the trick. Consider, for example, the Pattillo–Mackenzie typology, for their study is the most ambitious and exhaustive yet published. The first weakness in their presentation is the pejorative nature of the labels they choose, and their discussion of the three indicates that this is not accidental. "Defender of the faith" is meant to be mostly admired, though "there are relatively few institutions in the United States that fit this description."[4] "Non-affirming" has a negative sound, and the authors describe such a college largely in negative terms. "Free Christian" is meant to be affirmative, for this is the style they recommend. Such a college "is free because it does not control thought, Christian because it has a definite commitment."[5] In the authors' minds, it "combines the chief assets of the other two models while it tries to avoid their liabilities."[6]

They do not give examples. One gets the impression that their threefold arrangement is based more on the desires of evangelical churches than on the purposing of the colleges.

Yet the rough outlines of their three groupings are not altogether dissimilar, I must confess, to the three categories which I shall suggest. My titles, I hope, are nonpejorative, and the lineaments of each group differ in significant ways from the Pattillo–Mackenzie models. It is a spectrum along which these three are to be found, not a ladder of ascending worth. Many more than three groups, of course, could be identified, and they could be categorized in various ways. I choose these three, then, not because they are definitive but merely because they are handy and capable of being differentiated with some measure of accuracy and clarity.

The three groupings, each of which represents, in my view, a valid model of church-relatedness, are:

A. The Consonant College
B. The Proclaiming College
C. The Embodying College

Or in even shorter wording:

A. The Ally
B. The Witness
C. The Reflection

We shall look at each of these three in turn.

A. The Consonant College is an institution that, feeling independent in its own operations, is committed to the tradition of its related church and to consistency with that tradition in its own behavior. Its values are in the main its denomination's values. They are taken seriously and are evident in the life of the college and the lives of its alumni/ae.

Thus far the difference from our other two types is not pronounced. It begins to be shown in the way the college attests to its status. The Consonant College may talk very little about its church-relatedness, and this may be one of its marks of consistency with its church, which itself may · also be less concerned with public protestation. Only those who start by assuming that only loud profession is to be credited could conclude that quiet admission is a weakness. When a lack of fireworks is also characteristic of the denomination's behavior, then the college and the church can be said to be in harmony with each other. Thus this type is not the same as the Pattillo-Mackenzie "non-affirming college," for the college does not hesitate to affirm its nature as a church-connected institution. It's just that its style of affirmation is not according to some outsider's stereotype but is consistent with its own and its church's character.

This college, then, finds itself in the position of being an Ally with its denomination, bent on upholding the same values but not engaged in breast- or brow-beating on behalf of the denomination. To be an unassertive ally takes a good bit of sophistication; and this kind of college, therefore, and its church as well are likely to be self-confident, self-critical, and mature. Usually it matters not at all to the college and very little to the denomination whether there are certain forms of structure, organic ties, or religious requirements. A church affiliation, for the Consonant College, is not a matter of possessing or displaying traditional gimmickry. Yet I do not maintain that this category is therefore superior in its church-relatedness to the other two still to be described. Rather, I simply want to suggest that this bracket of institutions is not inferior to the other types, even though in previous discussions these institutions often have been made to appear to be less faithful to church, or Christianity, or religion in general. No disparagement of the Consonant College is in order, for as a mature and unassertive ally with its church it is true to its conception of what being church related calls for.

A few examples may help to delineate this category more fully. Take Haverford, for instance, an unobtrusively, yet committedly, Quaker institution of high quality. As both Kenneth R. Hardy and Douglas H. Heath have reported, their separate analyses of student and alumni attitudes show the power of its Friendly persuasion. "The college's Quaker values became the values of many alumni, although most of them neither identified themselves as Quaker nor thought of themselves as very religious."[7] Without the usual paraphernalia of religious emphasis, Haverford consciously provides a setting where "a specific Quaker influence is at work"[8] and thus fits the mold of the Consonant College.

Another but quite different example would be Salem College, in Winston-Salem, North Carolina, founded in 1772 as a lower school by Moravians who early were convinced of the importance of an educated womanhood. To this day the Moravian Church is small, nondemonstrative, intensely loyal. Less than 2 percent of Salem's student body and less than 1 percent of its faculty are Moravians. Yet the influence of the church is keenly felt throughout the college, especially at Christmas and Easter when the special observances of the church are deeply cherished by the collegiate community, overwhelmingly non-Moravian in composition. Much the same could be said for the only other college of this denomination, Moravian College of Bethlehem, Pennsylvania.

Still another illustration of this category might be Carleton College of Northfield, Minnesota. It comes to be related to the United Church of Christ by way of the Congregational stream, and it partakes of the early colonial understanding that had to do with a "covenanted society" consisting of "a tripartite social order based upon church, college, and commonwealth." As Wesley Hotchkiss has written, "These three basic institutions formed the society in a relationship of shared autonomy. No one of them was given authority over the others because all three existed under the sovereignty of God."[9] Carleton, therefore, understands itself to be free from the church as well as from the state, and this status frees it not to be either secular or sectarian but to be seriously concerned with religious study and worship in ways harmonious with its Congregational heritage and present relationship.

B. The Proclaiming College as the second category is an institution that joyously announces its affiliation with its sponsoring denomination at every appropriate occasion. But it does more than merely identify its connection; in its program it practices what it proclaims in ways that seem approvable to the two worlds in which it exists—education and religion.

These ways will differ from college to college and church to church. No one form of structural tie, no one provision for religious nurture, curricular or extracurricular, no one pattern of faculty, student, or trustee composition is requisite. Differences exist among colleges, among denominational groupings of colleges, and even among geographical groupings. For example, something like the old-style Religious Emphasis Week may still be found in one section, whereas some other part of the country will scorn that approach. No matter, the significant thing is that the Proclaiming College finds some way to affirm its religious commitment and then backs up the claim.

The bracket is wide. Somewhere in its broad confines are to be found the large majority of institutions that think of themselves as church related. Most of the pretenders are here, too, and the pretending may in fact be done either by the college or by its church. Let it be repeated: The Proclaiming College is the acknowledged academic partner of the church, taking seriously both its intellectual and its ecclesiastical character.

Thus it is the Witness. Once upon a time it witnessed to its own people, the faculty and students who were strong in the faith or could be made so by judicious internal evangelism. Or it may have been a witness to the world outside and sought to persuade its own to carry the gospel to the unwashed. Now it may seldom if ever be either the priest or the missionary; it knows itself first as a college, not a religious institution. It is its own master in deciding what it shall be and do, both academically and religiously. But as a college, it is in confederation with the church and is glad to admit it.

Examples of individual colleges that fit this loose description are hardly necessary. Most of the Catholic colleges belong here, especially as they have lately been winning increasing freedom for self-determination. Most Methodist colleges also fall into this category, using their long-won liberty to assert their connection. Likewise, here is where should be put the largest number of institutions bearing a Presbyterian label, or Lutheran, or Baptist, or any other mainstream Protestant group. The Proclaiming College is a free and credible witness to its being an academic partner of its proud denominational parent.

C. The Embodying College constitutes a third category distinct from either of the other two but closer to its Proclaiming cousin. Whereas it might be said that the Proclaiming College is one whose allegiance is to the norms of higher education with ecclesiastical overtones, the Embodying College would be one whose allegiance is to the tenets of its church with educational overtones. It is the mirror, almost the embodiment, of the denomination to which it gives fealty. Whether forced or unforced, it is the Reflection of the church, true in every major respect, sound in faith and observance. When one walks on its campus, one knows immediately where he or she is, ecclesiastically speaking.

Two terms have sometimes been used to denote such institutions, but they seem to me to be inadequate, even unfair. I refer to "believers' college" and to the Pattillo–Mackenzie phrase, "defender of the faith college." As for the first, either implication is unfortunate: (1) that other kinds of colleges are by or for unbelievers and (2) that this kind of college fosters gullibility. Neither is accurate.

"Defender of the faith" sounds a bit embattled. Even if its targeted group were to accept the moniker without umbrage, outsiders would likely be using it disparagingly. Actually, the folks who inhabit colleges belonging to this group don't feel they're on the defense at all; they're usually on the attack. The denomination involved has a clear orthodoxy to uphold, and the Embodying College is one of its means for doing so enthusiastically. Institutions of this type, as well as the other types, follow various patterns and indulge in diverse practices, but the differences here tend to be denominational not collegiate. That is, the colleges of any one church in this group would be less likely to differ one from another; the church itself would be more likely to set the pace and define the practice. The church is paramount. It is in this sense, therefore, that the college can qualify for the Reflection appellation.

Once again we must be careful with the flavor of the words used and the mistaken assumptions so easily made. As with what was called the Consonant College, so now with the Embodying College, people on the opposite end of the spectrum, or even in the middle, find it hard to give credence to the validity of the type. Yet the Consonant College deserves to be thought of as genuinely church related because, as we have already noted, its understandings and ways of behavior are consistent with those of its denomination. And exactly the same thing can be said for the Embodying College. That it is as it is stems from its being ecclesiastically what it is, and this category is no less a model of church-relatedness merely because its church's mores may seem strange to outsiders.

As for illustrations, most such colleges are the organs of churches that adhere to a sharply defined orthodoxy differing in some special regard from the general run of religious thought. Thus the colleges are Mennonite, Lutheran Church—Missouri Synod (all but perhaps Valparaiso), Church of Christ, Seventh-day Adventist, etc. Occasionally, the college of some large main-line denomination may also be properly located here, as the reflection of some special group or point of view within the church. In the chapter to follow, specific case studies of some of these colleges, as well as those of the other two categories, will be presented.

It is time now to take another look at the spectrum and begin to fill it out. On the left (but certainly not in any political sense!), let us place the Embodying College, a Reflection of the church; in the broad center, the Proclaiming College, a Witness for the church; and on the right, the Consonant College, an Ally of the church. We can sprinkle some names of colleges around—those that are to be written about in the next chapter, and a few others whose places are fairly obvious. Our spectrum would now look something like the chart of colleges on the adjacent page.

When we try to place institutions somewhere along the line, we begin to discover some interesting things about the line itself. For example, it has movement. That is, to the extent to which a college may change the nature of its church-relatedness from time to time, that change moves as the eye moves along the spectrum, from left to right, almost never from right to left. (Now you know why we put the Embodying College on the left.) A college may not change its position at all or at least not for a long time. Whether it does or doesn't change, or however much it changes, as long as it is still somewhere on our spectrum, it deserves to be spoken of as church related. It isn't more or less church related because of the change; it is just different. Thus no judgment is being expressed when movement from left to right is pointed out; it is simply the trend of history, a fact of institutional change, and we need to recognize it.

We need to observe some other facts about placement along the line. For example, if there were a directional arrow from left to right, it would indicate a fairly accurate progression from more to less rhetoric in regard to church-relatedness, from more to less evidence of organic ties with a church, and from less to more academic recognition. The institutions on the right-hand side of the spectrum tend to be higher-ranking colleges qua colleges. This is not to say, however, that they are more or less church related. This whole exercise is undertaken not to give grounds for saying some are "better" or "worse" than others, but to point out the presence of all of them somewhere on the scale.

Categories and Degrees of Church-Relatedness: The Colleges (examples)

(Those visited and described briefly in Chapter 3 are italicized)

(False claim) .... (No claim)

Concordia Teachers (Nebr.) *Goshen* Manchester David Lipscomb Andrews	*Morris Brown* *West Virginia Wesleyan* St. Thomas St. Olaf St. Andrews	*Austin* *Whitworth* *Seattle* Notre Dame Southern Methodist	*Furman* *Wittenberg* *Drury* Dickinson Wake Forest	*Kalamazoo* *St. Augustine's* Haverford Salem (N.C.) Carleton
Embodying College Reflection of the Church		Proclaiming College Witness for the Church		Consonant College Ally of the Church

It will have been noted that dotted lines separating the three chief categories are echoed by fainter dots within the large middle category. They are meant to call attention to the three groupings of the names there, left, right, and center. The Proclaiming College, the Witness, may lean toward being the Reflection of its church, may tilt toward being the Ally of its church, or may do neither; and surely three subgroupings are not too many into which to divide the huge number in the group.

If there were time or inclination, a number of other gradations and movements along the spectrum could be identified. For example, if only we knew enough, we might make distinctions or detect changes growing out of geographical factors, economic conditions, or characteristics of clientele. The variables are legion, and trying to identify the directions of change for them would be a fascinating exercise. If the effort were carried far enough, even perhaps to being computerized, one might develop a "natural history" through which all church-related colleges move, sooner or later. At this point in our knowledge, however, such a thing would be even more pretentious than the tentative placements on the scale already offered. It is important not to forget that the placings of colleges are personal judgments only, highly fallible, and, even if accurate at any one time, likely to change.

Tentative as the spectrum must be, however, it helps us to see things we may not have realized before. For example, each denomination might be said to have its own spectrum. That is to say, the colleges of any one denomination rarely, if ever, would occupy a single spot; rather, they would spread out along the line. Some denominational spectra—for example, the Catholics, the Methodists, and the United Presbyterians—would be so broad as to run across much of the spectrum's whole length. The Church of Christ would be a narrow band at the extreme left end of the scale; the United Church of Christ, considerably wider, would be toward the right end—which is just one more reminder as to how dangerous it is to pass judgment on the church-relatedness of any one college on the basis of the standards and expectations of some other than its own denomination.

Another version of the scale, with attention focused on the churches, might look something like the next chart.

The position of any one college on the spectrum would be found, one might suppose, within the bracket for its denomination. Yet that is not quite what the churches' brackets are designed to mean. Rather, each signifies how the church, rather than how one, many, or all of its colleges, looks upon the types and degrees of relatedness.

It is not impossible, therefore, that a college, on its own or its church's estimate of its church-relatedness, might be correctly placed outside the spectrum of its denomination. That is to say, a college might admit to some connection with a church according to its own understanding as to what such an affiliation ought to mean, but the church itself might be unwilling to claim the college. Or whether or not the church claimed and listed the college, the church's own definition of the meaning of relatedness might effectively exclude the institution from the company of those that accepted it. College and church don't necessarily see eye to eye on such a matter, and many an instance of discord between the two could be graphed by putting the institution's dot outside the denomination's line.

Then what happens? If the distance of the dot off the line is too great, the college may wish, or be forced, to leave the church. Usually when this is the case, the college may leave our spectrum altogether; it ceases to be effectively church related in its or any other's eyes. But an alternative development is at least conceivable and may in fact have occurred: A college may have moved beyond the right-hand boundary (movement is nearly always left to right, remember) of its denomination's spectrum and yet still desire and deserve to be known as related in some way. Is this the case with, say, Furman or Wake Forest vis-à-vis the Southern Baptists? How many Catholic colleges would fit this description? What about Valparaiso and the Missouri Synod Lutherans? Pepperdine and the Church of Christ? Whether or not these are valid examples, the point remains that a college may not need to cease being church related in order for the church to feel it has lost the college.

But we're dealing now with extreme and perhaps hypothetical cases since most church-related colleges are implanted easily in the structures of their churches. Both colleges and denominations cover a wide spectrum, all points along which can be said to be valid. Identifiable models are of at least three types, as we have noted. Now it behooves us to look at some actual institutions.

Categories and Degrees of Church-Relatedness: The Denominations

(No claim)

Consonant College
Ally of the Church

Proclaiming College
Witness for the Church

Embodying College
Reflection of the Church

(False claim)

African Methodist
Episcopal Church

Church of the Brethren

Christian Methodist
Episcopal Church

Church of Christ

American Baptist Churches in the U.S.A.

United Church of Christ

Christian Church (Disciples of Christ)

The Episcopal Church

Religious Society of Friends

American Lutheran Church

Lutheran Church in America

Missouri Synod—Lutheran Church

Mennonite Church

United Methodist Church

Moravian Church in America

Church of the
Nazarene

Presbyterian Church in the United States

United Presbyterian Church U.S.A.

Roman Catholic Church

Seventh-day Adventists

Southern Baptist Convention

NOTES—Chapter 2

¹Manning M. Pattillo, Jr., and Donald M. Mackenzie, *Church-Sponsored Higher Education in the United States* (Washington, D.C.: American Council on Education, 1966), chapter 12.

²C. Robert Pace, *Education and Evangelism: A Profile of Protestant Colleges* (New York: McGraw-Hill Book Company, 1972), pp. xii and 2. Used with permission of McGraw-Hill Book Company.

³*Ibid.*, pp. 104-105. The Carnegie Commission published also a *Profile of Catholic Higher Education*, whose author and main title were Andrew M. Greeley, *From Backwater to Mainstream* (New York: McGraw-Hill Book Company, 1969). Considerably better informed than Pace's volume, it too emphasizes the "immense diversity" of institutions ("from Immaculate Heart to the University of Dallas"), but it does not try to establish a typology.

⁴Manning M. Pattillo, Jr., and Donald M. Mackenzie, *800 Colleges Face the Future* (St. Louis: Danforth Foundation, 1965), p. 67.

⁵*Ibid.*, p. 68.

⁶*Ibid.*, p. 69.

⁷Douglas H. Heath, "Prescriptions for Collegiate Survival: Return to Liberally Educate Today's Youth," *Liberal Education*, vol. 63, no. 2 (May, 1977), pp. 338-350; see especially p. 345.

⁸Kenneth R. Hardy, "Social Origins of American Scientists and Scholars," *Science*, 1974, vol. 185, p. 502.

⁹Wesley A. Hotchkiss, "The Prophetic Academy: An Historical Perspective on UCC Related Colleges," *Journal of Current Social Issues*, United Church of Chirst, vol. 14, no. 2 (Spring, 1977), p. 66.

CHAPTER 3

Examples of
Church-Related Colleges

To talk of conceptual models of church-relatedness is ultimately self-defeating if no real-life, flesh-and-blood models exist. To set up categories and types is deceptive unless at least rough illustrations can be furnished. It is time to report on the visits to individual campuses undertaken for this essay.

But there were problems. Which colleges should be chosen? Who should do the visiting? What should be the agenda of inquiry? When? How long? And if things turned out to be different from what was first supposed about the institution, should a college stay in the list or be dropped?

To respond to the last question first, I decided to keep all the colleges in the review for the sake of representativeness. They were chosen in the first instance because the Study/Action Committee which conceived and is sponsoring this study, church executives, or others invited to nominate felt that these institutions were instructive in respect to church-relatedness. Academically they are neither the best nor the worst. In other respects—size, gender, race, creed, and economic condition—they are polyglot enough but not a true sample. Only in their church-relatedness was it felt that the chosen fourteen could prove helpful.

Many others were considered. Each executive of a denominational office of higher education suggested several colleges from his or her own group, though usually only one was included in the final list. Nominations from outside the churches' secretariats seemed to be based on different criteria from those of the church executives, and only a few such colleges could be included. When the total list had to be kept as small as a dozen or so—a decision necessary because of the limited time and scope of this study—it turned out that some denominations were not represented at all. Moreover, no one institution or even two can represent adequately those churches that have large numbers of colleges of various sorts and sizes related to them. The United Methodist group is too disparate to be exemplified by West Virginia Wesleyan; ditto the Southern Baptists by Furman, or the Roman Catholics by St. Thomas and Seattle.

True representativeness, then, could hardly have been gained by choosing less than a hundred or so. Yet the number chosen is larger than a representative cross section of a Gallup poll. When some colleges turned out to be less remarkable in their church relatedness than originally supposed, perhaps this made the whole group of fourteen more symbolic of the universe of church colleges than if all had proved to be worth visiting. In any event, all fourteen will be briefly described, and some others about which pertinent information was available will also be mentioned.

The visitors (see the List of Contributors to the Project at the end of this volume) were chosen and prepared for their task by the Society for Values in Higher Education. All of them were already broadly knowledgeable about higher education in general and church-affiliated colleges in particular. They were advised to center attention on matters having to do with the relationships of the colleges to their parent churches. Each college was visited by a team of two; each visitor was on two different teams. Lengthy sessions both before and after the period of visitation, at Zion State Park, Illinois, and Quail Roost Conference Center, North Carolina, gave ample opportunity for the fourteen visitors and representatives of the committee to rehearse what was being looked for and what was found. Though I must accept full responsibility for the inadequacies of the vignettes to follow, they have come out of a far-ranging, incisive process of investigation and discussion in which the other participants have been unusually candid, impartial, and patient with me.

The fourteen colleges visited for this study, with their denominational connections, are:

Austin College (Texas)—Presbyterian Church in the United States

Concordia Teachers College (Nebraska)—Lutheran Church—Missouri Synod

Drury College (Missouri)—United Church of Christ and Christian Church (Disciples of Christ)

Furman University (South Carolina)—Southern Baptist Convention

Goshen College (Indiana)—Mennonite Church

Kalamazoo College (Michigan)—American Baptist Churches in the U.S.A.

Manchester College (Indiana)—Church of the Brethren

Morris Brown College (Georgia)—African Methodist Episcopal Church

St. Augustine's College (North Carolina)—The Episcopal Church

College of St. Thomas (Minnesota)—Roman Catholic Church (Diocesan)

Seattle University (Washington)—Roman Catholic Church (Jesuit)

West Virginia Wesleyan College (West Virginia)—United Methodist Church

Whitworth College (Washington)—United Presbyterian Church U.S.A.

Wittenberg University (Ohio)—Lutheran Church in America

Austin College

The visitors "were impressed with the open and spirited way in which the school affirms the fact and meaning of its church-relatedness"* with the Presbyterian Church in the United States. Since its founding in 1849, Austin has been aware "of its role as an important expression of the mission of the church." In 1973 the relationship was redefined and strengthened in the "Covenant"—a good Presbyterian word—between the college and the Synod of Red River; it stated among other things, the intention

---

*Comments in quotation marks, unless otherwise attributed, are from the reports of the visitors.

That Austin College be an instrument of witness for the Christian Church in higher education as it offers quality education with a concept of the wholeness of life as interpreted by the Christian faith, and that the College, exercising its responsibilities to be free to pursue truth under God, be a resource to the Presbyterian Church for creative leadership and for interpretation of the implications of new discoveries for the Church in its mission to a changing world.[1]

This is brave talk; for many another institution one might well wonder whether, first, the words had been carefully and soberly chosen and, second, the intention bore any resemblance to the campus fact. But such doubting would be out of place at Austin. Before the covenant was adopted, the college prepared an "Institutional Profile" which affirmed that

there is no neutralism in education; every educational institution consciously or unconsciously embodies in its life and curriculum some religious stance, some institutional consensus of value judgments. For Austin College that stance is consciously and unashamedly the Christian faith.[2]

Yet Austin doesn't believe in or practice indoctrination. The "Profile" stresses with equal force "the seriousness of the commitment as an educational institution," including such elements of a quality program as "scholastic integrity," "academic innovation," and "freedom in the pursuit of truth." This is clearly a college that honors excellence. It thinks it's "the best liberal arts college in Texas," and it probably is.

Though Austin's church affiliation is "forthright" and "articulate," it does not clutter its program with supposedly supportive dos and don'ts. For example, there is no required chapel or church attendance or even a required course in religion. Rather, all students take an interdisciplinary core, such as a series of courses in the Western heritage, with the subject of religion being a prominent part of the syllabi. Since the college's concern is "the liberally educated mind" and "the pervasive role of values," emphasis is placed on such features as the honor system (taken with great seriousness), the "dignity of each student," and the faculty mentor program, much more highly structured than the usual student advising. "Personal development," including the nurture of "a sensitized conscience," is the genuine, yet not heavy-handed, aim for the students. It turns out, therefore, that the college's "straightforward avowal of its Christian orientation" is a matter not so much of document and pronouncement as of the effort to establish a pervasive atmosphere in campus life.

Much the same sort of thing has been attempted in other Southern Presbyterian colleges—for example, Eckerd and St. Andrews: a covenant with the church, the inclusion of religion in interdisciplinary courses, an emphasis on total atmosphere, etc. From one institution to another, however, differences exist in terms not only of the degrees of relative success but also of the persons and forces responsible. In Austin's case, many knowledgeable people give large credit to longtime President John Moseley, who himself points to the Board of Trustees. The faculty, too, have undoubtedly played a positive role. All together, it adds up to Austin's being a free, effective witness to its understanding of the way the Christian faith impinges on higher education. It is neither church distant nor church dominated; it belongs to a new and lively breed of church-related institutions.

Concordia Teachers College

Concordia Teachers College in Seward, Nebraska, is one of several Lutheran Church—Missouri Synod Concordias. Its well-defined relationship to the church "is probably as close as can be imagined," for it is "owned and operated" by the denomination, whose control extends even to quite specific matters of administration. For example, no teacher may be appointed for as much as a year without being cleared not only by the college's Board of Control but also by the church's Board of Higher Education. The relationship is described in detail in the *Handbook of the Lutheran Church— Missouri Synod,* and all constituencies seem to accept the college's subservient status without dissent.

The educational purpose of the institution is equally clear: "to train elementary and secondary teachers for Lutheran parochial schools" or for some other form of church-sponsored work. Something "over 90 percent of the students come from Lutheran parishes," and a like proportion intend to enter professional religious occupations. The faculty are as single-minded as the students; "they must affirm the Confession and would not come here if they were not in accord."

The "remarkable unanimity" at Concordia shows itself in various aspects of campus life. Among those cited for our visitors was the "widely utilized" practice of faculty members stating "their own personal value convictions in the classroom," coupled with a lack of encouragement to students "to explore and evaluate their own theological and moral convictions." Two other areas that reflect the intimate church-relatedness of Concordia are "the liturgical life of the college," including "seven worship services a week," and a lively community service program called "Impact" (Immediate Mobilization of Persons Agreeable to Committing Themselves).

Whether all of this would make for peace and harmony at some other time is anybody's guess. At the present moment, however, Concordia is inevitably affected by the turmoil in the Lutheran Church—Missouri Synod; and even though the college has "remained entirely loyal" to the synod, and thus to its conservative leadership, it has earned the displeasure of "the radical conservatives," a term our visitors heard on campus for the extreme right wing. The recent resignation of the president was brought about, it seems, by charges of "doctrinal deviation" emanating from a reactionary periodical.

In spite of the current upheaval, or perhaps because of it, Concordia gives the impression of being relatively confident about the outcome, gracious and cooperative in manner, unsophisticated, and nondefensive. It deserves to be accepted, of course, for what it is: a church-related college of *its* church, not of some other; a faithful reflection of what most leaders of its denomination want it to be. One of our visitors wrote that Concordia, "however threatened at the moment, seems anything but defeatist, constrained, or joyless."

Drury College

Drury owns to a double connection with both the United Church of Christ and the Christian Church (Disciples of Christ). The former through its Congregational antecedent founded the college in 1873, and the latter established a School of Religion, now a department, there in 1909. This twofold tie is at least one explanation for "the nonsectarian intent and spirit of the college," which emphasizes "Christian orientation" rather than church affiliation. The interest of both churches remains strong, however, and it seems likely that the Christian Church will soon come to share with the UCC a relatedness with the total institution.

Yet Drury's Articles of Association, in line with its whole tradition, "appear to avoid precision and illuminating detail in defining its church relation, for fear of misinterpretations suggesting ecclesiastical control." In this respect the college's geographical location is not an insignificant factor: Springfield, Missouri, plays host also to Southwest Missouri State University and to Evangel College of the Assemblies of God, and Drury is pleased to be philosophically in between.

Since the usual style of its two church sponsors is not to intrude, Drury pursues "its own internal mandate" to be small, devoted to the liberal arts, and "value oriented." The last of these could mean becoming innocuous, but this seems not to be the case. Our visitors came to the conviction "that, however well or unwell value-judgments get their play in this course or that, value consciousness is somewhere and somehow being nurtured in the student's educational experience at Drury." Moreover, these are not just vague secular values in general; this is "a continuing and relatively effectual sensitivity to the place of religious thought and perspective in liberal arts education."

Where does this valuing take place? Hither and yon, as at most colleges; perhaps anywhere some of the time, and perhaps nowhere all of the time—for students won't always be persuaded and faculty can't always persuade. Two places, however, seem to be especially influential and stable in their influence—the Department of Religion and Philosophy, and the chaplaincy. It is fortunate that they are strong, for the college has had seven presidents or acting presidents in the last eight years.

But isn't it a bit risky to allow an institution's sense of church-relatedness to consist largely in an emphasis on value consciousness and then to let that rest on the accident of having effective people in some one or two departments? Yes—just about as risky as letting its genuine religious zeal depend on a signed piece of paper or a presidential ukase or required chapel. Different denominations do things differently, and so do their colleges; and there is no panacea.

Furman University

The recently completed *Study of Southern Baptist Colleges and Universities, 1976–77,* directed by Earl J. McGrath, comes to the not-surprising conclusion "that Southern Baptist colleges have maintained a much closer relationship than many other denominational schools"[3] to their parent church. But since the evidence for this is gleaned from factors that are subject both to change from time to time and to varied interpretation, it is equally not surprising to find that such a conclusion may not apply to all fifty-odd Southern Baptist institutions alike. Each needs to be examined by itself because not even a church as professedly free as the Southern Baptist Convention is monolithic.

Furman is Southern Baptist, no doubt about it, and most of its organic or visible ties are of the usual close order—the South Carolina Baptist Convention's election of trustees, generous annual support (over $800,000!), concern for rules governing students, etc. But Furman has carved out its own character and its special relationship with the church, and in these regards it is atypical. In trying to understand what type of institution Furman is, one needs to be wary both of those who think its being Southern Baptist tells everything worth knowing and of those others, slightly more knowledgeable, who see only its differences.

The dramatic thing about Furman in the last ten to fifteen years is its drive toward academic excellence. This campaign, including efforts to upgrade faculty and student body, to increase outside sources of support and inside educational demands, and to win greater scholastic recognition, has been and continues to be successful. Most experts would probably rate Furman at least Number Two academically among all Southern Baptist institutions, an advance from its earlier standing, and would give primary credit to the recently retired president, Gordon Blackwell.

The university's relationship to the church needs to be seen in the light of its present emphasis on academic freedom and excellence. Our visitors reported that "there are two images of church-relatedness" that they discovered on the campus. "The first image is that of the church as a potential threat to liberal education or to freedom." Furman has had its share of heresy hunts and social restrictions and seems to have come through them remarkably well. But there is enough residue of feeling on such matters, especially the latter, to explain how the topic of church-relatedness may sometimes conjure up the specter of indoctrination or old-fashioned moralism. The university is not likely to bow to such pressures ("Two years ago the Convention passed a resolution against dancing in its colleges . . .

[but] Furman kept on dancing."), but the juxtaposition of Furman's commitment to freedom and excellence and the church's actual or supposed opposition gives a defensive cast to the question of denominational affiliation.

Lest it appear that only Furman is caught in such a quandary, let it be noted that, like loyal, high-spirited children in a loving family, colleges sometimes have a falling-out with their ecclesiastical parents which mars the usually happy understanding. To illustrate from the other leading Southern Baptist institution: The student newspaper at Wake Forest recently quoted a prominent church official as saying that if one had to pick between "academic freedom" and "religious heritage," Wake Forest should choose the latter, a comment hardly calculated to endear the church to the college. In the same issue, September 9, 1977, was reported an effort by a committee of the Baptist State Convention to prevent Wake Forest from using, or to force it to return, part of a $300,000 grant to the Biology Department from the National Science Foundation. At first the question was supposedly the separation of church and state, but as the months passed it came to be the right of self-government—for the university's trustees voted to accept the grant in toto. Wake Forest and the Convention are now engaged in a serious running debate on whether or in what ways the two should or can remain connected. The moral is: Restiveness with, or even rebellion against, a sponsoring denomination has often been a normal part of being church related, although for a season it may indeed make things more difficult.

Back to South Carolina: The second "image of church-relatedness" at Furman is strongly positive. It has to do with the affirmation of the university's character and values as a church-related college, as described in a widely circulated brochure. The first commitment reads in part as follows:

> 1. Furman is a person-centered community, emphasizing the prime worth of persons and encouraging concern for others. . . . Christian love requires us to view others as persons to be respected rather than as objects to be used. . . .[4]

It is through fostering the Christian life, in personal and social terms, not through any peculiarly Baptist activity, that the university seeks to fulfill its church-related obligations. Not until the last item does the brochure mention its specific Southern Baptist rootage, and even then, with an unaccustomed ecumenical flavor:

> 4. Furman is a college which acknowledges its denominational and regional heritage and responsibility. Furman as a Baptist college belongs to the free-church tradition among Protestants. Honoring belief in the competency of the individual before God, it cherishes the right of each person to reach his own decisions about life's meaning without interference or coercion.[5]

Ways of affirming Christian values and the importance of persons are similar to those employed on many other campuses: care in choice of faculty, strong courses on religion and the humanities generally, well-planned opportunities for worship, and innovative efforts such as a series of Values Seminars and a program for entering students called Dialogue. The most unusual feature of Furman's campus life is the Collegiate Educational Service Corps, or CESC, a massive project of voluntary community service, initiated and run by students. CESC is the embodiment of caring for other persons, and over 50 percent of Furman's student body of 2,300 participate in it. Recognizing that it has problems of limited perceptions and techniques, our visitors were "tremendously impressed with what CESC is accomplishing."

The university is instructive because it shows how mistaken a stereotype can be. Many Southern Baptists would find it hard to feel completely at home, academically and religiously, at Furman, as at Wake Forest, but many others like what they find and are proud of their two front-runners. The institutions themselves are no less Southern Baptist because they take their intellectual life seriously. The Furman brochure on *Character and Values* . . . sums up this way:

> As a church-related college Furman commits itself to academic excellence without compromise of its Christian heritage. Furman affirms the worth of both the life of learning and the life of religious faith and morals.[6]

Goshen College

Goshen is the name of the town as well as the college, a favorite practice of founders. In Goshen's case the founders were Mennonite, and the college has remained staunch in the faith to this day, with "a full-bodied, unapologetic church relationship."

The marks of this relationship are conclusive. The Mennonite Board of Education and the college's Board of Overseers constitute the two governing bodies in a dual system for coordination, reminiscent of the way some state systems are set up. "Most of the faculty are Goshen graduates." All tenured faculty must be Mennonites ("or share the spirit of Mennonites"—but none has yet passed that test); by board policy the student body is expected to be around 65 percent Mennonite. As our visitors heard more than once on the campus, "Mennonites are an ethnic group" and a non-Mennonite "feels faintly outside."

It would be a mistake to suppose, however, that theirs is a fortress mentality. On the contrary, "they are open and at ease with a visitor," are by no means all of one mind ("more diverse than Amherst students," said one of our visitors), and practice an enthusiastic outreach to the community nearby and the world at large. The program in international education is one of their gems, and around 90 percent of the faculty have lived abroad. "Because the college believes that people in all countries are of one humanity," says the Goshen *Bulletin,* "it believes that study and work in other parts of the world give students better preparation for membership in that one tribe. . . . " Mennonite as it proudly is, Goshen is not divorced from the life of the society at large.

In fact, the college means to redeem society. Goshen exists, says a statement of purpose adopted in 1976 by the faculty and Board of Overseers, "for the transmission, enrichment, enlargement and embodiment of the Believers Church vision," and its forthright aim is "to develop informed, articulate, sensitive, responsible Christian disciples." Again: "Our objective is to have faith permeate the entire life of the campus." The college goes about this in the usual ways—study, worship, service, counseling—with some success.

Yet the apparent homogeneity of its student body, in origin if not always in point of view, gives Goshen little chance to tackle the unbelievers. Asked why they chose Goshen, some students "said they wanted a college where they would be supported rather than beleaguered in their faith." And one student opined, "Goshen doesn't preach Christianity enough; it only practices it." Like many another campus quite different in orientation from Goshen's, the revival of student evangelistic and fundamentalist groups has resulted in the criticism that "the faculty are not confessional enough." You can't win!

One further point is of special interest. Part of Goshen's understanding of its church-relatedness is that it minister to the church, not merely indirectly by training students to be its future leaders, but also directly by supplying both helpful advice and constructive criticism. The college organized the Center for Discipleship in 1970 to bring faculty and students into fruitful contact with pastors and lay persons of congregations throughout the church through various workshops, seminars, and conferences. At the very least, this has proved to be important for the sake of communication, and it may indeed, as Goshen claims, have "tied the college and the churches together. . . ."

Kalamazoo College

Kalamazoo is a good example of the danger of describing any institution's church-relatedness in terms of the expectations of some other denomination than its own. The college is American Baptist. This church group has traditionally allowed its colleges great freedom, and what might seem indifference or even intentional disengagement in some other circumstance may be a quite appropriate posture in this situation.

Illustrations, therefore, can be misinterpreted. Our visitors began by wondering whether people at Kalamazoo were "incredibly confused" about its relation with the church, or whether they simply practiced "studied ambiguity"; but before the visit was finished, it became clear that "they think pluralism and denominationalism are compatible." Neither faculty nor students are "chosen for their religious interest," and church affiliation is seldom discussed. The Admissions Office doesn't mention denomination, for it feels it hurts recruitment. Some friendly local Baptists "think Kalamazoo doesn't care about them any more." These are the things that get noted when a denomination or a college is "reluctant to coerce."

The reality includes much else that is unambiguous. The signs of a lively regard for religion are numerous: Voluntary chapel is well planned and attended, and the Department of Religion is strong. Our visitors were impressed with the temper of human contacts—student-student, faculty-faculty, and student-faculty—that seemed to achieve "a significantly higher quality of personal relationships" than most institutions, public or private. These relationships, they thought, "still linger from the religious base" of the college. Moreover, Kalamazoo seems to provide "a context where fundamental value questions can be unapologetically raised" and where "Jews and Catholics are comfortable."

But is this traceable to the college's church relationship? Or is it merely evidence of a basically humane atmosphere, a vague value consciousness nurtured earlier by a more visible church tie but now pretty much on its own? One person observed that "religion is like a thread going through the fabric of the college's life. It is difficult to identify but it nonetheless has an effect on the whole." Though this is so, it still may not be a peculiarly denominational thread; but that itself may make it true, not false, to the American Baptist position.

Diversity and openness are so accepted that the college's concern for denominational presence could easily be underestimated. In a recent address, President George N. Rainsford, an Episcopalian, made clear that "our Baptist roots are important to us." When the annual Armstrong Lectures bring "relevant religious voices to the college for worship, study, counseling, and dialogue," the Baptist churches of Michigan join with the college in sponsoring a "Ministers' Workshop" for Baptists and others in the region. Kalamazoo's director of church relations not only cultivates a receptive posture as befits the associate director of development, his secondary title, but also mounts a substantial and varied program of help to the churches. All of this is adding up to "a new, mature relationship" in which the college will be "able to give to, as well as receive support from, the churches," thus achieving an "interdependence," a "partnership," that goes far beyond mere mutual freedom.

In this connection it may be well to note that Kalamazoo did not go the way of Denison, another high-quality college of American Baptist lineage. In 1973, Denison was in serious upheaval about its church connection and religious character, which were regarded by many at the college as being wholly in the past. The provocation was an effort to remove from its centennial gates the mild description, "A Christian College of Liberal Arts." For some students and faculty, the loose tie seemed much too tight. The trustees, however, reaffirmed "the Christian principles which guide our college," including "personal freedom grounded in personal responsibility," "the individuality of faith," and "religious pluralism." The American Baptist Churches'

Division of Christian Higher Education still lists Denison as one of its colleges and feels it is making progress in the reestablishment of some genuine relationships.

Manchester College

Manchester is one of six colleges sponsored by the Church of the Brethren and "is considered to have the closest ties with the church." The Articles of Association provide explicitly for church ownership, and through election of trustees to the board, the districts of the church can exercise control if they are so inclined. Over half of the faculty are Brethren, and a third of the student body.

Is this, then, a tight, even rigid, relationship in which the church-and-campus faithful gather for mutual protection, embattled against an alien world? Such a statement could hardly be further from the truth. Manchester feels it is open and free, and church and college give every appearance of a happy and productive partnership, nondefensive in their attitude toward the society they serve.

Some of the college's strengths bear out this feeling. Opportunities for worship and scholarly study are of high caliber, and the Convocation Series, an "extensive yearly schedule . . . sponsored by the college as part of its liberal arts emphasis," is impressive. Contacts with the churches are frequent and intimate, and their support is generous. "Interest in social service dominates the Manchester campus," and the almost-thirty-year-old Peace Studies Program is nationally known, having become "a model for similar programs in other colleges."

One of the favorite words at Manchester is "caring": students use it to describe the campus life and its "personal support system," and the college itself, in its statement of purpose, speaks of managing both its educational and business affairs "in a humane and caring way." Emphasis in the statement is placed on

> . . . the importance of acquiring an appreciation for those values which have always been traditional in the Church of the Brethren, such as social justice, a "caring" community, tolerance and international interdependence.[7]

Yet Manchester has a few problems in church-relatedness and its implications. First, structure: Those who feel "that the church's involvement . . . should be one of 'partnership rather than control'" have worked "toward the loosening of legal ties," and several of the Brethren colleges have recently made charter revisions. "This was interpreted by some as a pulling away from the church," but in the past two years denominational conferences on higher education have softened the issue and encouraged "more involvement" but less control by the church.

"One of the major concerns of Brethren people who support the college is the life-style of the students": drugs, sex, alcohol, and the usual sins that collegiate flesh is heir to. But the incidence of these indiscretions seems considerably less than at most other colleges, and a more serious question is the relative lack of student initiative and leadership. There is, for example, "no student government"; there is, instead, a Community Council, on which students serve in majority but don't feel they run. Nor do they run the Community Court. Our visitors reported that two officers of the college laid this lack of initiative (although, they said, not apathy or lack of participation) to "the nature of the Brethren . . . not to 'accept honors'" or to raise themselves above others, though they will perform "a specific task exceedingly well."

The ethos of Manchester, then, is determined in considerable part by its intimacy with the church, but it is not easy to know whether that relationship is independent of, or how much it has been molded by, the longtime president, Blair Helman. His is a strong rule, though benevolent, and he "sees his role mainly as an interpreter of the church to the college and of the college to the church." The "lengthened shadow" style of academic administration may make for problems of continuity, but there is no gainsaying the success of Dr. Helman, and of his wife, often mentioned, in keeping Manchester and the Brethren in close, informed, and mutually beneficial alliance.

Morris Brown

Morris Brown, academically, is part of the Atlanta University complex of institutions and ecclesiastically is related to the African Methodist Episcopal, or AME, Church. Now and again the question may arise as to whether Morris Brown will stay in the Atlanta University consortium, but no serious doubt has arisen about its remaining a keystone in the AME structure.

The reason for this is not hard to find historically. It turns, among other things, on the level of sacrifice of the supporting constituency. Other denominations more affluent than the AME Church may give larger sums to their colleges, but in Morris Brown's case the church as a whole and especially the Georgia congregations have tradition-ally been generous in regular giving according to their means ($200,000–$250,000 annually) and quick to respond to crises, such as a recent dormitory fire.

The college "expects homely love offerings" from the church, and "everybody felt good about" the church's gift of $22,000 to pay for the temporary housing of the students in a local hotel after the fire. In response, the college accepts the burden of educating overseas students, many of whom are "sent, unfunded," by their AME bishops. An open-door admissions policy that leads "church members [to] expect the school to absorb the cost of education" puts an even greater strain on the budget. Ninety-five percent of Morris Brown's students are on some financial aid, and 50 percent receive total aid.

The church seems to be "generally satisfied" with the existing relationships—or so officers of the college believe. The usual provisions are present: courses in religion, Religious Emphasis Week, worship services. Impositions are few: the chairman of the board no longer has to be (though he still is) the resident bishop, the bishop no longer lives on the campus, and quotas of AME's are not set for faculty positions. If church officers are sometimes "concerned with . . . student yells at the football games" or even more serious shenanigans, surely this is nothing new. Our visitors were struck more by the seeming disinclination of either party, college or church, to examine the matter of church-relatedness in depth. The fundamental relationship seems to have changed very little in recent years.

But this state of affairs is not apt to continue. Pressures for change are coming, indeed have already been felt, from at least four sources: the Southern Association of Colleges and Schools, the federal government, Ford and other foundations, and "student militancy." In diverse ways their growing influence will probably work toward lessening the influence of the church, unless some revitalization takes place. The most promising recent development is the formation by the ten AME post-secondary schools (including seminaries and junior colleges) of the Association of Institutions of Higher

Education (AIHE), which is a coordinating agency under collegiate control. If the AIHE does its job, Morris Brown and the others are likely to be better financed, better managed, more independent of the church, but still loyally affiliated.

St. Augustine's College

St. Augustine's is an institution of the Episcopal Church, though one would not know it from the composition of the student body (about 18 percent Episcopalian). It might escape notice on other grounds as well. For example, the college has no Department of Religion and thus no major in the subject; courses on religion are tucked inconspicuously into other departments. The relationship is "tenuous," "traditional," and seemingly not demanding in any form.

Yet the college "recognizes its historic ties to the Episcopal Church" and feels it "would be the loser if the ties were severed." The church makes an annual gift of around $300,000; but more, it serves "as a buttress against complete encroachment by the federal government, the largest source of . . . support." Perhaps the greatest loss, if the two became separated, would be the feeling that the underpinnings of the college's "family style," "the sense of belonging," and other treasured values would be weakened. As the vice-president for academic affairs put it, "The value-oriented system would be lost," in curriculum and in campus life.

In spite of "appreciation" for the relationship, however, the prevailing view at the college seems to be that closeness of association with the church is a thing of the past, never to be revived. St. Augustine's sees its future as depending on government funds, largely federal; and if it had to choose between church and state, as it thinks it may, the choice might go against the church. "The college has gone beyond the point of no return with regard to public funding; it could not survive long at all without it." The sad conclusion our visitors reached was that, though the vestige of a connection is still "useful" and "prudential," there seems to be little evidence "that this College is consciously taking sustained account of its church-relatedness or giving very much thought recently to the question."

College of St. Thomas

The College of St. Thomas is an institution of the Roman Catholic

Archdiocese of St. Paul and Minneapolis, governed by a self-perpetuating board of which the archbishop is the ex officio chairman. Of the roughly two hundred and fifty Catholic colleges in the United States, St. Thomas is one of only twelve diocesan establishments.

That the college is "intimately related to the life of the archdiocese" there is no doubt, but the nature of this relationship is variously understood among various members of the two organizations. As our visitors reported:

> There were some who were confident that the archdiocese did (and, in the minds of some, should) exercise authority over all aspects of the life of the college, and that any attempts by the college to develop independently could (and, in the minds of some, should) be quickly halted. . . . On the other hand, there were persons—especially but not exclusively within the faculty—who described the control of the church as "nominal" or "irrelevant," and the archbishop as chairman of the board a "figurehead. . . . "

In the main, prevailing opinion seems to be that church control, though "real," is "general in nature" and "sporadic."

Differences in regard to the nature of the church-college connection take on sharper edges with respect to the related question as to whether and in what ways St. Thomas is perceived to be Catholic in program and spirit, not just in government and structure. The range of opinions is considerable. The main-line position of "those in authority" is represented by a recent well-publicized statement of the Long Range Planning Committee, which reads in part:

> As a Catholic institution . . . St. Thomas offers, as one of its major purposes, formal instruction in Sacred Scripture, Catholic theology, and religious education. Centrally allied to this purpose is the coordinated effort to involve all members and friends of the College community in creating a stimulating environment for experiencing through worship, through fellowship, and through service, the teachings of the Gospel and the mission of the Church.[8]

To people who agree roughly with this statement, therefore, the college is Catholic in all the usual ways: origin, legal status, composition of faculty and student body (largely but not over-whelmingly Catholic), curricular requirements, liturgical services, and public image.

Those who are dissatisfied are not of one mind. At one extreme are a few who feel that St. Thomas is "sadly deficient as a Catholic college" because its orthodoxy is suspect. In this view, a true Catholic institution "teaches the doctrine of the church and does not teach the contrary." St. Thomas, therefore, is too liberal.

Most of the dissidents are in the opposite camp, feeling that the college is too conservative. Though theology is "loose," philosophy is "extremely rigid, with only courses in St. Thomas Aquinas available." Yet "liberal" and "conservative" are relatively meaningless terms in this connection, and points of view are not polarized around them. Take, for example, the opinion that St. Thomas's Catholicity "is traditional only": it may be held alternatively by those who approve and those who deplore.

A Committee to Examine the Religious Nature (CERN) of the college "is now operating actively," produced by and producing in its turn a "healthy, creative" ferment of diverse attitudes and desires. The aim of the committee, however, is not to determine whether St. Thomas is too much or too little of this or that but to express "a concern for general spiritual renewal," in accord with the above statement of the Long Range Planning Committee. The conclusion of this matter is simply that St. Thomas is patently and proudly Catholic, but there is a wide spectrum of opinion as to what this means.

"This confusion about the Catholic nature of the college was particularly marked when related to two specific areas, the selection and reappointment of personnel and the development of new educational programs." When faculty are hired, are their "religious and moral convictions," or even "ecclesiastical relationships," examined carefully? Are new programs established primarily to serve the church and the community or to balance the budget? Such questions receive varying answers from responsible college officials.

Here, then, is an urban institution, three-fourths of whose students are commuters, which is having to face most of the secular pressures of the day and some difficult ecclesiastical or religious ones as well. Its being puzzled by many of the problems of church-related institutions generally has not led it to seek an illusory escape; and as St. Thomas continues to strive for clarification of nature, goal, and program, it has the promise of attaining new strength.

Seattle University

Seattle University, back to back with St. Thomas as the other Roman Catholic institution in our list, is thought by a few purists to be not church related at all, at least in the usual sense. It is Jesuit; and having what some regard as "no structural relationship to the Catholic Church," it falls into a category different from diocesan colleges and perhaps from those of other religious orders. A high-ranking lay administrator at Seattle described the university as, in turn, "private, Christian, Catholic, and Jesuit"; but our visitors felt that "those terms overlap and are not clearly distinguished in anyone's mind."

The "Jesuit mystique" shows itself or is explained in a variety of ways. Organically, Seattle "communicates with its church primarily through the rector of the local Jesuit community and the Jesuit provincial. It has virtually no contact with the local bishop." Thus it has a sense of freedom in its organization and program "from orthodox shackles" and "from a narrow Catholic education." "The strong liberal arts tradition of the Jesuits" is the basis of the curriculum, and our visitors could find no evidence "of coercion or restriction of thought." Something less than 20 percent of the faculty are Jesuits, although they occupy most of the power positions in the administration and the key posts in the philosophy and theology departments. Ten hours of course work in religious studies are required of all undergraduate students. The aim of the university, as our visitors reported, is

> . . . to carry out the difficult task of providing young people with an educational experience which combines intellectual development of high quality with maximum opportunity for spiritual growth in a Christian atmosphere.

"Jesuit," "Catholic," and "Christian" all come into play, therefore, in defining the religious character of the institution. A narrowed focus of sponsorship may make for a broader perspective. In other words, Seattle's relationship with the Society of Jesus may explain why some observers feel the university "is more conscious of itself as Christian than as specifically Catholic" and why the more imprecise term is often used to describe the institution's nature or program. Such a tendency is probably encouraged by the fact that over half of both the faculty and student body are non-Catholics and by the presence down the street of a mammoth, secular competitor, the University of Washington. The atmosphere of the place, however, is not one of neutrality or unspecified piety; it is "Jesuit Catholicity with its characteristic humanism that makes Seattle 'distinctive.'"

The danger, as some Jesuits see it, "is that the pendulum swing might go too far, . . . might result in complete secularization." The proportion of Roman Catholics in both student body and faculty is falling, and financial stringencies will hardly halt the slide—except that getting more Jesuits on the faculty would be fiscally desirable if it could be managed, because they do not receive lay salaries. Finances may also explain why, in the view of some campus leaders, "the university is being forced to be more vocational" in courses of study offered—business, nursing, engineering, journalism, etc.—thereby weakening the longtime liberal arts emphasis.

This opinion, however, is vigorously resisted by Seattle's new president, William J. Sullivan, S. J., from St. Louis University. He argues that the university has not sold out to vocational interests but is engaged in that kind of "professional and career-related education" that is quite consistent with a liberal arts core. Our visitors reported that "this is surely the biggest conflict on campus": whether the "liberal arts emphasis," the "cultural tradition," and the "sense of community," in all of which the Jesuits take pride, can survive and perhaps redeem the financial exigencies ahead.

"The word 'community' was on virtually everyone's lips," according to our visitors, and the university works hard to make it something more than mere camaraderie. The campus ministry, staffed only by Catholics, is highly praised; and though it suffers the twin handicaps of a "minuscule budget" and a student body two-thirds of whom are commuters, it is playing a major rule in giving a Catholic tone to the campus. Such things as liturgical experiments (e.g., "a highly touted Saturday midnight mass"), the "Search" program for students, a "renewal" program for faculty, a community service program called "Reach Out" are evidences of the vitality of the campus ministry. "The issue of the Catholic character of Seattle University," says Father Sullivan, "is very much alive," and if there are clouds in the future, there are also signs of bright promise that the university will continue to represent creditably the church and the order.

West Virginia Wesleyan

West Virginia Wesleyan is United Methodist in its ecclesiastical allegiance, but that by itself tells as little about the college as does the general Catholic label for St. Thomas or Seattle. Neither ecclesiastical camp flies a single delimiting banner to which all institutional followers must repair, and the liberty for self-definition is, if anything, greater among the Methodists. But if the ends of the Methodist spectrum are far apart, the Wesleyan of West Virginia is pretty close to the center, all things considered.

The chief facts of the structural relationship are quickly told. The West Virginia Annual Conference of the church elects the college's Board of Trustees in meetings that take place on the campus. Half of the forty-member board are laity, which leaves a full twenty who are clergy. Since the recent defection of Morris Harvey from the Methodist fold, West Virginia Wesleyan is the only institution of the church in the state. It receives something over $200,000 annually from the conference's subvention, together with a $20,000 nugget from the Pittsburgh conference as well. There are plenty of organic ties.

There are plenty of atmospheric relations, too. In recent years "the campus has twice . . . been made aware of the role of the Board of Trustees." One of these occasions had to do with the "alcohol issue," long an inflammatory subject in Methodist circles. A recent president felt it would be helpful to clarify the rules, for "there had been considerable confusion among the students as to just what was and what was not allowed." The board went along, but the Annual Conference raised questions; and the outcome was that a committee of college and conference personnel "after long hard work" produced an acceptable policy. The undeserved result seems to have been that many students and faculty got the impression that only such things as drinking are "religious issues" of sufficient importance to catch the church's attention.

The other recent occasion for campus realization of the importance of their trustees had to do with pressures brought upon various public and private institutions to compromise their academic freedom in favor of one or another witch-hunt of the moment. Some other schools succumbed, but the college's "board acted as a strong bulwark for academic freedom." Moreover, it was the group of ministers particularly who "represented the liberal element" on the board, and their "defense of academic freedom was rooted in the clergy's religious training." At least in West Virginia, Methodist clergy "tend to be liberal politically, even though they are conservative socially." The Wesleyan community is sophisticated enough to applaud the one and deplore the other. Unfortunately, however, the church, or at least the board informed and prompted by the church, doesn't get credit for the one but bears the blame for the other. In this regard it should be noted that there is "an atmosphere of free inquiry" at the college (and along with it a "warmth in dealing with members of the community as individuals") that stems consciously from the religious rootage of the institution.

The "recent president" mentioned above is Jay Rockefeller, the present governor and, as John D. IV, scion of that remarkable American family; and he was Wesleyan's president from 1973 to 1975, one of six chief executives of the college in the past eight years. Whether Rockefeller sought "to change WVWC into a more secular, more diverse institution" is moot; but it seems clear that the effect of his regime was to "put the question of church-relatedness front and center," so that his successors became and are dedicated to the strengthening of "its close ties to the Methodist Church [and] its role as West Virginia Methodism's own college." The incumbent, President Fred Harris, is especially well fitted for this task, for he has just come from being the denomination's chief executive officer for that part of its Board of Higher Education and Ministry that deals with its colleges and universities.

Yet the college can't be what it once was. After all, it had only 500 students twenty years ago and has 1,800 now. Changes have been immense, rapid, and not fully digested, and leadership has often been "inchoate." Although the Department of Religion is first rate, perhaps "the strongest . . . on campus academically," it is sometimes criticized "for being too liberal amid conservative pietistic students." On some points, the college seems ahead of its constituency; on others, behind. More non-Methodists in the faculty and student body, the search for "new student sources and new kinds of funding," the need for "a stabilized administration"—these aspects of the present scene could represent "secularizing trends." The chances are strong, however, in spite of serious problems now and over the horizon, that one of the college's characteristics of the new day "will be . . . a Methodist church relationship as fundamental."

Whitworth College

Nearly every institution that owns to some church relationship will speak of itself at least occasionally as a Christian college. Whitworth does so consistently. In fact, it proudly proclaims its "theme" to be Jesus Christ:

> When we state that Whitworth's "theme" is Jesus Christ, we mean far more than having an institutional tie with the United Presbyterian Church, USA. As a college community, we seek to affirm by thoughtful inquiry and responsible action the Biblical and historic faith proclaimed by the church. . . .[9]

The college means for "the Christian faith and its expression [to be] understood in all its richness and variety," to the end that "every student should have an opportunity seriously to consider the Christian faith during his or her college years."[10]

The rhetoric is backed up with action. Curricular provisions include two requirements, "a core course . . . on the Judeo-Christian tradition" and one in biblical literature, and "other disciplines also attempt to bring in Christian values and perspectives." Perhaps the most unusual feature of the Christian emphasis is the work of the chaplain. His office has seven full-time employees for a student body of approximately 1,200, and it runs a varied and well-received program, which does not include required chapel, given up several years ago. The chaplain is "minister to the whole college, not just to students." All in all, our visitors felt that "there is a strong sense of Christian faith on the campus."

Such a development elsewhere has sometimes been at the expense of close relations with an individual denomination. Whitworth, however, wants to be genuinely church related as well as Christian; and President Edward B. Lindaman, a layman and formerly head of the National Council of United Presbyterian Men, has been "clearly wooing the church more than the church is seeking Whitworth as its partner." The reasons are not limited to getting students and financial support, though the college can use both. (The formal tie is with the Alaska-Northwest Synod, over 200 of whose churches give around $200,000 annually.) Lindaman and others want Whitworth to be a partner with the Presbyterians because they believe the college has much to offer to the church—preparing future lay people, teaching, lending faculty expertise, sponsoring special programs—and in its turn the college "needs a theological base" which only the church can provide.

Alongside the college theme is its "goal," which is "human development." A promotional brochure explains:

> The College directs its entire program to help learners attain their maximum potential as healthy, competent individuals. As in the past, this primarily means intellectual competence. But Whitworth also emphasizes learning experiences which foster emotional, physical and spiritual growth. . . .[11]

Thus the college marshals all the student-service and campus-betterment efforts into one concerted push. Understanding and cooperation were sought at the beginning, with a two-week, all-faculty workshop in the summer of 1973. Since then the Student Development Center, which quarterbacks the program, has increased in size and budget comparably with the chaplain's office. Goal and theme march forward together.

But as on all campuses there are, predictably, tensions. Some that seem to have force or substance or both:

1) Human development vs. Christian faith: Does the former make the college "too humanistic"?

2) Human development and Christian faith vs. academic and intellectual interests: Has the academic program been neglected because the new and better-financed emphases have been "oversold"?

3) Whitworth has a goal and a theme but no "mission"—"an educational response to the needs and problems of society."

4) "Conservative vs. liberal expressions of Christianity" in faith and morals.

5) The "financial crunch": There is wide consensus that ". . . most of the disagreements and unhappiness are caused by a difficult financial situation."

To about 1962, Whitworth was "very conservative" for a Presbyterian institution, being said to have had "a fundamentalist image." Between then and Lindaman's coming in 1970, "the college took on a more secular direction." Now the effort is to find a right balance, neither to let secular drift go unchallenged nor to return to an outmoded conservatism. The task is not easy. It means strengthening old ties, embarking on new programs, resolving tensions. But Whitworth is determined to show it can be done.

Wittenberg University

In recent years the Lutheran Church in America "has made a concerted effort . . . to clarify and where possible to strengthen the relationship with LCA colleges." One important evidence is the establishment of covenants between the colleges and their supporting synods, which in Wittenberg's case are two, Ohio and Indiana-Kentucky. The covenants "are meant to be reviewed at regular intervals," says the church, for they define the current "expectations" of each party to the pact.

> The Indiana-Kentucky and Ohio Synods accept and sustain a supporting relationship to Wittenberg University . . . as a recognized College of the Church, with a three-fold concern for its character as a Christian institution of learning, its academic excellence and its material welfare. Wittenberg University acknowledges and welcomes this supportive relationship. . . .[12]

Whereupon the document proceeds to list eleven commitments of the college and seven of the synod in service to each other. For those who are interested in the data of support, let it be noted that about 25 percent of Wittenberg's students are Lutherans, and gifts totaling more than $250,000 annually come from the two synods or related Lutheran sources.

When a college is close to its church, it turns on more than merely a solemn covenant solemnly arrived at. At the present time, Wittenberg "is working hard at . . . rebuilding its ties to the church." However it happened, "there was too much drift and uncertainty on this question in the recent past." But though "it is not easy to rebuild a strong church relationship," President William A. Kinnison is exercising vigorous leadership to that end, in all the usual ways of increased contact and mutual appreciation.

Even if "the drift is over," it is instructive to take note of its nature. Ten years or so ago the college adopted "a deliberate policy to enhance the academic quality of the institution." This meant, among other things, the encouragement of "a diversity of viewpoints among the faculty" and the appointment of teachers without regard to their religious affiliation or concern. "In one year alone forty new faculty members were added to the university." The result was that "this striving toward academic excellence was done at the expense of a strong church-college orientation among the faculty." Our visitors reported that "a number of faculty still see a dichotomy between a religious stance and high academic quality." But the danger seems not to be great, for now that the college has indeed strengthened its intellectual life, it is "more self-confident about emphasizing its religious basis."

Whether or in what way the desire for academic distinction has affected the performance of the Religion Department is uncertain. The department "is regarded by most as competent but not outstanding" and "has bent over backwards to assume an academically respectable posture." One course in religion, with a wide choice, is the requirement. It is well in the past that "the department considered itself an arm of the church and operated something like a high level Sunday School." Now the complaints are different: that the department has "no regard for . . . the fragmentation of students' faith" in its courses and that the meager requirement, which can be met by a course in some non-Western religion, fails to guarantee that students "can . . . become theologically literate in the Christian religion."

It is also true that "the role of the chaplain at Wittenberg is not an easy one." His assignments are heavy and include "the duty of representing the church to various groups within the college, often by himself." That he is widely respected is a considerable tribute.

Wittenberg, then, struggles to be both church related and academically strong, and it believes these two should not be in conflict. To move ahead in both respects takes careful thought. This has recently been given by the Commission on Mission and Priorities, with the president's firm backing and broad membership from the campus community. The report says:

> Wittenberg University accepts partnership with the church as proposed in the LCA rationale and embraces the church's commitment to academic freedom, to religious diversity, and to academic excellence.[13]

Then the report quotes approvingly from the LCA rationale statement, *The Basis for Partnership Between Church and College,* a statement which can apply to more than the Lutheran Church in America and Wittenberg and thus perhaps can serve as an appropriate end to these fourteen college examples:

> There is substantial advantage . . . when the church as an institution can join with another institution, such as a college, which has its own demonstrated competence and stability. This steady collegiality allows for continuing dialogue, interaction, and mutual service. There is also the advantage of the colleague institution's own access to and impact upon society. It is good not to be alone, and to have more than transient allies, when participating in a complex world.[14]

Is any one of these fourteen a model of church-relatedness? Not exactly.

Yet lest that negative judgment suggest a loss of heart, let it be quickly noted that it really isn't negative at all. One does not need to call upon the old saw that a model is "a small imitation of the real thing." Rather, one simply remembers that every college is *sui generis*. No campus in this country is like any other, not even some fast-growing community institution that seems to have been stamped out of a collegiate assembly line. Least of all is a college a private creation, independent of city, state, and nation and often straining at the leash of its ecclesiastical founder. Let it not be imagined, therefore, that the point of this chapter is to say to go and do like Goshen or to simulate one of the Saints. Such an effort won't be worth a whit.

But from any one of our fourteen, and from many another church-related institution as well, much can be learned about what it means to try to establish and maintain a vital church connection. And from noting even briefly a wide diversity of institutions, we begin to get some hints of what are the essentials of church-relatedness, as distinct from the superficialities and irrelevancies. To try to record those impressions is the task of the next chapter.

NOTES—Chapter 3

[1] "The Covenant Relationship for Austin College and the Synod of Red River Presbyterian Church in the United States," mimeographed, undated, p. 1.

[2] "Institutional Profile."

[3] Earl J. McGrath, *Study of Southern Baptist Colleges and Universities, 1976–77* (Nashville: Education Commission of the Southern Baptist Convention, 1977), p. 20.

[4] *The Character and Values of Furman University,* undated brochure.

[5] *Ibid.*

[6] *Ibid.*

[7] "Statement of Purpose," Manchester College.

[8] "Statement of the Long Range Planning Committee," College of St. Thomas.

[9] *Whitworth College Catalog—1977-78* (Spokane: Whitworth College, 1977), p. 61.

[10] *Ibid.*

[11] Promotional brochure, Whitworth College.

[12] "Covenant," Wittenberg University.

[13] *Report of the Commission on Mission and Priorities* (Springfield, Ohio: Wittenberg University, June 24, 1977), p. 15.

[14] *The Basis for Partnership Between Church and College: A Statement of the Lutheran Church in America* (New York: Division for Mission in North America, Lutheran Church in America, 1976), p. 3.

CHAPTER 4

Essentials of
Church-Relatedness

It may not be amiss, at the outset of this chapter, to remind ourselves of the aim of this whole exercise. We aren't arguing the superiority of one type of institution over another—private over tax supported, or church related over independent, or any one of three kinds of church-related institutions, the Ally, the Witness, or the Reflection, over the others. We take as given, though not immutable, the fact that a college is church related, already identified or claimed as such; and we ask: What is it that makes this so? What are the essentials of church-relatedness, lacking which the identification or the claim turns out to be false?

Now that we have cleared some nonessentials out of the way— superficialities, irrelevancies, myths (Chapter 1)—and now that we have looked at categories (Chapter 2) and even at a few individual specimens of church-relatedness (Chapter 3), it is time to put down what seems to be requisite. Because we are dealing with two organizational entities, the college and the church, we will need to note the essentials for each in turn and then, in conclusion, for both together.

The number is small. After all, not many elements are absolutely indispensable for the whole company of church-sponsored institutions, though a much larger number might be desirable, or fairly widespread, or even necessary for one or another denomination. Not everything that can be imagined or that some churches require will be noted. Even for those few items listed, we shall necessarily deal in generalized statements, the particularities of which will often differ from one to another institution or group. It is a minimum list; but don't let the generality of language with which the elements are described fool you; it is also a demanding list. The number of determinants to be mentioned is only eight.

Essentials for the College

Back when we were setting up the spectrum of church-related colleges (Chapter 2), the minimum definition with which we got started was that "it needs to be an institution that, first, puts forth some sort of claim to being connected with a church and, second, supports that claim with some sort of observable action that makes the claim credible." Now we need to put meat on those bare bones.

1. *To be church related, a college must want to be* and aim to be so related. There must be on the part of the college a *conscious intention* to achieve and maintain a continuing relationship with a church or perhaps churches and a significant measure of *congruence* among the constituent groups of the college in their understanding of this intention. This is the necessary point of beginning; and no matter that a denomination were to covet a college deeply, if that college wants none of it, that is the effective end.

The relationship, as we have already noted, can be of various sorts. It may, but need not, be an organic or structural tie. The particular embodiment of the relationship that one college might want, or accept, might be anathema to another. The institutional sketches in the preceding chapter illustrated the possible diversity. The thing that matters is that it be a genuine, valid relationship, irrespective of the form it takes.

If genuine, then the college will communicate its desire to the church. That is, it would be expected that the college would express clearly in official documents and publications its *intentionality of relationship*. Further, it goes without saying that the college's willingness to own to a connection should make it respectful of the church and its representations. How strange it would be, though not impossible, for a college to cherish an affiliation with a church for which it had no respect.

It would be expected, further, that if the college is sincere, it would find an appropriate way to proclaim its intentions not only to the church but also to the general public. Here, of course, is the problem of rhetoric, for many a church-related college methinks doth protest too much. The rhetoric must be of intention, not of achievement, or else it is likely to lose its touch with reality. Nothing is more suspect than the institution that wears its Christianity on its neon sign if not on its sleeve.

Using verbs of agency for the college raises the inevitable question of who is in fact the agent. When the institution desires, communicates, proclaims, who does it all? The president? The board? And what is the role, the share in the doing, of other individuals and groups?

The facts provide a quick answer to such questions. A vital connection with a church may indeed be, but isn't always and doesn't have to be, the work of the board, or the president, or the chaplain, or any other one person or group. Note, again, the preceding campus sketches. The conscious intent is, in fact, strongest when it is shared in at least some degree among all the constituent groups of the college. There needs to be a *congruence* as well as an intentionality about a college's church-relatedness. The indices and perceptions about being connected with a church will change from place to place and time to time, but the common commitment must remain.

2. *To be church related, a college must make proper provision for religion in all its dimensions*, in at least rough harmony with the views of its sponsoring denomination.

This summary sentence will strike any strong partisan as bland. It doesn't specify how much, what kind, by whom, when, and where; and many church-related college people are of a mind to argue the particularities. Argue is the right word, for the particularities would differ from church to church and school to school. Consensus on the details of religious provisions would be almost impossible to reach.

But the basic proposition must still be affirmed: A college can't pretend to be church related if it doesn't provide for the presence of religion in all appropriate ways in the campus life.

Perhaps the premise of this position should be made explicit: that churches and thus *church-related colleges* have or *ought to have something to do with religion.* It is not undebatable, I suppose, in either fact or theory; and I enjoy my own biases sufficiently to be moved to confess that there are *some* churches, together with their colleges, that have little to do with religion, as I would like to define it. But this isn't an exercise to suit my taste, and we're looking instead for the point of view that can bring people together.

In regard to religion, at least two affirmations would seem to be common to all churches and their colleges: that *there is an ultimate source* of all life, and that *all humankind are kin.* Put into the form of a minimal religious directive, with traditional language, these insights become the twofold command to love God and neighbor. Some institutions think the government won't let them love God—at least not if the deity is called that—and others seem not to want to love neighbor. Well and good, if that is their choice. But they can hardly claim church relationship unless they can show that their churches, too, support the unloving stance—which surely is nonsense, isn't it? Religion will mean much, much more to any believer, even those on college campuses, but it dare not mean less.

The newswriter for a group of self-styled "evangelical" schools called the Christian College Consortium saw a brief release of the National Council of Churches that mentioned the eight "characteristics essential to church relatedness" here being discussed and noted that "not one of them mentions God or Christ."[1] Even if he had read this chapter, however, he and his cohorts would still not be mollified, for they want to exclude, whereas the aim of this essay is to include. A theological or Christological point of view peculiar to some one or another denomination may indeed be reflected (though sometimes may not be) in that church's colleges, but the effort to make all "Christian" colleges fit some particular God-and-Christ formula ends by merely being divisive.

Our basic proposition about provisions for religion has some inescapable implications. First, and as was noted in an earlier chapter, the church-related college will *take the study of religion seriously.* This one ought not to be too difficult as a general item in our catalogue, for after all a college's business is study and its subject matter includes all main disciplines of thought and work, of which religion is one in nearly everybody's reckoning.

But here is one of the chief temptations to particularity. One college says, "The department must be as good as any other"; another treats all subjects alike and may not even have a specific department of religion. One says, "We gotta have requirements"; another says, "Requirements don't fit our curricular pattern." One says, "The Bible must be studied with the most advanced scholarship available"; another says, "The Bible is to be believed as it is, without interpretation or embroidery." The nub of the matter is this: So far as I can see, there is no one formula for the study of religon that all church-related colleges could ever agree on or that would fit all traditions. Look again at the diversity displayed in Chapter 3. The only universally applicable proposition is that some kind of study befitting the denominational bent and / or the college's understanding is essential. To say less is preposterous if church-relatedness is to mean anything at all. To say more is impossible, in light of the diverse points of view of colleges and churches.

Yet we aren't quite done with the study of religion, for a strange kind of ghost needs to be put to rest. It is sometimes said that the greater the theological sophistication of the department, the lesser the strength of the church tie. So what is taken as strength? Subservience to an unsophisticated stance in the church? But if a church wants first-rate scholarship, then surely its presence in one of its colleges makes the church glad. In some one instance, to be sure, the statement might be true; but in some other, even in the same denomination, it might be false. In any event, if the church-relatedness of the institution is to be valid, the facts don't seem to justify our adding to our propositions either "The department must be strong," or "The department must be weak."

A second implication of the insistence that a church-affiliated college must provide properly for religion is that it will *take worship seriously*. Again, specifics as to time, leadership, desirable decibel level, or anything else are out of place. Our fourteen examples do a bit of everything, including almost nothing—and a college that itself does nothing might still be taking worship with proper seriousness if a local church of its denomination (or of some other approved stripe) is close enough at hand to minister to the campus and if the college is encouraging that church's activity.

The point is, the college must see to it that there is such a thing as a *campus ministry* or ministries, if the institution's tradition makes it desirable. Worship and related expressions of faith may be as distantly different as are the Quakers from the Holy Rollers, but their progeny, institutional and individual, should be moved to quake and roll as their definitions of holiness require. A church college may not legitimately take a none-of-my-business attitude.

To keep from dragging this out, a third implication may as well be a grab bag: the church-related college must *take seriously other customary expressions of religion* that fit the purpose and mores of an academic institution. With this proposition (and examples in Chapter 3) in mind, colleges variously might subsidize or otherwise foster voluntary student religious activities, support positions of professional religious leadership, and develop programs of ameliorative service in the community. The possibilities are legion. Their appropriateness would need to be tested in each case. Such testing would be part of a church-related college's proper business.

Two further comments remain to be said about this second essential. First, making fitting provision for religion in the collegiate enterprise is a suitable purpose for any type of institution, including independent and even tax-supported schools, but the rationale for a church-related college must go beyond that of its secular counterparts, beyond simply wanting students to be better informed. The school that owns to a church tie must care about *preparing students for a later life* of fruitful participation *in that or some other congenial church*. Membership means different things in different traditions, of course, but the common denominator for the church-connected campus should be that its students also will continue to be church connected.

The second comment has to do with a distressing fact of the present scene, which constitutes another reason for giving religion its due. The datum is this generation's *abysmal illiteracy about Christianity* and other faiths, *about the Bible, and about the impact of religion* on society past and present. No church college ought to be expected to become its denomination's last-ditch Sunday school, but by virtue of its own institutional nature it must seek to relieve the gross religious ignorance and inexperience of its constituency.

3. *To be church related, a college must put its values and those of its church into recognizable operation* in every aspect of the life of the

institution, including the functions of scholarship, teaching, and learning, as well as in personnel practices and the campus ethos. Or, since most of us aren't anticipating the millennium anytime soon, the college must *try* to do so and give evidence that it is trying.

Two parts of this proposition need brief exposition. First is *the presence of values* and *their integration into the normal behavior* of the school. Hardly any other topic makes academic people so nervous and silent or, conversely, so pretentious and blatant. Part of the trouble is that values, conceptually, are slippery, and we hotshot academic types like to pretend that we don't know what we mean. Another part of the trouble is that, when we do get over that hurdle, we find it easier, because safer, to profess than to practice. But a church-related college, just because it is church related, has somehow got to rise above this morass and begin to ask the value-laden questions of its own performance. As the vignettes in Chapter 3 suggest, answers may differ; but the questions need to be the same or at least similar. Such as:

—What are the intellectual values that should undergird the teaching of all disciplines, not just religion? How can they be properly brought into the course of study—not hidden or ignored, not cheaply advertised?

—What are the creedal values, if any, to which the denomination feels its colleges should subscribe? Can the college do so? How?

—What are the humane values that the church and the college must espouse? Does the college live up to those values in, say, its business operations, or its policies of hiring and firing, or its dealings with parents and alumni—not to mention faculty and students?

—What are the moral values that govern the character of campus life? Are they adopted out of a concern for students, or townspeople, or the church? Out of fear, or justice, or hope of gain? Are they honored in the breach or the observance?

The questions literally are endless. The ways of responding to them are multifarious. Whatever, the church-related college can't duck.

Moreover, it must take the follow-up step of fashioning a *personnel policy that supports the college's commitment to values.* One does not need to hold, though many do, that a genuine church relationship is more dependent on persons than on policies or structures in order to believe that the quality of persons is crucially important. An institution is not really very good at valuing, any more than it is at loving or praying. It takes people to pray, to love, and to value.

But which ones? How many? How should they be chosen? And in the choosing or thereafter, can the conflict between freedom and commitment be resolved? Questions such as these divide the company of church-related colleges into diverse patterns, so that the only safe commandment for all is that a value-conscious personnel policy designed to foster the institution's most cherished principles is requisite.

We mustn't leave the matter here, however; we need to note at least some of the boundaries of the debate. For example, take the question of who are the key people for building a college's commitment to values. We need to go no further than the visits to the fourteen sites (Chapter 3) to know that the answer can be, variously, the trustees, the president, the administration in general, the faculty, and even the student body. As noted earlier (in Chapter 1), the insistence may be that all, some, or none of these persons should belong to the college's church. A recent conference on "the mission of church-related institutions," at which representatives of fourteen churches were present,

> . . . raised the issue of the percentage of students or faculty of the sponsoring denomination necessary to maintain the essential character of the institution. Some participants felt that fifty percent was the critical point at which denominational commitment was threatened. On the other hand, some felt that an institution's most Christian existence was among those not sharing its faith. . . . While most agreed that numbers are important, the majority of the group seemed to feel that attitude or sympathy toward the mission of the college was more important than strict accounting of formal affiliation.[2]

The most awkward question arises when a college determines both to seek committed people and to foster an atmosphere of freedom. Which gives way? Superficially, the Embodying Colleges, those that are the Reflection of their churches, would seem to have the advantage; for, being more tightly defined in their church relationships and usually being less concerned about academic distinction, they simply opt for homogeneity and apply the tests necessary to achieve it. Actually, however, winning the battle may mean losing the war; for what does it profit if the institution is all of one mind and thus ceases to be a college?

In this connection it may be helpful to take note of a notion current now and then, if for no other reason than to cast doubt upon it. The absurdity runs to this: that the greater the diversity—religious, ethnic, philosophical, or what-have-you—in the student body, or the faculty, or the administration, the weaker is the link between the college and the church. Maybe this is true for some monolithic agency, though even there it is debatable; but for institutions, both colleges and churches, that honor freedom and delight in it, the link might well be stronger.

A personnel policy that supports the college's commitment to values, including the value of freedom, is not easy to set up and maintain. Each college has to be pretty much a law unto itself. But it can be done. Simply as an illustration, notice how a spokesman for St. Olaf, proud of its relation to the American Lutheran Church, describes its situation. After sketching out the college's various provisions for religion and values, he concludes:

> Most importantly of all, we hire people who are committed to these matters. All the programs and money in the world cannot help us achieve our stated ideals unless most of our faculty and administration embrace them out of conviction. When we hire, we try to hire the most capable chemists, artists or deans we can find; but we hire only those who convince us that they believe in our distinctiveness as a college of the Church, and who persuade us that they cherish our ideals even if they don't share our religious and ethnic heritage.[1]

Essentials for the Church

Though our primary concern is with the college, we need to pay some attention to those essentials for church-relatedness that the denominations have within their power to control or provide. Even if colleges were to fulfill their requirements amply, the connections might not be either close or cordial if the churches failed to do their part. For any one denomination, many items would need listing; for all alike, only three essentials will be mentioned.

4. *To be church related, a college must be able to count on its church's understanding of the educational task* in which the college is engaged. This is different from whether both church and college have a well-formed rationale for their mutual relationships; that item will

be discussed in the next section. The emphasis now is on the necessity that the denomination *know* what a college is all about.

Some denominations don't seem to know, and many church men and women in other denominations are likewise laboring under false apprehensions and expectations of their colleges. The problem is so widespread that strains can and do develop in almost any church at one time or another.

The present friction in the Associate Reformed Presbyterian Church is a case in point. This small denomination has only one college, Erskine, and understandably feels quite protective of it. Recently the General Synod of the church asked the college's trustees "to require that those teaching Bible will personally affirm and teach the Scriptures as the infallible and inerrant Word of God." The Bible Department replied that to hold to inerrancy "or any other position rigidly and exclusively, not subject to study and revision, is idolatry." The faculty as a whole stated that to implement

> . . . the directives of this Synod would destroy its traditions by making adherence to a particular theological position more important than the search for truth. Neither faith nor reason could flourish in such an environment.

The college's board voted to "express to the 1978 General Synod . . . its inability to comply." The trustees "affirmed their autonomy, . . . pointing to the Synod's function as that of naming the Trustees who then must bear the responsibility for the College."[4] The moral of this: If a college can't count on its denomination's sympathetic understanding of what that particular institution feels it must be and do, then the ecclesiastical connection is in trouble.

5. *To be church related, a college must receive tangible support from its church.* Such support, as Chapter 3 indicated, is of more than one sort. It is money, to be sure, but it may also be gifts in kind, or recruitment of students, or scholarship and loan funds, or even action as *amicus curiae.* No precise amount, level, or percent of material support is mandatory. But if a church wants its protest of regard for the college to be credible, it should make enough support available to escape a charge of penury and to qualify for being thought of as generous.

6. *To be church related, a college must be made to feel that the denomination also gives it intangible support,* when needed and

justified by the institution's pursuit of its proper purposes. Intangible support is also of more than one sort. It can be both for and against; that is, it may consist variously in helping the college to serve society more effectively (e.g., encouragement to go into some neglected area of social need) or in standing firm with the college against outside militant pressures (e.g., from the John Birch Society). Whatever its peculiar purposes and self-image, a college has a job to do vis-à-vis that part of society for which it feels some sense of responsibility—a region, an age group, a minority, a profession, the adherents of a point of view. Most of the time, presumably, it can get ahead in its work without undue handicap or interference. But when difficulties and pressures arise from government, foundations, business, pseudo-patriotic groups, or a host of other sources, the affiliated church ought to be there in moral, intangible support lest the college find that understanding of the educational program and monetary support are not enough.

Essentials for Both the College and the Church

A further desideratum in church-relatedness is a mutuality of interest and supportive action between the college and the church. The two are engaged in reciprocal enterprises, and each is appreciative of the other's activity. Two of the essentials of church-relatedness are of this sort.

7. *To be church related, a college must inform and illumine its denomination* on all matters that would appear to be relevant or useful *and must welcome being informed and illumined in return.* The heart of this proposition is the simple expectation that the college should have some amount or kind of *beneficent influence* on its sponsoring church and vice versa. What's the point of a connection between the two if this much, this little, is not to be characteristic of their relationship?

As with the other items already discussed, this one is resisted by some as being unnecessary and inadvisable and is made much more extensive and explicit by others. Those academics who want none of it feel that the assumption of a special role of keeping the church fully informed puts the college in a subservient position; and, conversely, they don't much care to hear about the church. Those who want to expand the idea would be prepared for stronger language: the college should educate, or criticize, or revitalize, even redeem, the church; and, conversely, they would probably recognize that fair play dictated that the church have a similar shot at the college. The prevailing impression I get from the examples in Chapter 3, however, and from other contacts with church colleges is that most such institutions give less thought to this proposition than to any other essential mentioned and, further, that most of the limited contact is for financial and other self-serving reasons, not to inform, illumine, or exercise beneficent influence.

Yet the situation could and ought to be different. One of the case-study visitors asked, "Why is Roman Catholicism the most vital and changing denomination in contemporary America?" His answer was that Catholic colleges are responsible; they have "prepared for the renaissance by creative criticism," by producing "counterpressure groups," by leading the way in "theological sophistication" and "liturgical experimentation." Whether or not he is right about "the most vital and changing denomination," or about Catholic colleges as a whole, he has called attention to an important role of the church-related college in almost any denomination and, by implication, the college-related church.

8. We have come almost full circle. For essential number one we said that to be church related, a college must want to be. Now we say: *To be church related, a college must know* why *it wants to be so related,* and to complete the reciprocal arrangement, *the church must know why* it *wants connections with its colleges.* In other words, *each must develop a rationale for its relationship with the other.*

As we have had to recognize so many times before (and as Chapter 3 shows), the reasoned exposition would differ considerably from school to school and church to church. Thus no effort will be made here to construct a least common denominator, for if all were to have no objection, it would then be certain that none would be willing to adopt it. In any event, first-rate analyses for individual colleges are now being produced in considerable number, and first-rate minds are at work on behalf of their churches' positions. Such statements as those of Andrew Greeley for the Catholics, Thomas Trotter for the Methodists, and Wesley Hotchkiss for the United Church of Christ are adding new depth to the ongoing discussion of the meaning of church-relatedness.

Although no encompassing rationale will be attempted, a few things in general can be said. First, for something that shouldn't have to be said: Clichés, platitudes, and other superficialities will not be convincing. Any persuasive exposition by either church or college ought to be grounded in educational philosophy and theological understandings. For many, the idea of a covenant will be attractive. If few can sustain for the college the missionary or the monastic role, fewer still may be able to support the function of the college to be the humanizer of secular society; yet each of these roles may be valid for some groups and institutions. Whatever is felt to justify the ties between college and church, the distinction between a genuine rationale and a rationalization will need to be kept. Old commitments will hardly suffice, for if church-relatedness is to continue in strength, there must be a new pledge and a new involvement of the church in education and of the college in religious life. Finally, one sentence in utter sincerity is better than a treatise with tongue in cheek.

A Closing Word

These then, it is suggested, are the essentials: To be church related, a college must

1) want to be;

2) make proper provision for religion in all its dimensions;

3) put its values and those of its church into recognizable operation;

4) be able to count on its church's understanding of the educational task;

5) receive tangible support from its church;

6) be made to feel that the denomination also gives it intangible support;

7) inform and illumine its denomination and must welcome being informed and illumined in return;

8) know *why* it wants to be so related, and the church must know why *it* wants connections with its colleges. To repeat: each must develop a rationale for its relationship with the other.

Do we have any colleges that live up to this minimum prescription?

Before we attempt an answer, perhaps a translation into other categories would be useful. Suppose we were listing qualifications for educational distinction: To be academically excellent, a college must be several things, *a, b,* and *c.* Or qualifications for public support: To be tax supported, a college must do several things, *x, y,* and *z.* Each list of propositions would probably be more specific than our list, for eligibilities for tax support and even for academic excellence are subject to more precise definition and measurement than are those for church-relatedness. Yet in each of these imaginary cases, if one were to ask whether any colleges qualified, it would have to be pointed out that many of the listed items were matters of degree, not kind. There are degrees in academic excellence; there are even degrees in respect to what being tax supported means.

Is it to be wondered at, then, that church-relatedness is a matter not of absoluteness but of degree? A college is never absolutely, completely church related. It is always less or more church related

than it was last year;

than it intends to be next year;

than its denomination thinks it is, or wants it to be;

than is some other college of its denomination;

than are colleges connected with other denominations, etc., etc.

It should not pain us to realize that no college complies fully with the list of essentials we have drawn up. They *are* essential for a genuine church-related college to aim for, but they are likely always to elude complete fulfillment.

Is church-relatedness, then, a good thing? Surely the answer is yes. America wants and needs a pluralistic system of higher education, a sensitivity to moral and religious values, a commitment to freedom, an emphasis on personal worth. Church-related higher education cannot claim sole ownership of these benefits, but it can show its devotion to them. Whether the Ally, the Witness, or the Reflection of its denomination, the church-affiliated institution deserves the support of its church, its community, and the general public.

It was at this point that the first draft of this manuscript ended. Under the aegis of the sponsoring Study/Action Committee of the National Council of Churches, a weekend discussion of the first drafts of all chapters commissioned for this volume was held at Wingspread, the quarters of the Johnson Foundation outside Racine, Wisconsin, on November 18-20, 1977. Representatives of the boards of higher education of all participating denominations and officials of all colleges to which site visits were paid swelled the group of critics to approximately fifty, and I fully expected some fireworks.

But mighty little happened, as far as my draft was concerned. Needless to say, some dissatisfaction was expressed here and there about choice of wording or of illustration; and I have not uniformly ignored all such sensitivities: several colorful phrases and anecdotes have been cut out. The presidents or other officers of a few of the colleges visited have questioned, either at Wingspread or by letter, some points of view of their visitors or interpretations of my own; and in most instances a happy resolution of the difference was arrived at and incorporated in the essay. So far as I know, grousing around the fringes of the meeting seems to have been at a minimum, and I can only report my astonished gratitude for the generous reception my first draft received.

This is not to suggest that the respondents and others had nothing of substance to say. On the contrary, they made some important emphases or fresh observations, such as:

—To speak of church-relatedness largely from the point of view of the college is to leave out an important ingredient of the whole question, namely, the church's understanding of the educational task. Since this was not the assignment for my paper, it remains as a challenging question for the next stage of the inquiry.

—What is the relevance of church-relatedness for the college's survival? Any generalization would be extremely shaky, for even with the fourteen institutions to which site visits were paid the answers would have to run all the way from "none" to "complete."

—What is the relevance of church-relatedness for the college's being able or willing to play a role of leadership in its community or toward the solution of some of society's grave problems? The answers would have to be similarly broad and indeterminative.

—What is the relevance of church-relatedness for a college's having now and then to fend off various pressures from the surrounding society? This is somewhat the obverse of the preceding question. When a college must assert its academic freedom, or that of its professors, does its church-relatedness affect the issue one way or the other? The answer seems to be: Sometimes pro, sometimes con, most often neither way.

—The "vision of partnership" between college and church must be sufficiently realistic to take into account and seek to overcome the "vision of adversariness" that sometimes exists.

—As Wesley Hotchkiss said at Wingspread, "We have learned to live with our pluralism." There is "one continuum," one line on the chart, and we are happily seeing an end to the time when all church-related colleges were not on one line. Strong examples and weak examples can be found all along the spectrum, of course, and gradations are ever present; but only a small number of extremists are any longer trying to reserve the line for themselves alone.

A query of a longtime friend, made privately, provokes me to one last comment. He said, "What made you change your attitude? In your little book, *The Protestant Stake in Higher Education,* you were quite critical of church-related colleges. Now you seem to think they have a chance. How did you get converted?"

It drove me back to my brochure written in 1961. One answer to his question is that I think his memory failed him. *The Protestant Stake in Higher Education* came out with an affirmation, albeit somewhat muted; its conclusion was that church-related colleges

> . . . can serve as forerunner for all the rest; they can go further and be more explicit about the fundamental premises. . . . can become the conscience for the totality of higher education; . . . can be truly faithful to the meaning of education itself—that it is devoted to the discovery and spread of knowledge, to the activity of the mind, and to the relevance of knowledge and thought for the whole life of man.[5]

But a more thoughtful answer would be that both the times and I have changed, the times considerably and my opinions at least in degree. Since the early sixties, nearly every denomination has reviewed its collegiate progeny both critically and helpfully, and nearly every church-related college has been challenged, bribed, or shamed into looking candidly at its church connection or has done so on its own without outside stimulation. Things, therefore, are different.

And the differences, I think, are largely for the better. The denominational executive who clucks protectively over his or her vulnerable chicks and makes feathers fly when the henhouse is invaded is now the rare exception, not the rule. Much more frequently the church-related colleges stand up today to the world around them—to institutions of other types and sponsorships, to the government, to disbelievers outside and gullible believers within, to the church itself when necessary. It is just barely possible today, though such a thing might have been unthinkable a fairly short time ago by any but the most devout partisan, that the future both for post-secondary education and for religion lies in the hands of the church-related college that knows itself to be, first, a seat of higher learning and, second, a home of spiritual values. This I have come to believe.

NOTES—Chapter 4

[1] John Novotney, "Criteria of 'Church-Relatedness' Drawn from Examination of Colleges," *Christian College News Service* (February 10, 1978), pp. 4-5.

[2] "Achieving the Mission of Church Related Institutions of Higher Learning," report of a conference held on November 29-30, 1976 (Washington, D.C.: Association of American Colleges, 1977), pp. 10-11.

[3] *Ibid.*, pp. 6-7.

[4] All quotations are taken from "Erskine Policies Draw Attention," *The Presbyterian Outlook*, vol. 159, no. 32 (September 12, 1977), p. 4.

[5] Merrimon Cuninggim, *The Protestant Stake in Higher Education* (Washington, D.C.: Council of Protestant Colleges and Universities, 1961), p. 66.

RESPONSE

William A. Kinnison

The author's purpose is stated as finding models of church-relatedness that are credible to church men and women and educators, to determine what makes these models church related, and then to ask if such church-relatedness makes any difference to church men and women or educators. I would insist, in addition, on asking if it makes any difference to *students* or to *society* at large.

Dr. Cuninggim begins with the college and insists upon viewing the topic from the college perspective. He says that he is not talking about a function of the church, although the denomination might need to look at the matter from its own perspective on occasion. The essence of the church-related college, however, is the result of the symbiosis of the church's view and the college's view. It seems to me that this symbiosis, plus the level of maturity in the relationship and the degree of independence of each partner, accounts for the categories and degrees of church-relatedness which are delineated for us in this paper.

Although the author begins in Chapter 1 with a position that seems unidirectional, in Chapter 4 he corrects the position. But there is the possibility that a stronger case needs to be made from the beginning that the church-related college differs from others because, unlike the non-church-related college, it interacts primarily with a major religious institution of our society rather than with a government or with a private secular establishment.

Church-related colleges, like all other institutions, have not been total masters of their own fate. They have had an interrelationship that is different. They are what they have become because of a variety of external, as well as internal, factors. Chief among these is, or was, their specific denomination. Robert Parsonage's paper is thus an important companion to this one, but the analysis of the interaction needs to be made.

The first chapter is a serious effort at clearing away the misconceptions and misapprehensions of insiders and outsiders— those who serve within or support church-related colleges, and those who serve in or support non-church-related institutions. The author ends the first chapter with an appeal that all forsake the myths of insiders and outsiders and begin afresh in pursuing the reality of what is a church-related college.

This is an altogether helpful beginning. Yet I would raise the historian's caution that myths, in fact, function as realities in the behavior and motivation of people and raise the political scientist's view that what is true matters less than what people believe to be true when they are to take political action.

To cite and deplore mythologies is one thing; to uproot them is clearly another. While it would be good to dispel the myths and pursue a clearer reality, that reality will perhaps always be surrounded to some degree by the old myths and deflected by them. Perhaps in a real sense, the mythologies of insiders provide a rationale that is in some way essential in the harmonizing of a precarious and changing relationship between church and college. The myths of outsiders, on the other hand, provide a validity for the group by challenging its legitimacy. The challenge is proof of a meaningful role, because only if the church-college role were meaningful would others bother to challenge it. Such a theme has been shown to be recurrent in our history and our politics by Richard Hofstadter, Richard Brion Davis, and others. Too much understanding that both sets of myths are myths might well create a house where worse demons come to occupy the space where earlier demons had been driven out. The tensions created by the old mythical viewpoints may be better than a clear, sacred/secular, church/state confrontation over proper ownership of the educational turf.

The second chapter on categories is challenging and even exciting to those of us who have sought to make reason out of the multi-variant group called church-related colleges. It poses a range of institutions exhibiting varying degrees of church-relatedness, determined presumably because of (1) their intention to be such and (2) the degree of intimacy and congruence they feel for their ecclesiastic sponsors. Note that it is feeling *for* and not *with* a sponsor, not a *colleague institution*. The model, which continues to emphasize the author's intent to preserve a collegiate focus, excludes some rather more interactive relationships of colleague institutions, is unidirectional, and appears to be more static than the relationships of colleges and churches actually are. The basic concept, however, is enlightening and helpful.

The author justifies a clear criterion for determining the non-church-related college in order to exclude it from the range. He also reviews previous efforts to categorize and label the remaining institutions, including those of the Pattillo-Mackenzie study and Pace's study for the Carnegie Commission, and dismisses them as pejorative, negative, and not readily applicable to any specific institutions that one wants to categorize. He then poses three classifications or compartments of his own to measure a group of institutions in motion over time from one institutional definition to another. This is a very helpful and much richer conceptualization, but the titles assigned here, while less pejorative and more useful, are still subject to misunderstanding, partly perhaps because the mythologies we set aside in Chapter 1 still lurk in the recesses of our minds and partly because there is a lingering feeling that the categories may occur as a result of other factors than those specified.

The "Proclaiming College" sounds more like Pattillo's "defender of the faith" or Pace's "evangelical-fundamentalist college," particularly for those who have a Christian view of the word "witness." There is clearly room for misunderstanding the word as the author intends its use. Those who with zeal pursue the "proclaiming of the gospel" would certainly misunderstand it. The concepts and ideas represented in the proposed classification, I would repeat, are valid and helpful, but I would suggest different titles and a reexamination of the causative factors at work.

I would reassert the point made earlier about the essence of the church-related college being a symbiotic relationship of colleague institutions: a relationship that requires that the church's view of education be as critical to the relationship as the college's view of its degree of "intimacy or congruence." The degrees of difference in this relationship, influenced by the church's perception of itself, underlie the differences in all three of the classifications proposed here. All three categories, I think, represent three varying degrees of consonance between the college and its church.

The colleges are like they are not so much because they reflect the nature of their churches, although they do that. They are like they are because of degrees of interaction with their churches over time. The structure, polity, and beliefs of one church enable its colleges, depending upon their strength and vigor, to evolve one kind of relationship, while others find, create, or stumble into other kinds of relationships. They may tend toward three major classifications, but the reasons they do so are more complex than the analysis in the chapter suggests.

Chapter 3 deals primarily with descriptions of the fourteen colleges selected for this study and is of genuine interest to anyone impressed by the varieties of church relationship. Let me add a further word about the value of the case studies and the references to other church-related and formerly church-related institutions. The breadth of the author's definition of church-relatedness and the inclusiveness of the concept, limited only by intentionality and evidence of congruence, is very well illustrated by the case studies. The specific cases begin to add up to the philosophical construct in a very meaningful way.

In the final chapter the author more clearly recognizes the duality of the subject at hand. "Because we are dealing with two organizational entities," he says, "the college and the church, we will need to note the essentials for each in turn and then, in conclusion, for both together." Such a posture, while not anticipated in light of Chapters 1 and 2, is clearly foreshadowed in the case studies of Chapter 3.

The essentials, however, are somewhat out of balance, which is typical for most discussions of mutual responsibilities for church and college. In a measurement of proportions, Dr. Cuninggim devotes 63 percent to essentials for the college, about 17 percent to essentials for the church, and 17 percent to essentials for both. It is a truism that all such studies devote more time and space to a description of what the colleges must do than they do to a description of what the churches must do. One wonders whether such a discrepancy tells more about the tendency of our relationships than anything else. It clearly suggests that the more serious considerations of the issue originate among the colleges themselves. Perhaps more detail on the nature of the educational task which the church must undertake and more detail about the evidences of its acceptance of that educational task would be helpful and enlightening.

The basics which are presented in Chapter 4 are clear, unmistakable, and undebatable, but perhaps not sufficient. While some would add more, these basics do, or should, represent a common denominator for the church-related college and the college-related church. They will be more helpful, however, and in a sense more compromising for the colleges than for the churches. I would have hoped that such a study as this would be more specific in outlining the obligations of the churches which are blessed with colleges with intentions to be clearly church related. The best of intentions will not preserve the strength and integrity of our colleges in the years immediately ahead. Clear understandings between church and college will be essential for the welfare of both in an increasingly secular and state-dominated society. Separately, each shall surely perish; together, the chances of survival for both may be slightly improved.

RESPONSE

Shirley M. Jones

As one of those charged with specific responsibility for relating the church, in my case the American Baptist Churches, to its colleges, I could spend the time allotted me lamenting the current state of church/college relationships. But, rather, I would like to focus on the positive notes in this paper which I believe will advance the possibilities for an environment in which church and college can move into the future in a supportive partnership rather than in an adversary style.

While there is a danger in starting on a negative note, as the author did in Chapter 1 with the mythology surrounding church-related colleges, it appears to be a good strategy in this instance because a new grasp of essential elements must begin to lay to rest some of the misconceptions about church-relatedness. I am willing to venture that many of these myths are the creations of church-related colleges themselves and that any change of perception among the churches must begin with a change of consciousness among the colleges. The competitive model which is normative in our society, and in our churches, all too often motivates an institution to communicate half-truths or downright untruths about sister institutions in an effort to "look better" in the eyes of the supportive constituency and prospective students.

Moving to the categories of church-relatedness and the case studies presented in the second and third chapters, I respond very positively to the three groupings advocated by Dr. Cuninggim. The categories seem to me to capture the essential marks of the varying models and in a positive affirming mode. The case studies help, in most cases, to put some "flesh on the bones" of the descriptions in Chapter 2. Likewise, the graphs are helpful in understanding the institutional categories and denominational profiles. I feel the categories provide positive content for dialogue between church and college and, among the colleges, about relationships, unlike the earlier Pattillo-Mackenzie types which tended to pit college against college and church against college.

Now to the essentials of church-relatedness. There are several assumptions about the present state of the church (at least in my denomination and some others represented here about which I am knowledgeable) that need lifting up before I comment. *First,* the American Baptist Churches in the U.S.A. is a pluralistic denomination—multicultural, multiethnic, multilingual—with broadly ranging theological persuasions and a bent toward rugged individualism and local church autonomy. The difficulty for a college to develop a meaningful relationship with these varying church constituencies, let alone other publics, is apparent. *Second,* the shift of power and responsibility from national to regional units of the church significantly affects the way in which a college relates to the church. Regionalism is a reality for the church and the college.

The first proposed essential, that of conscious intention, is the most straightforward and yet most complex of the factors mentioned. Simple expressions of intentionality about church relationships in official documents and publications of the college would certainly make clear its position to the church and wider community, but without support from all the constituent groups of the college, this is likely to bring about reactions that range from meaningless to disruptive in the campus community. Also in some states, such as New York, this would likely mean that state support would cease and that the college would have to (and in fact it would only be fair to expect that it would) appeal to the church or churches for increased financial support.

While I have some difficulty with the rather empty sound to the second proposition—that of making proper provision for religion—the three "inescapable implications" spelled out by the author make that more palatable, i.e., that the college will take the study of religion, worship, and expressions of religion seriously. It would be helpful for the third subpoint to read something like "community of faith in action," since the definition of usual religion refers more to a set of beliefs and ritual observances than action growing out of faith.

While it is clear that the church-related college should and can deal with biblical illiteracy among the student body, it is less clear to me that it is the college's responsibility to prepare students for fruitful participation in a church. I would hope that the college could do so—for the church is surely not doing a very good job of nurturing its young people into responsible adult Christians—but I am not sure this is a primary role for the college. Perhaps it is an area where church and college need to join hands.

When we approach the issue of expecting the total life of the college to exemplify its church's values, we are at the very heart of the issue of the church/college relationship. Not only has the church done poorly in articulating its values to the college, but also it has not done very well in living out its stated value system within its own structures. Responding to the fads and pressures of the moment may appear to move the "kingdom" forward, but as William Sloane Coffin has said, "If you don't stand for something, you are likely to fall for anything." Without struggling for a renewed sense of mission and for the values that grow out of commitment to that mission, the church will become vacuous and irrelevant to the needs of society.

Likewise, the church's college must engage in a self-conscious struggle to discover new models for acting out Christian values in a rapidly changing society, starting with its own setting, but not restricted to it. Colleges ought to be about the business of thinking about and planning for a future that is life affirming. That requires a toughness of mind and commitment that is found in precious few institutions today, but I am not without hope.

It is my conviction that church and college must engage in this struggle together. The issues raised in the latter half of Chapter 4—that the college must be able to count on the church's understanding its educational task and receive tangible and intangible support—will find their own resolution, for support always follows meaningful struggle and engagement in mission. One could hope that church and college could move beyond merely "informing and illumining" one another to a process of encountering the issues as partners, for neither is immune to the God who is at work in the accelerating societal change process.

RESPONSE

John D. Moseley

Merrimon Cuninggim has provided new insights and analysis to help us think about what it means to be a college related to a church. He has made an excellent contribution to the perceptions of church-relatedness in higher education, and he has done so in a precise and readable paper.

My response starts with a fundamental assumption about the paper: that it is not just an academic exercise but a resource for action. From this whole project we should draw guidelines and assistance for both the church and the college as they work to clarify relationships and roles. I want to make three comments related to using this paper as a resource for action.

First, the American higher education system has so changed in the last twenty years since Sputnik—in size, in kind, in society's expectations of education, in public policy—that new questions emerge about the nature of the educational task and what that means for the church college.

The changes can be documented at length, but perhaps two "explosions" summarize the situation: the knowledge explosion and the explosion in the number of students brought about in the 1960s with the concept of universal post-secondary education. These two explosions are having their effects. The knowledge explosion is placing new pressures on the student's capabilities to learn what is even minimally required for life and for work, and the student explosion is placing new pressures on the teacher's capability to deal with the learner in a reasonable and beneficial way. The result may be a new educational task, one that centers not on facts and answers but one that centers on perspectives and processes for lifelong learning to cope with the rapid changes and ambiguities of life.

The changed educational context has implications for the church. Many church people and others are involved in post-secondary education, lifelong learning, striving to stay up with the demands of their jobs, aiming for career changes, enriching their lives. As another has characterized it, these people—church member and nonmember alike—are "in transition," often with many new questions about themselves, their future, their relationship with the world in which they are trying to cope. Many of these people need, perhaps long for, the ministry of the church. They are open to the Good News of the gospel to help in the quest for a meaningful and purposeful life. Yet at the very time of this significant need for ministry to people, there seems to be less understanding, less programmatic endeavors, and less financial support for these opportunities of ministry to individuals in transition in the educational establishment.

Thus I feel that the larger context has changed, creating new tasks and encompassing new people with needs the church and church college can address. This changed context must be considered by church and college as they work to define their individual roles and joint relationship.

Second, action must be based not only on the changed context of the present but also on trends and conditions of the future. The tough question must be asked: "What *ought* to be the role and function of the church and the college in the remaining years of the twentieth century?"

History, tradition, and current relationships are instructive, but we must not rely on them alone. Essentials of church-relatedness drawn from case studies might tell where we are now, but they do not necessarily tell where we *should* be. We must be careful not to project the present state as the role of the future, for if we do, we may miss the point and the opportunity for new and even greater mission and service, both for the church and for the college.

As one projects the new universal post-secondary education system, one cannot help but realize that the future context will be as different from the present as the present context is from the past. The changing makeup of the student population; the different institutional delivery systems of the state college and university sector, the community college sector, the independent higher education sector, and the proprietary, technical, and vocational sector; the growing importance of communication and cultural media on the way people learn—all have their impact.

What "ought" the church to do to minister to the *people* in such a system, the great majority of whom will be outside the realm of the church college? With pressure from various other fields of ministry for priority funds, the church will surely need new roles and strategies. Moreover, the old response of sending professionals to state campuses to do the church's ministry is no longer feasible, given all the new state campuses. Is one answer to have a new involvement for the local church, the individual congregation, to minister to these people?

And what "ought" the church do to minister in and with the college of the church? Originally in this country the church saw the need for education and established colleges on the frontier to meet that personal and societal need. Although the church pioneered and showed the way, the state gradually became involved and now does the volume business. What should church and college alike do to meet the needs of a constituency and to be a viable part of the universal post-secondary educational system where they are the minority?

These are just examples of questions that focus on the future and what *should* be done. There are others, and they should be examined in relation to what we perceive the future will be like as each institution, college and church, fashions its relationship. And the questions should be examined with the understanding that there is no one pat answer to what should be done. Just as the paper points out that there is a broad spectrum of church-relatedness, so too there can be a broad spectrum of responses to what should be done. But merely examining the possibilities may sharpen the need for certain emphases in the "essentials of church-relatedness."

Third, I am persuaded that the greatest need of colleges and universities today is for each to have a clearly defined role. This role must include an understanding of how the institution fits into the needs and diversity of the total post-secondary education system and how it serves both the educational need of its specific constituency and of society. The institution must then have the courage to fulfill that role with integrity, discipline, and quality.

Thus the points in the paper of intentionality and of rationale are right on target. I think, however, I would want to emphasize the centrality of these issues, especially as one considers the context of the changed present situation and questions relating to what should be in the future.

These have to be central because, for me, they are the starting point. From the intentionality and rationale develops the educational philosophy that serves as the foundation and guide for the educational program and the activities of the college. If one has a basic commitment, it is easier to discipline one's self and the institution to do well what the committed role is and not to be everything to everyone.

In closing, let me relate an experience I had studying this whole issue of church-relatedness. I served on a church committee that tried to find a biblical and theological basis for the church to be in higher education. After long examination, we finally recognized that the biblical and theological basis was for "the church" and not for education or the college per se. But the pervasive concern and commitment of the church took it into the field of education, just as they also take the church into health care, international missions, and other fields. This approach frees the church to make its priorities of mission and resources in each generation. Accordingly, the church's strategy and investment for education in the twentieth century may not be the appropriate ones for the twenty-first century. The basic commitment and philosophy may be the same, but the strategies and priorities may be quite different, both for the church and for the college. Thus, the rationale *has* to be central, for the strategies emanating from it are changeable to conditions.

The action of working out a rationale and strategies may be done any of a number of ways: superficially and with the assumption that "we all know what we mean" by a college of the church; philosophically in a way that kills the effort by talking and debating the issues to death; or intelligently and committedly in a way that faces the issues and deals with them. I hope that includes recognizing the changed context of the present system, the possibilities for what *ought* to be done in the future, and the centrality of intention and rationale.

RESPONSE: EXCERPTS

William R. Johnson, Jr.

It is interesting to note that those schools founded by predominantly black denominations are placed in the "embodying" and "proclaiming" categories, which is probably where most of them should be placed. It is interesting to note, however, that to the average church person and leaders of these denominations, particularly of the Christian Methodist Episcopal Church, most of these schools are neither reflections of nor witnesses for the church.

The predominantly black colleges are as varied as the entire sampling of fourteen schools. They vary according to the different histories of founding or philosophies of the founders, on the basis of location, and in terms of enrollment—the percentage of students, faculty, and staff of the sponsoring denomination. . . .

I am grateful to Dr. Cuninggim for recognizing the need to speak to those essentials that are within the power of the denominations to live up to and adhere to. I believe that church-relatedness is a two-way street. As Dr. Cuninggim has said, it is just as important for the school to feel, to respond to, and to act out its church-relatedness as it is for the church to feel, to respond to, and to act out its college-relatedness. Too often church-relatedness in my own history has referred to the giving of money by the church and the receiving of money by the schools.

RESPONSE: EXCERPTS

Ben C. Fisher

I think there is another kind of very destructive myth that needs to be challenged. That is, that church-relatedness and academic excellence are really not compatible or are inconsistent. . . . I believe during the past decade that the majority of church-related colleges have been greatly underestimated both as to their academic integrity and, if you want to use the term, excellence. If this is not true, then there is something missing in the standards of our five regional accrediting agencies. It may be a horrible weakness of any study of this sort that we do not give sufficient attention to the stated educational purpose of the institution. The stated purpose of the institution is the criterion by which every standard necessarily is measured. Therefore, if we speak of excellence in broad, general terms, it must be somewhat related to what the institution says it is trying to do. And I don't believe there is just one kind of excellence. Thus, to speak of the presence or lack of presence of academic excellence without these other factors being taken into consideration can result in some very seriously distorted conclusions.

The church-related college has been greatly underestimated not only in the quality of its academic program but also, I believe, in the freedom which its professors have in teaching their discipline and in dealing with controversial issues. Certainly now, there are some exceptions. But I believe . . . that in some ways the church-related institutions may be some of the freest institutions in our society. . . .

I would like to speak to what I believe is another myth. And that is that church-related colleges stand in constant danger of falling into the error of indoctrination. . . . I do not believe that our mission is to indoctrinate, but I do not believe that, by and large, indoctrination is the real problem. I think we are more in danger of a bland mental, spiritual, moral, and social neutrality in which we never really take a stand anywhere on anything. . . .

RESPONSE: EXCERPTS

William J. Sullivan

There's also a question that I think could be explored. If there is movement on that map of Merrimon Cuninggim's, what are the drivers, what are the motors of that kind of movement, and, also, what are the inertial forces involved in either preventing institutions from moving or making it difficult for them to move? . . .

There are three things that I would simply observe in conclusion. . . . If you put the twenty-eight Jesuit schools on Merrimon Cuninggim's map, they would run over a very, very wide range . . . several of them probably running into his right-hand category and the middle one. . . . Second, I think at this time you would find fairly heavy resistance to further change. That's not to say that change isn't going to occur, that there's not going to be movement. . . . I think at the present moment you would have a pretty hard time trying to get one of these institutions to change its statute or charter to move it farther to the right [of Merrimon Cuninggim's chart]. And third, . . . I think the activity of the Jesuit communities in defining their purposes and making clear what their interests in the university are is a very healthy and a very legitimate action which will make it easier for the Jesuits to continue to relate to those institutions and ultimately also to help the institutions themselves to clarify their religious purposes.

RESPONSE: EXCERPTS

Albert J. Meyer

One variable that we have to consider when we talk about church-relatedness is the degree of consonance of the church in question with the surrounding society. This is a significant variable. It is a determining variable. . . . And we could draw a chart on which we would plot distinctiveness in this dimension if we wanted to use Dr. Cuninggim's scale of distinctiveness to consonance. . . .

There is a second variable upon which church-relatedness is dependent. It seems to me that the typology has to be based on a two-dimensional space, not a simple, one-dimensional continuum. . . . Even granting that we have the location of the church along a continuum of distinctiveness to consonance, even though we have a church located on that continuum, there is still another variable that is significant. A given church may have institutions with entirely different missions in education, and different models would be needed to represent those missions.

One model, for example, is a school or college with students and faculty almost entirely from that church, committed to the simple life, low in tuition, emphasizing peer learning, the community, and the nature of that community in interaction with the larger society. But the same church may sponsor other schools or colleges where very few of the students come from that church; sometimes these institutions are in other countries. These represent a different model or mission where the institution provides a service to the larger society and does it very much as a church-related institution.

Questions for Institutional and Denominational Self-Study

As was stated previously, the purpose of the study has been to seek answers to some fundamental questions about the distinctiveness, mission and purpose, priorities, and possible future of church-related higher education. In its deliberations, the Study/Action Committee sought to give general shape and focus to these questions (see Introduction). As the project consultant, Merrimon Cuninggim, gave further definition to the task; he, members of the committee, and staff began to formulate the specific questions which would need to be probed during campus visits. During a two-day meeting with the fourteen campus visitors, the project consultant described their search task, outlined the questions which needed to be discussed with constituents of the colleges and universities in order to proceed with the project, and, with the assistance of those present, prepared a final schedule of questions. It will be readily noted that these questions were not intended to form a quantitative and objective survey instrument; rather they were meant to be a common guide to assist visitors in perceiving the character and purpose of the institutions they visited.

Following the campus visits, the visitors met again with the project consultant to report and discuss their findings. Additionally, they shared other questions that had arisen in the course of their visits and had been prompted by their reflections on those experiences.

Following is a composite list of questions, including those which the project consultant and the visitors added after the campus visits were made, the answers to which inform Merrimon Cuninggim's observations. The questions are presented here as background to the study and in the hope that they will stimulate further deliberation within church and college. As the reader will observe, the questions are stated in such a way that they can readily be used by all manner of church-related institution and in every denomination, although, of course, not all questions will be relevant in every situation.

AREAS OF INQUIRY

A. Intentionality of Relationship—in the College

1. Is there a clear statement in the official documents and important publications of the college of the college's relationship to the church and the effect of that relationship upon the character and program of the college?
2. Is this statement consonant with the denomination's view of the relationship and the meaning of it? With the college's understanding of the denomination's view?
3. Is the college's relationship to the church defined and represented chiefly or only by the president of the institution, or is it represented by other elements in the institution as well, including trustees, faculty, and students?
4. To what extent is church relationship dependent upon persons rather than structures?
5. What congruence is there in the perceptions of church-relatedness among the different constituencies in the college? Does church-relatedness have a different importance for staff than for students?
6. Are there evidences that the college is respectful of the church's representation, positions, demands, and requests as appropriate to that denomination?
7. What forms of communication are there between the college and the church?
8. Do the purpose, form, and effect of the church relationship

receive the continuing attention of the faculty, administration, and board of the college, and do these groups perceive that they significantly determine the relationship themselves?

9. Is there current public discussion on the nature and appropriateness of church-relatedness within the campus community? By whom?

10. To what extent do the different constituencies of the college—faculty, students, administration, trustees—perceive that their expectations regarding the meaning of church relationship are being achieved?

11. Is it in the interest of the college to explore new and richer ways of relating to the denomination?

12. Do student-led organizations understand their responsibility in fostering a student culture or atmosphere which supports the denomination's concerns?

13. Does the college's practice and culture foster lay initiative by students and faculty or hierarchical trickle-down of values and tradition? What mode of response is expected from them?

14. Are there ways in which college constituencies engage in constructive criticism of their churches as well as in collaboration with them in matters of common human and social concern? Does the college help the church to understand and further its mission?

15. Does the college have a significant and continuing relationship with other colleges related to that denomination that is not maintained with institutions in its own geographic area?

16. What does church-relatedness mean for the college's ability to withstand political, social, and economic pressures and to retain independence in the face of recurring orthodoxies?

B. Intentionality of Relationship—in the Church

1. What is the denomination's view of the mission of the college and of the way in which church and college are related?

2. Is this view consistent with the college's understanding of the relationship?

3. Is there a clear statement in official church documents and important publications affirming the relationship of the college(s) to the church?

4. To what extent is the relationship to the colleges dependent upon persons rather than structures?
5. What are the theological and educational foundations of the statement?
6. Does the church and its various constituencies see the college as a valuable and complementary colleague in service to persons and society?
7. Does the church assist the college in withstanding political, social, and economic pressures and to retain independence in the face of recurring orthodoxies?
8. How are congregations informed about the program of the colleges?
9. Does the church provide financial support and members of college trustee board(s), and does it recruit students for the college(s) in ways that are appropriate to the college-church relationship in that denomination?
10. To what extent do the different constituencies of the church— lay people, pastors, denominational board members, and staff—perceive that their expectations regarding the college and the church relationship are being achieved?

C. Program of the College

1. What is distinctive about this college? Where are the creative edges in that distinctiveness? Who is advancing or blocking that creativity?
2. Is there freedom for study, inquiry, and thoughtful expression, creating a forum for honest and careful scholarship and divergent views?
3. How do Christian perspectives regarding the reverence for truth and a transcendent source of life and creation, as well as care for persons, make themselves shown in the institution?
4. What integration of values inherent in the church relationship occurs within the curriculum itself?
5. What is the role of core/interdisciplinary courses in bringing about integration?
6. Is there a commitment to stimulate students to a consideration of ultimate values for themselves?
7. Do the faculty and administration give concentrated attention

to the growth and developmental needs of students?

8. Is the concern for students paramount, taking precedence over the interests of faculty, administrators, or others?

9. Does the institution make provision for a significant engagement with the Christian faith in ways that are appropriate to the college's denomination?

10. What responsibility do students see as theirs to make the college Christian?

11. Does the college provide opportunities for worship and voluntary religious life? Are these consistent with the denomination's understanding and desires?

12. Does the college seek to prepare students for life in the church as desired by the denomination?

13. Is the area of religious studies the peer in strength and respect of the other disciplines?

14. Do the other academic disciplines have a concern for theological issues and the interaction of Christian thought with the cultural and intellectual currents of the times?

15. Is there any evidence that the greater the theological sophistication of the religion and philosophy department(s), the weaker is the church-relatedness of the institution?

16. Is there any evidence that the push toward "academic excellence" and the upgrading of faculty in terms of academic achievement as measured by degrees, publications, and academic reputation tend to weaken the church-relatedness of the institution?

17. Is there study and lively concern regarding the issues of social justice, the environment, global interdependence, etc.?

18. Is there an institutional commitment to serve the special needs of the institution's own region, a minority population, or a disadvantaged constituency and to provide community service experiences for faculty and students?

19. Does the college make a conscious effort to see that its policies and practices in regard to governance, management, administration, fiscal, and material matters follow ethical norms expressive of Christian faith? Are these policies and practices consonant with its denomination's expectations?

20. Does the college make a conscious effort to see that the

character of campus life reflects a sensitivity for persons, for justice, for freedom as well as for other perceived qualities of Christian community? Are these consonant with the denomination's expectations?

D. The Personnel of the College

1. Does the institution seek to have a significant number and/or core of persons from its denomination and/or other professing Christians in the student body, on the faculty, in the administration, and on the board?
2. If so, what does it regard to be a "significant number and/or core" and how is it assured?
3. Are there key positions on the faculty or in the administration which the institution believes should be held by persons of that denomination and/or other professing Christians?
4. In what sense are faculty expected to be role models?
5. Does the institution seek deliberately to have a diversity of religious commitments and perspectives in the college community? Is this policy seen as a part of its understanding of a church college or running counter to it?
6. Is there a chaplain who has the solid support of the college and effectively uses his or her position at the center of the college's life? Is this role consonant with the denomination's expectations?
7. Does the institution believe that the greater the religious and ethnic diversity of the student body, the weaker the link between the denomination and the college tends to become? Is it concerned about it?
8. Does the institution believe that the greater the religious and ethnic diversity of the faculty and administration, the weaker the link between the denomination and the college tends to become? Is it concerned about it?

E. External Determinants on the Church Relationship of the College

1. How do increasing financial pressures affect the college's ability to fulfill its mission, as it sees it and as the denomination sees it, as a college related to the church?
2. Does the increase of state authority, in the policies of awarding

scholarship funds, approving new degree programs or other expressions of central authority, affect the college's ability to fulfill its mission, as it sees it and as the denomination sees it, as a college related to the church?

3. What are the effects of the power of the federal government as to the choice of personnel, the construction of facilities, the keeping of records, etc., as expressed through such measures as the equal opportunity/affirmative action laws, the Buckley amendment, etc.: Is there any evidence that the college is using these requests to pull away from its church relationship?

4. Does the college believe that foundation grants represent an external influence that tends seriously to determine the character of the institution?

5. Do enrollment pressures bear on the church-related character of the college? Cf. catalogue material, admissions officers, etc.

6. Do other external influences seem effectively to condition the character of church relationship of the college, such as its geographic location, unionization practices, etc.?

F. Cultural Issues

1. Does the college believe that there are dimensions of a Christian understanding of higher education that go beyond the prevailing view of higher education in the larger community?

2. Does the college believe that being a Christian college limits its freedom to be a servant of the larger community?

3. Are the ethnic, geographical, and economic backgrounds of the students important or discernible in the recruitment, admissions, and life of the college? If so, in what ways?

The Embodiment
of Church-Relatedness:
Creative Illustrations

Merrimon Cuninggim has argued that church-relatedness cannot be measured by such traditional indices as the number of trustees elected or appointed by the sponsoring church, the extent to which students are required to take courses in religion, the presence or absence of requirements regulating chapel attendance. Rather, he has made a compelling case showing that church-relatedness inheres in certain "essentials"—such as conscious intention to maintain a relationship with a church or churches, making provision for religion in all aspects of college life, receiving tangible support from the church—the specific character and expression of which differ according to denominational history and practice. And in discussing specific institutions, Cuninggim has provided some valuable illustrations of the diverse ways in which these colleges and universities are attempting to give form and content to their particular understanding of church-relatedness in governance, curriculum, student life, and relationships with church and community.

Participants in the Wingspread Consultation expressed appreciation for Cuninggim's discussion of these specific illustrations—and asked for more. Additional, more detailed knowledge of ways in which churches and colleges are trying to make church-relatedness a practical, vital, daily reality could, they said, be useful to other institutions struggling with the same task. Therefore, the Study/Action Committee determined that a further discussion of creative illustrations should be appended to the study.

Illustrations are drawn from different churches and colleges affiliated with a variety of denominations. The use of the particular illustrations should not be construed to mean that they are necessarily the best examples to be found or that the churches or colleges mentioned were the first to adopt a particular program or emphasis. However, they are valuable examples.

Another preliminary word needs to be said about the illustrations. Church-related colleges do not have a monopoly on the programs and emphases discussed below. In many instances, strikingly similar illustrations could be drawn from other independent and from public institutions of higher education. The difference in such cases, we would hold, is more in motivation and intention than in kind. The church-related college might likely enter into a neighborhood tutorial program and be able to sustain the interest and energy needed to see it through on the basis that it fulfills the commandment to love one's neighbor, as well as for general humanitarian reasons. Likewise, it might well interpret the significance of such involvement on the part of its students in religious as well as secular terms. This explanation is not offered in order that invidious distinctions can be made between religious and secular motives and intentions but only to suggest that similar activity may legitimately be prompted and sustained and its significance interpreted for different reasons and on the basis of different values.

Though church persons might hope that some such programs and emphases as the following would have a place in other independent and public institutions of higher education, it is evident that they believe such concerns to be central to the life of the church-related college and expect that the college will give specific attention to one or more of them, depending on the particular religious tradition of the school.

Covenant-Making: Austin College

In his discussion of fourteen colleges in Chapter 3, Merrimon

Cuninggim notes that covenantal agreements with their denominations play a significant role in defining church-relatedness for a number of them, including Austin College. Austin was one of the first institutions to develop a covenant, has periodically reviewed and revised it, and recently prepared a commentary on the covenant-making process for the benefit of interested institutions.

In the document, "Insights for Writing Covenants Between Church Bodies and Institutions or Agencies," issued in first draft by Austin's Center for Program and Institutional Renewal, it is suggested that covenants address five subjects: the nature of the covenant, parties to the covenant, responsibilities under the covenant, the process of review and renewal, and formal approval.[1] "The Covenant Relationship for Austin College and the Synod of the Red River," revised last in the spring of 1978, shows how these two institutions are choosing to deal with the five subjects.

The document sets out in careful detail the nature of the covenant—"this Covenant is a voluntary agreement between Austin College and the Synod of Red River to affirm a current and historic relationship in which there is a mutuality of purpose."[2] The intentional reaffirmation of the historic church-college tie has been necessary, according to the covenant statement, "to make explicit what previously went unexpressed and to clarify a relationship that had become uncertain and confused."[3]

The covenant defines and describes the responsibilities of each party for the other—college and synod each has a unique role, both share a common ground of Christian faith and commitment, both must remain separate, independent corporations in order to fulfill their distinctive goals, and both shall look to a Covenant Liaison Committee to facilitate the institutional relationship. The common ground shared by college and synod is explicitly stated in terms of what both parties affirm about the nature, perspective, mission, and educational goal of Austin as a college of the church. And the key role of the trustees in maintaining the institutional integrity of the college and fulfilling the conditions of the covenant is summarized in this statement, ". . . the commitment of the individual Trustee is two-fold: to the Covenant and its affirmation and to the Charter and its corporate responsibilities."[4]

The covenant affirms the mutual support of college and synod for one another—each shall provide services for the other, the synod shall provide financial support for the college, the covenant shall be reviewed and, if necessary, revised every four years. While the program relationships are broadly defined in the covenant, specific details and procedures are left for development in a supplementary Statement of Understanding to be renegotiated every four years. Financial obligations are specified in the covenant to insure clear understanding by each party; likewise, specific procedures are set forth to insure the systematic review of the covenantal relationship.

Finally, formal approval and the pledge of the Synod and of the Board of Trustees of the college to carry out the provisions of the covenant are recorded in the document.

While Austin College and the Synod of the Red River affirm the necessity of dealing with all five subjects in the development of a viable covenant, they are equally adamant that a covenant must reflect the specific character and needs of the parties involved and seek above all else to nurture the relationship into which they voluntarily enter. In covenant-making, "there is no one 'right way.' The only truly 'right way' for each relationship is that which facilitates best that particular relationship."[5]

Peace Studies: Manchester College

The relationship of Manchester College and the Church of the Brethren is described in some detail by Merrimon Cuninggim in Chapter 3. One important way in which that college seeks to respond creatively to the church's historic concern for peace and the commitment to serve human need is through its program of peace studies, begun thirty years ago.

A publication of the college describes Manchester's particular approach to peace studies.

> Since 1958 this program has provided interdisciplinary studies in the understanding of war and peace, social change and conflict reduction. Bringing together the expert knowledge and experience of special guests and faculty, Peace Studies relates the findings of political science, history, ethics, religion, sociology, psychology, economics and the philosophies underlying various civilizations to humanity's major problems of order and justice in the twentieth century. Major attention is given to questions of values and historical perspective as well as to the more technical aspects of cultural analysis, political theory and practice, how to respond to

violence and hostility, and social psychological factors underlying strife. Concrete case study is devoted to such problems as population control, resource utilization and the determination of national interest in the light of international perspectives. Environmental Studies courses provide perspective on global capabilities for meeting problems of hunger and economic justice.[6]

In recent years, a growing interest has led to a particular focus on conflict resolution within the interdivisional major in peace studies.

To broaden their student's experience and understanding of the issues addressed in formal peace studies, Manchester encourages majors to participate in overseas and volunteer service experiences. The Brethren Colleges Abroad program and the church's volunteer service programs provide many of these opportunities. To extend the impact of the peace studies program to others in the college, church, and community, Manchester maintains the Peace Studies Institute and publishes the *Manchester College Bulletin of the Peace Studies Institute*.

The Peace Studies Institute plans retreats, classes, and college-wide conferences—to which the wider college constituency is invited—to hear noted speakers, debate related public policy issues, and explore issues of peace and justice specific to various areas of the world. Further, the institute has sponsored nonviolent training labs for the campus community, church, and peace groups; has provided evening and summer courses in peace studies for area teachers; and has conducted short-term programs and research in conjunction with the Central States Colleges' Association and with the American Friends Service Committee.

The *Manchester College Bulletin of the Peace Studies Institute* is published twice a year and contains a wide range of scholarly articles on issues of peace and justice, reviews, information about related conferences and study opportunities, and news of faculty and alumni/ae of the Manchester peace studies program—many of whom are at work in programs of peace education and action.

Commenting on the current state of peace studies at Manchester College, Allen C. Deeter, associate dean of the college and director of the Peace Studies Institute, writes,

There is strong institutional commitment, at least as far as administrators, many faculty, alumni and trustees are concerned. A surprising number of endowed peace studies scholarships of modest size have been started. We have more students in peace studies and a more diverse student and faculty group than ever before. A number have been attracted to peace studies, and thus to Manchester, who are clearly outside our normal constituency . . . we are just at the beginning of a *Re-evaluation Period* whose directions are impossible to guess. If peace studies would emerge less strong and less significant from our continuing rethinking, it would surprise me greatly.[7]

Collegiate Educational Service Corps: Furman University

Merrimon Cuninggim writes in Chapter 3 that "the most unusual feature of Furman's campus life is the Collegiate Educational Service Corps, or CESC. . . ." Cited on two occasions by the National Center for Volunteer Action as among the top four volunteer programs in the nation, CESC deserves a further word of elaboration.

The Collegiate Educational Service Corps was begun ten years ago by six Furman students. In its first year, CESC placed 75 student volunteers in 18 community serving agencies; currently some 1,200 persons—more than half of the Furman University student population—are involved in more than 60 agencies through CESC. The volunteer program is funded by the university, coordinated by a member of the staff, and receives the assistance of faculty and administration, yet is sustained through student initiative.

According to a descriptive brochure aimed at Furman students,

> Service Corps is based on the belief that the greatest gift a person can give another is the gift of himself and his time. CESC is as strong and diverse as the hundreds of volunteers who share their time, concern, and consequently their lives with those who are in need of care. The only prerequisite for student participation in any program is the desire to be involved with the lives of others.[8]

CESC is organized into nine divisions or areas of service—adult programs, child enrichment, church ministries, etc. Each division maintains liaison with three to fourteen community agencies. Student coordinators for each agency help to enlist volunteers, arrange their placement, and oversee the program through the school year. Student volunteers in the highly individualized program must make a commitment to regular involvement—"CESC is not an organization to relieve the student's occasional altruism, but a serious contract to participate weekly with other people in their life situation."[9]

To launch the program at the beginning of the school year, CESC conducts a human relations workshop for community agency personnel and Furman students. Emphasis in the forty-eight-hour workshop is on developing greater self-awareness, interpersonal skills, understanding of the opportunities for service, and commitment to one another.

Commenting on the significance of the program, its leaders state:

> Perhaps the CESC spirit can best be described as that force which binds the student volunteer, the agency director, and the people of the community together in a sense of Neighborhood. A Neighborhood is more than a location; it is a community. It is a community of shared needs and concerns where the individual, the basic unit and most valuable resource of the Neighborhood, is recognized and affirmed. This is exactly the point where Service Corps enters the picture. CESC provides opportunities for the student to share in this sense of Neighborhood through positive action in the community. . . .
>
> The Service Corps volunteer is effective because when he encounters the warm and responsive human being who comes to his agency offering his hand, the student is never alone. Our love teaches us that the question to be asked is not "Who is my neighbor?", but "Who can I be a neighbor to?"[10]

World Hunger: A Denomination's Program for Involving Higher Education

Initiative for strengthening old patterns and devising new modes of church-relatedness may emerge at various points within the church-college community. The following example illustrates one denomination's role in this process.

In the spring of 1976, the General Conference of the United Methodist Church made the alleviation of world hunger a mission priority, granted the yearly expenditure of a minimum of $5 million of additional church money to combat hunger, and directed the various program boards of the church to develop "programs, services and resources in areas such as lifestyle, public education, policy and legislation."[11] It also directed that 58 percent of the special funds be used to alleviate hunger directly and deal with its root causes and that 6 of the remaining 42 percent be allocated to the Board of Higher Education and Ministry to provide training opportunities in United Methodist institutions.

Based on the premise that "we must utilize the problem-solving capacity of higher education if we are to get at the underlying causes and work toward long-range solutions" in the battle against world hunger, the Board of Higher Education and Ministry decided to offer its share of the priority funds as grants "to stimulate and support activity within universities, seminaries, colleges, and campus-related groups addressing the problem of world hunger, with the hope that Christian concern and technical expertise may be harnassed."[12] Further, the board determined that grants would be made for projects which dealt with (1) higher education and U.S. policies, attitudes, and behaviors impinging on world hunger; (2) higher education and better production and distribution of food; and (3) stimulation of world hunger/research by academic communities. It also set forth the following general criteria to be used in determining which proposals would be funded:

—clarity and helpfulness in identifying the problems to be addressed

—recognition of complexity and interrelatedness of problems

—commitment to social justice

—indication of biblical/theological awareness and perspective

—capacity to envision new structures and patterns of interaction

—attention to the needs of those who most need help

—sensitivity to varying cultural patterns and needs

—willingness to share learnings through the church[13]

In the first year of the program, fifty-six completed proposals were submitted to the grants committee. Since that time, more than two dozen grants have been made—a number of them to church-related colleges. Monies have gone to church-related colleges to support such programs as the training of student teams to work in churches to help people understand and support the church's priority on world hunger; to support internships in which local people are trained to conduct community study groups and develop practical methods to combat hunger in their own state; and to mount a program in which persons trained in consumer and producer cooperatives will work to provide adequate food for the urban poor at good prices for farmers.

Grants which are made by the Board for Higher Education and Ministry are done so in consultation with the church's coordinating committee on hunger, and review and accountability requirements are built into the grant-making process.[14]

Writing about the project, Cecil Findley states:

... willingness to share learnings through the church" is a general criterion for all proposals. This task of helping the church become better informed and more effective in its response is a major portion of what the Board of Higher Education and Ministry is committed to in this effort. As followers of God in Jesus Christ, we care intensely that a hungry world may eat, but we would have this caring in touch with higher learning so that we as a church may avoid the danger of being "all bleeding heart and no bloody head." [15]

Continuing Education for Church Leaders: Lakeland College

Many colleges seek to make their resources available and relevant to the churches which surround, and in many cases, help to sustain them. Lakeland College, related to the United Church of Christ, is such a school and is attempting to respond specifically to the need of the churches for adult continuing education.

In 1976, after discerning a need among persons in Wisconsin churches to explore the nature and meaning of a variety of contemporary faith issues, Lakeland faculty and staff developed the Comprehensive On-Going Leadership Training (COLT) program— a series of "mini-courses" in religion designed for adult lay leaders and clergy to be offered in local churches. The general objectives established for the program were:

1. To develop an awareness of the biblical heritage in the context of contemporary biblical theology
2. To develop an understanding of the history of the Church and its faith
3. To initiate a discussion of the principal issues confronting the Church in contemporary society
4. To examine the role of the Church in the local community, and
5. To examine the role of the church-related college as a learning resource in the mission of the Church
6. To study the Polity and constitution of the United Church of Christ
7. To study Church management and finance, and
8. To study strategies for a vital ministry of the local church [16]

Additional objectives relate to the nature of Christian education and effective church school teaching.

Supported by a grant from the Council for Higher Education and the Board for Homeland Ministries of the United Church of Christ, and endorsed by the Wisconsin Conference of the UCC, the COLT program offered twelve courses in eight locations the first year, attracting more than 560 adult learners. Lakeland faculty and laity and clergy of the Wisconsin Conference served as instructors.

Courses were offered in local churches on the basis of an assessment of needs and interests. Evaluation sheets were distributed midcourse, and subsequent sessions were adjusted in light of the responses of participants. Finally, participants in the initial mini-courses were asked to suggest what new courses they would like to see added.

At the conclusion of the first year, the COLT program was invited to return to all eight locations in 1977-78. Moreover, Lakeland has been asked to begin offering courses in seven additional areas of the state. An evaluation of the program notes that, "since the program is academically oriented, it does not compete with other educational programs in the church but provides church members with an opportunity for reflection and dialogue concerning the Christian faith." [17]

A significant number of parish clergy participated in the COLT program during its first year. Subsequently, they asked that Lakeland College develop a similar program specifically for them. An on-campus continuing education program for clergy serving small churches who cannot afford sabbatical leaves has been planned by the college, approved by the Wisconsin Conference of the UCC, and will be offered as funding is available.

Theological Development of College Faculties: A Denominational Emphasis

At its general convention in 1976, the American Lutheran Church established the "Third Century Fund for Theological Development of College Faculties" and allocated $50,000 to the church's Division of College and University Services to underwrite the project in its first year.

The program is based on the following objectives and rationale:

> On the assumption that the contribution of individual faculty members of our colleges/universities would be enhanced by their entering into substantial theological learning and reflection, the objective is to provide opportunities for such an experience for as many faculty as possible.
>
> In developing these opportunities we want to go beyond reflection upon humanistic and ethical considerations such as medical ethics, war and peace, genetic manipulation, etc.—important as these issues are. We want to understand "theological" in this instance to refer to the classical Christian heritage and its distinctive themes surrounding an understanding of God as Father, Son, and Holy Spirit, His work of grace and

judgment, a Christian understanding of humanity and society, the Christian Church as the people of God. We intend to provide an opportunity for reflection upon the points at which that heritage intersects and interacts with contemporary views of meaning and non-meaning.[18]

According to the study plan, each ALC college or university may receive up to $2,000 yearly to fund proposals for theological development which have been initiated locally, satisfy the objectives stated above, and have been approved by the division. In its inaugural year, two colleges have used the funds to hold a joint faculty retreat (involving thirty-five persons from each campus for a weekend discussion of such topics as "The Role of the Church in the Twentieth Century" and "Is There Human Nature?") and to host follow-up discussions involving the total faculties of the two institutions. A third college has used the special funds to enable faculty and spouses to come together with a noted theologian and author for discussion of his latest work.

As a second phase of the project, a week-long theological workshop is to be held on a campus which houses an extensive theological library and "will require substantial involvement (reflection, study, writing) on the part of each participant."[19] Colleges may select up to five persons to participate in the workshop, with preference to be given to teaching faculty with high potential, women and minorities, lay persons with little formal theological education, persons who have not previously had much contact with faculty of other ALC institutions of higher education, representatives of more than one denomination, and persons who have participated in the local theological development program.

Yet a third aspect of the program may be developed. It would identify persons who have participated in the local discussions and/or the summer workshops and desire continuing theological discussion with their peers and bring them together on a quarterly or semiannual basis for regional conversations.

The project includes evaluation of all phases by participants and skilled observers.

Student "Search": Seattle University

Merrimon Cuninggim has called attention in Chapter 3 to the fact that the campus ministry at Seattle University plays a significant role in giving a "Catholic tone" to the campus. Through a variety of programs, campus ministry reaches out to students and faculty and, through them, to the wider community. But the key program, central to the creation and expression of Christian community at Seattle, is one called "Search."

The purpose of Search, according to Seattle Chaplain Charles Schmitz, is "to create an atmosphere in an off-campus setting in which young adult Christians can deepen their faith and experience a call to Christian commitment." The program, now in its seventh year—and being replicated on other campuses—is student run and advised by the campus ministry office.

The Search is offered three times a year at Seattle; each time forty students are recruited for the experience on a first-come, first-accepted basis. Five weeks prior to the event, three communities of past Search participants are formed. The first group of seven students, known as the "Team," meets weekly to prepare the talks which will be given during the weekend and to share in prayer and the Eucharist. The second community of sixteen persons, called the "Crew," meets weekly to plan the logistics and details for the weekend, to solicit letters of support and prayers from family and friends of the new Searchers—who are not aware of this activity on their behalf—and to engage in worship. The third community, or "Vigil," meets weekly to pray for the new Searchers and to plan an around-the-clock prayer vigil to be conducted during the Search weekend on behalf of the new group.

On the Search weekend, the participants are taken to a well-prepared campground where they are conducted through the retreat experience by the three communities. After becoming acquainted with one another, the participants are addressed by their fellow students on the subjects of Why I Am Here, Hiding and Opening, Sin and Forgiveness, The Person of Christ, Personhood, and the Challenge of Christianity. Following each talk, participants and the Team members engage in a period of creative response and on Saturday evening, after the sixth presentation, are feted to a thanksgiving dinner, replete with turkey, candlelight, and music. After dinner, the participants adjourn to the chapel and engage in the rite of reconciliation. Afterward, they return to a room where the letters of friends and relatives and handmade gifts have been laid out for them. The evening ends with fellowship, prayers, and exchange of the kiss of peace.

While Saturday night marks a high point in the weekend, Sunday morning is a carefully planned low point. Participants are rudely awakened and herded into the dining room, which the Crew has "destroyed"—as a symbolic representation of the "real world" which the Searchers must now reenter. However, cleaning implements have been placed in the midst of the chaos, and once participants discover these and organize themselves to clean up the mess, breakfast is brought out and served. Following breakfast, the Searchers, Team, Crew, and Vigil—who have engaged in prayer for the Searchers at another location throughout the weekend—join together in the chapel for the Liturgy of the Word and the Eucharist. At the offering, each Searcher is invited to place some sign or symbol of his or her weekend experience on the altar and to comment upon its meaning. Following lunch and presentation of the seventh talk, "The Christian Community of Love," all return to the Seattle campus.

One week later, those who have just participated in the Search, and all who have previously engaged in the same experience, are invited to the "Final Breakthrough Liturgy" held in the university chapel. Usually 200 to 300 students participate. A final talk, "Christian Commitment," is given, the Eucharist is celebrated, and students are invited to commit themselves to and sign up for peer ministry; community service with youth groups, the handicapped, the elderly; prayer groups; and/or the three communities which will lead the next Search. The final liturgy symbolizes the rhythm of the Christian life—it marks both the end of the search for self and the beginning of service to others.

Institutional Self-Study of Mission and Priorities: Wittenberg University

In his discussion of Wittenberg University (Chapter 3) Merrimon Cuninggim notes the "careful thought" which the school's Commission on Mission and Priorities has recently given to the concerns for church-relatedness and academic strength. The commission represents Wittenberg's significant attempt to engage in a comprehensive and systematic study of its purpose and role and to plan for its future.

As early as 1970, the need for an ambitious institutional self-study was acknowledged by Wittenberg University, and in 1976 the Commission on Mission and Priorities was established to carry it out. Commitment to the project was first made by the school's Board of Directors; subsequently it was discussed and endorsed by students, faculty, and staff. Membership on the fourteen-person commission was determined by the president on the recommendation of the constituencies to be represented—students, faculty, staff, and the Board of Directors. The three board members were chosen to represent the church, alumni/ae, and community constituencies of Wittenberg. Funding to hire a director and to support the work of the commission in its task was secured from the Division for Mission in North America of the Lutheran Church in America, the Aid Association for Lutherans, and the college budget.

The rationale for the study, the charge to the commission, and the outline of its task were issued by the president in a document entitled "Facing Reality." [20] The president outlined the specific tasks of the commission, set out a timetable for its work, and charged the commission "to begin pursuing the consensus and mutual under- standing that would enable the university to face its future with a clearer sense of its goals and priorities." [21]

During its tenure, the commission developed its own study and research procedures; devised plans to involve the entire Wittenberg community and constituencies in discussion and deliberation of the commission's proceedings; established special task forces to study campus life, educational mission, enrollment, facilities and environ- ment, finances and resources, religious environment, and structure and. governance; and held open hearings to allow all groups and individuals associated with Wittenberg to present their concerns.

At the end of eighteen months, the Commission on Mission and Priorities published its report which restates Wittenberg's mission, identifies seven priorities for the institution, summarizes the reports of the task forces, and lists commission recommendations and points of consensus.

In clarifying the total mission of Wittenberg University—"to help educate 'the creative minority of a civilization,' to develop in harmony the intellectual, spiritual, social and physical qualities . . ." —the commission was able to give clearer definition to the spiritual task of the University.

Wittenberg, related to the Lutheran Church in America, seeks to manifest its Christian commitment and Lutheran heritage. For academic and social integrity, Wittenberg encourages an environment of respect for all people and diverse beliefs. However, the University also encourages critical assessment of personal faith, beliefs and ethics. The University community challenges its members to perceive themselves as servants in society through clarification, assessment, and development of their spiritual beliefs and ethical values as these are manifested in academic, personal, and social pursuits.[22]

Additionally, on the basis of the assessment made by the Task Force on Religious Environment, a number of specific recommendations for strengthening the religious life and commitment of the institution were generated.

Reflecting on its own work, the commission concludes:

The process through which the Commission and its task forces sought answers provided a valuable beginning for the open and honest airing of opinions that is so vital to communication among Wittenberg's constituencies. Their ability to continue to talk openly with one another, their willingness to assume and grant leadership, their commitment to excellence, their belief in the University's mission and their focus on its priorities will enable Wittenberg to translate its purpose into saga and to survive the difficult times ahead with significance and distinction.[23]

Education for Justice and Peace: A Pilot Project

In 1975 the College and University Department of the National Catholic Educational Association (now the Association of Catholic Colleges and Universities) established a Task Force on Education for Justice and Peace to explore ways in which member colleges might become more involved in such education. At first, the task force was primarily interested in curriculum development; but later it became interested in articulating a process of institutional self-examination and self-definition with respect to justice education which might afford many different approaches to the subject.

Thus, in 1977, the task force outlined a "Proposed Process" to the 220-member institutions of the association which would lead to the identification of some institutions in various parts of the country in which specially called committees on each campus might identify issues and concerns relating to justice; assess local resources for dealing with these issues; and in dialogue with staff of the association assess what it would take to move ahead on a model project.

Further, the proposed process called for the planning of a summer workshop "designed to help two or three key people from each model site plan the process needed for their own model and to get needed critique and guidance from each other."[24]

Thirty to thirty-five colleges volunteered to serve as "pilot schools," and seven were selected for participation. Following their selection, staff for the project visited all seven institutions to help initiate the process. As a result, "each institution was helped to surface the 'justice issues' of most significance and urgency to them and given some help in establishing priorities, evaluating resources and planning action steps."[25] Among priority issues identified by the pilot institutions were the need to rethink and redesign existing courses so as to address justice/peace issues; the need to apply conflict resolution methods to the problems between U.S. and international students on campus; the need to focus study and action on such problems as the criminal justice system and international disarmament.

After the pilot projects were well under way, the task force was dissolved and an Advisory Council on Justice Education was established in its place. Comprised of representatives from various constituencies—college presidents, task force, pilot schools, and national Catholic organizations involved with peace and justice issues, the Advisory Council met for the first time in February, 1978. The initial act of the Advisory Council was to request progress reports from the pilot institutions, and on the basis of those reports, it has recommended that representatives from the seven colleges come together in the summer of 1978 to develop an evaluation process for regular assessment of the model projects.

Because there is a growing interest among other Catholic institutions in mounting or strengthening programs of justice education and action, the staff of the association is providing counsel and service to a growing number of colleges and universities interested in peace and justice studies and the Advisory Council is currently considering how the association might better serve the widening network of interested institutions.

NOTES

[1] "Insights for Writing Covenants Between Church Bodies and Institutions or Agencies," Center for Program and Institutional Renewal, Austin College, Sherman, Texas, Spring, 1978, pp. 2-15.

[2] "The Covenant Relationship for Austin College and the Synod of Red River," rev., 1978, p. 1.

[3] *Ibid.*, p. 2.

[4] *Ibid.*, p. 5.

[5] "Insights for Writing Covenants . . ." p. 16.

[6] "Peace Studies," Manchester College, North Manchester, Indiana.

[7] Allen C. Deeter, "Pioneering in Peace Education in the Church College," *Manchester College Bulletin of the Peace Studies Institute*, vol. 7, no. 1 (January, 1977), p. 33.

[8] "Collegiate Educational Service Corps," Furman University, Greenville, South Carolina, brochure.

[9] Statement on church-college relations, Furman University, p. 12.

[10] "Collegiate Educational Service Corps."

[11] *Our Missional Priorities 1977-80,* The United Methodist Church (Evanston, Ill.: United Methodist Communications), p. 5.

[12] Cecil Findley, "World Hunger and the Board of Higher Education and Ministry," *Higher Education and Ministry Report,* The United Methodist Church, April, 1977, pp. 1-2.

[13] *Ibid.,* p. 2.

[14] *Ibid.* and *Higher Education and Ministry Report,* The United Methodist Church, January, 1978, p. 3.

[15] Cecil Findley, *op. cit.,* p. 2.

[16] "Council for Higher Education of the United Church of Christ, 1976 Program Grants, Progress Report," Lakeland College, Sheboygan, Wisconsin, February, 1977.

[17] *Ibid.,* Final Report, May, 1977.

[18] "Theological Development of College Faculties," Division of College and University Services, American Lutheran Church, descriptive brochure, 1977.

[19] *Ibid.*

[20] William A. Kinnison, "Facing Reality," mimeographed paper, Wittenberg University, Springfield, Ohio, 1976.

[21] *Ibid.*

[22] *Report of the Commission on Mission and Priorities* (Springfield, Ohio: Wittenberg University, June 24, 1977). pp. 1 and 5.

[23] *Ibid.*, pp. 35-36.

[24] "Report for the Advisory Council on Justice Education," from the NCEA College and University Department, mimeographed, January 20, 1978.

[25] *Ibid.*

SECTION II

Perspectives: Past, Present, and Future

CHAPTER 5

Roads to
Our Present

James H. Smylie

In *Giles Goat-Boy or, The Revised New Syllabus,* we find this parody on the Lord's Prayer offered to the Grand Tutor:

Our Founder, who art omniscient,
Commenced by Thy Name.
Thy College come, Thy Assignment done
On Campus as beyond the Gate.
Give us this term Thy termly word.
And excuse us our cribbing,
As we excuse classmates who crib from us.
Lead us not into procrastination,
But deliver us from error:
For Thine is the rank, tenure, and seniority, for ever.
So pass us.[1]

Written in 1966 by novelist John Barth, this fictional bit of nonsense illustrates not only disdain for higher education but also the important role institutions of higher education have come to play in our lives and the society.

What is an institution of higher learning? We thought we knew as we surveyed proudly our church-related institutions.[2] Yet some observers have moved to identify institutions of higher learning as the churches of our time. Hazel E. Barnes, writing of the English scene and citing Barth's parody, did this in a volume, *The University as the New Church* (1970). Well aware of that literature which attacks the university as a sacred cow, Barnes undertook an evaluation of institutions of higher learning and emerged from her analysis reassured. "If to point out to man the path to truth and enable him to grasp it is the function of the Church," she wrote, "then the University is and ought to be our new church." She warned against the dangers of a new establishment of religion and the mistakes made by the medieval church—assertions that human beings may be saved only through its offices, reliance on past revelation and unchallenged spiritual authority, and practices which produced a gap between the overprivileged clergy and underprivileged laity. Despite these dangers the university has to be willing to "accept responsibilities of guardian of the public conscience." Moreover, concerning itself with the problem of values and the realization of values, the university could hope to "supply the grace necessary for salvation."[3]

This language may be inflated, but it illustrates a euphoric attitude which some people have had in our recent past about higher education. While not speaking in salvational terms, John E. Cantelon wrote in *College Education and the Campus Revolution* (1969) in a similar vein. Institutions of higher learning were performing tasks in some ways more than the church. They were taking on

> such basic religious tasks as answering for an increasing majority of the better educated questions regarding the nature and destiny of man and of what constitutes highest value and meaning.[4]

Harry E. Smith celebrated *Secularization and the University* (1968), using categories of Friedrich Gogarten and Dietrich Bonhoeffer, and suggested that in a world come of age, institutions of higher learning could now seek the truth and take on responsibilities for personal and institutional aspects of life necessary for human existence.[5] Given massive governmental support to institutions of learning, we can see dimly perhaps the outline of a new church, a new class of holy men and women with benefices, established to save us, although it should be noted that neither Cantelon nor Smith identify the university with the church in their arguments. They did argue the importance of the institutions about which they were writing.

What is the church? What Barnes, Cantelon, and Smith do is suggest how a section of our population has turned away from the church as a community and how many people in academic life no longer look to the church for the truth about human existence, about the nature and destiny of humankind, and of what constitutes highest value and meaning. Julian Hartt put the matter simply. In his *Theology and the Church in the University* (1969) he suggested that the church might be defined in terms of these root theological convictions:

1. Acceptance of the revelation of God in Jesus Christ is an acceptance of a way of knowing God that is normative for all other knowledge of God.
2. Acceptance of the revelation in Jesus Christ is an acceptance of a way of serving God that is normative for all other ways of serving God.
3. The connection between knowing God and properly serving him is so terribly close and demanding that apart from divine grace we could not endure it.[6]

The church is a community of believers dedicated to bringing root theological convictions into a sharpness of formulation which makes their moral implication unmistakable. This is certainly a reductionist way of defining the church. But it has the merit of reminding us about the unique thing which Christians have to say and do in the world, for which others will not take responsibility. Indeed, Julian Hartt claimed in his book that it was the responsibility of Christian institutions of higher learning to help the church carry out the mandate as suggested here.

We are discussing the relationship of the church to institutions of higher learning at a time when Protestant denominations (many of those associated with the National Council of Churches) and the Roman Catholic Church are undergoing something of an organizational and identity crisis. Many church-related institutions of higher education are also undergoing a crisis, under the pressure of mounting costs and the competition of tax-supported schools, sometimes forcing the closing or the separation of these institutions from the church. F. Thomas Trotter, of the United Methodist Church, has written about the problem of denominational officers concerned with education. They have to count their institutions at the end of the day to see if they are all in place, and sometimes find they have to announce: "One of our colleges is missing." Because of this pressure, some people argue that the church ought to get out of the business of higher education altogether. Others maintain that it is important for the church to stay in higher education in order to provide a different kind of learning, an option to that offered in many state and privately sponsored and supported schools.[7]

My responsibility is to serve as historian, to refresh the memory about where we have been as the church, the community of believers, and how we have carried our educational responsibilities in the past. First of all, I plan to go down some main-traveled roads in the history of church-related higher education and to recall some of the important landmarks along the way. While our special concern is church-related higher education, the investigation shows that church-relatedness has been defined in many different ways and that it has been and still is difficult to separate this particular concern from the work of Christians engaged in higher education in general. Second, I want to call attention to some important roads taken in the history of higher education which we tend to neglect, that is, the education of women, blacks, and Roman Catholics. Then I want to recall some conversations which we have had along the way about the Catholic substance of the faith, Christian commitment, and the responsibility of the church-related institution to serve a prophetic purpose in the society.

Main-Traveled Roads and Some Familiar Landmarks

A journey through the history of higher education in the United States highlights the fact that the church has had a formative influence on its development. Christians related themselves as persons and through their institutions to the mind's adventure in many constructive and creative ways. An abundant literature illuminates this past for us. It includes familiar volumes, such as Donald G. Tewksbury, *The Founding of American Colleges and Universities Before the Civil War* (1932); Paul M. Limbert, *Denominational Policies in the Support and Supervision of Higher Education* (1929); Clarence P. Shedd, *The Church Follows Its Students* (1938); Merrimon Cuninggim, *The College Seeks Religion* (1947); Manning M. Pattillo, Jr., and Donald M. Mackenzie, *Church-Sponsored Higher Education in the United States* (1966); and Kenneth Underwood, *The Church, the University, and Social Policy* (1969). This literature, supplemented by many denominational, institutional, and conference studies, provides for us a map of the territory and interpretations of landmarks along the road.[8]

Higher education began in colonial America at a very early time. To begin at the very beginning, we note that the universities of Peru and Mexico were established by the Spanish government and the Roman Catholic Church almost a century before such institutions began to take shape in the English colonies. Harvard was founded in 1636 and William and Mary in 1693 to help Congregationalists and Anglicans carry out their English errand in the Massachusetts and Virginia wildernesses. These institutions were followed by Yale, Princeton, Brown, Pennsylvania, King's College (now Columbia) in the eighteenth century to meet colonial demands for education. These colleges may not be labeled easily as state colleges, church colleges, or private colleges, since the commonwealth, the church, and private persons played a part in sponsoring and supporting them. Brown and Columbia had ecumenical boards, and students from various denominations and colonies attended these schools. The colleges preserved aspects of medieval Catholic education with Protestant modifications, with an emphasis upon the learning of the classics and a study of the Bible in whose spirit many colonists lived and moved and from which they gained their Christian identity. Harvard stressed the explication of *veritas*, interpreted through the mottoes of the school—*In Christo Gloriam* (1650) and *Christo et Ecclesiae* (1692).[9]

Douglas Sloan has investigated broadening approaches to education in the eighteenth century in his study of *The Scottish Enlightenment and the American College Ideal* (1971). Americans began to supplement the older classical and biblical learning with more practical courses and learning experiences, to provide for instructors who were subject specialists, and to experiment with closer relations between gown and town.[10] College education was primarily preprofessional, and students went on to apprentice in theology, law, and medicine. The Christian character of these institutions was guaranteed by the Congregationalist, Anglican, Presbyterian, and Baptist clergy who presided over them, the trustees who controlled them, and the professors who introduced the students to the republic of letters and to republican responsibilities. Lest it be thought that this early period was a nonsectarian golden age, we might recall all of the denominational squabbles and the fact that William and Mary was founded so that young men would not have to go north to a Puritan College and that the College of New Jersey was founded so that the young enthusiasts of the Great Awakening would not have to go north or south for a non-Presbyterian education. And Yale preferred *Lux et Veritas* in Hebrew as well as in Latin.

The final ratification of the Constitution of the United States of America in 1789 and the passage of the First Amendment in 1791 are convenient and significant landmarks along the way since they signaled the beginning of the constitutional debate over the nature and extent of religious liberty which would affect higher education in years to come. The federal government had not as yet sorted out its educational obligations and could not make up its mind about the establishment of a national university, which had been advocated by some clergy and laity.[11]

In the new nation, Christians and the churches faced up to an obligation to train a literate national citizenship and leadership. This second part of the road extends from 1789 to 1862, with the passage of the Morrill Act and the establishment by the federal government of the land-grant schools. This was a period of "freedom's ferment," as Alice Felt Tyler called it, a time of a bewildering proliferation of denominations, societies, and institutions of higher learning. Denominations, which had begun a process of organization in the 1780s, continued to spread and refine their structural patterns. At the same time Christians were often confronting one another, they were also exploring ways and means to express the unity of evangelical Protestantism, especially in common causes. This exploration culminated in an attempt to organize the American branch of the Evangelical Alliance in the 1840s. One way in which Protestants cooperated was in organizing such societies as the American Bible Society, the American Tract Society, the American Sunday School Union, all of which were intended to provide an education for Americans.

Christians approached their obligations in higher education in several ways. They began a wave of residential college building with Hampden-Sydney, Franklin, Dickinson, and Hamilton, in the Revolutionary Era. They also participated in the establishment of state universities in the South and in the West, many Christians believing that this was a better way to provide higher education than through the church-related college. Tewksbury charted the founding of 516 colleges and universities by Christians and their churches

before the coming of the war between the states. The University of
Georgia was one institution not founded under denominational
auspices but under Christian influence which, for all practical
purposes, became a Presbyterian institution. Abraham Baldwin, a
Connecticut Yankee in Georgia, a Yale graduate, and a lay
theologian, helped draw up the charter for the University of Georgia
in 1785 which put the purpose of higher education this way: Since the
happiness of free governments, the charter read, depends upon a civil
order based upon "the result of choice, and not necessity," and since
the "common wishes of the people become the laws of the land, their
public prosperity, and even existence, very much depends upon
suitably forming the minds and morals of their citizens." [12]

One of the tensions which developed between the state-related
schools and the church-related schools, as Albea Godbold has
pointed out, was the feeling that the former were really not concerned
with public education but rather with training the few with tax
support, whereas the latter were attempting to educate the many
without the financial assistance of the state. In both instances, clergy
served as presidents and professors and shaped the nation's mind and
morals. [13]

This was not the period of "great retrogression" in American
education. Our predecessors were attempting to send the nation to
school. Jerald Brauer may have been exaggerating in his essay for the
Second Quadrennial Convocation of Christian Colleges in 1958, but
his comment is worth remembering. The Christian churches "did not
play a unique role in American higher education—they *were*
American higher education." [14] There was considerable sectarian
competition and bickering in the building of colleges and over the
control of state institutions. But this competition and bickering
should not be allowed to obscure the achievements. In 1929, Limbert
showed that church-relatedness was determined by many factors, the
nature of ecclesiastical polity (congregational, presbyterian, or
episcopal), the concern of a denomination for education, the
availability of funds for sponsorship and support of education.
Congregationalists deliberately encouraged a model of independence, on the one hand, and fellowship, on the other hand, whereas
presbyterian and episcopal polities attempted more control, though
not with any degree of uniformity or success. Recently, David Potts

has stressed the significance of the local control over these institutions and the local popularity of and pride in these colleges.[15]

The curriculum in the colleges and universities also varied. Shaped largely by the mothers of colleges, Harvard, Yale, and Princeton, the modified classical system came under increasing criticism by those who thought the nation needed a more utilitarian course of study. The famous Yale report, "Original Papers in Relation to a Course of Liberal Education," was published in 1827 and was intended to bring some order out of the growing chaos in higher education. It analyzed what it was that made an educated person. It encouraged classical studies with moral philosophy for the discipline of the mind and character, while suggesting the possibility of a broader course offering for students. Philip Lindsley, a Princetonian, a Presbyterian preacher, and a perceptive educator, showed some disdain for the "Hic, Haec, Hoc-*ers*," but he was probably as unfair to them as they were to him in his education experiments in Tennessee.[16]

With the organization of the American Education Society in 1815 and the Society for the Promotion of Collegiate and Theological Education in the West in 1843, interdenominational cooperation in higher education started. These national societies, supported primarily by the Congregationalists and Presbyterians, helped sponsor and support institutions and served as early accrediting associations.[17] It should be noted that denominations, following the pattern set by Andover in 1808, organized theological seminaries— "hot houses," Peter Cartwright called them—for the training of ministers and that these were institutions over which churches had far greater control than over their colleges and universities.[18] Although not slow to organize colleges, Methodists and Baptists, among others, did show considerable suspicion of professional theological education for clergy.

At the close of this period, Harvard's President James Walker maintained that the college had to make a distinction between "Christianity considered as a means of enlightening and civilizing men in their relations to each other and the world, and Christianity considered as a means of eternal salvation to individuals," both legitimate functions of Christianity. He did not want the college to become the church. In reminding his hearers in 1855 of the enlightening and civilizing work in which all Christian colleges were engaged, he also reminded them of the larger obligation, as he saw it, of Christians.[19] So important was this work considered that one Methodist clergy maintained that "the President of a superior college has it in his power to do more harm or good thàn the President of the United States."[20] Standing *in loco parentis* and *in loco dei,* the college president did have an awesome responsibility. And Natalie A. Naylor, in suggesting a revision of Tewksbury's study, suggests that so pervasive was the common purpose of the schools organized in this period that it deserves to be called, not the era of the denominational, but that of the Christian college.[21]

Consolidation of national denominational policies in the field of higher education and the search for interdenominational cooperation are important developments along the next stretch of this main-traveled history. The landmarks to set this period apart are the Morrill Act of 1862 and the Servicemen's Readjustment Act of 1944, better known as the "GI Bill of Rights," which provided assistance for veterans of World War II seeking higher education. The founding of land-grant colleges did not bring about the demise of church-related education, nor did it suddenly end the influence of the pattern of education established in the first half of the century. But this period does mark the serious entry of the federal government into the field of higher education and the growth of a university system, state related and private. Often the older college of arts and sciences became the heart of the university, and the newer institutions continued to have a general Protestant orientation.[22] To be sure, in 1869 the University of Wisconsin did away with compulsory attendance at chapel services but not with chapel services themselves.

This was a period of consolidation and change in church-related higher education. As Robert H. Wiebe has shown in his study, *The Search for Order, 1877–1920,* the industrialization and urbanization of American life brought on a quest for new organizing principles and the bureaucratization of life. This impulse in the larger culture touched denominational efforts in higher education and had a decisive effect on church-related schools. Denominations experienced considerable growth in bureaucratic structure at the same time they were entering into closer cooperation at every level of Christian faith and life. Particularistic tendencies in Protestantism were countered by those of a more cooperative nature. Sloan's suggestion that it was this later period which was marked by "incredibly fierce sectarian strife" rather than the earlier period should be reexamined without neglect of the strife or ecumenical spirit which we can trace throughout the nineteenth century.[23]

We have already observed the early beginnings of this process before the Civil War, with societies and boards organized to assist those in the field of education. Congregationalists took over these early societies in which they had been engaged with the Presbyterians—a falling-out which symbolizes independent developments in this period. Congregationalists, organizing themselves as a denomination, formed the American College and Education Society in 1874 and continued to aid educational institutions. Presbyterians in the United States of America organized the Presbyterian Board of Aid for Colleges and Academies in 1883, an agency reorganized as the College Board in 1904. The Methodist Episcopal Church, heavily into higher education by now, established a University Senate in 1892. Other denominations followed suit in an attempt to exercise more control over the institutions. The Methodist University Senate performed pioneering work in setting standards for Methodist institutions and in working out a process for accrediting schools which wished to be related to the Methodist Episcopal Church.

These boards were often more liberal in their view of higher education than were the denominations they represented; nevertheless, some colleges and universities resisted attempts of these denominational boards to extend control over academic life.[24] Francis L. Patton, president of Princeton University and himself a Presbyterian preacher, told a group of alumni in New York during the latter part of the century that he would do all he could "to keep the hand of ecclesiasticism from resting on Princeton University," thus distancing himself from the denomination which had been related to Princeton from its earliest years. A Protestant Episcopal study of church colleges in 1895 also showed resistance to more formalized church-relatedness. Let the president and a majority of the trustees and a number of faculty be church members, the study said, and the institutions would be church schools and better off without diocesan meddling.[25] Limbert found in 1929 that these agencies offered spotty financial support of educational institutions.

During this period of consolidation under school boards, the denominations further shaped their understanding and definitions of church-related schools. The Episcopalians thought their schools should be known by the product. Just as did Oxford and Cambridge, so American colleges and universities under Episcopal auspices should turn out "not learned devils, not walking dictionaries, nor impracticable doctrinaires, but gentlemen."[26] Other denominations made more official statements than the author of the Episcopal study of church colleges quoted above. In the early part of the twentieth century, some of these statements of purpose were quite specific. Most boards called for the study of the Bible and of the Christian religion and placed an emphasis on the training of Christian character as well as on the pursuit of truth in a spirit of freedom, as did the Methodists in 1926. The Northern Baptist Convention maintained in 1920 that the fundamental thing in Christian life, and therefore for Baptist higher education, was "the experience of grace in God in human hearts."[27] The United Lutheran Church stated that along with the teaching of the Bible, other qualifications were necessary for a Christian college in 1920:

> . . . that every such institution shall maintain a Department of Bible Study, with cognate courses in Christian Religion and Ethics, with a full-time professor or instructor, and shall agree to use part of the funds received from the Board for the maintenance of this Department and it shall require for graduation three periods of study a week in these subjects during at least two College and Academic years.[28]

The Board of Christian Education of the Presbyterian Church, U.S.A. was very specific about what constituted a Christian college in its *Annual Report* of 1925. Chief characteristics were:

1. The professors and instructors professing Christians and members of some evangelical church.
2. Teaching of the Bible organized into the regular curriculum with a ranking professor as a faculty member.
3. Regular services of public worship in which student attendance and faculty participation are expected.
4. Positive Christian point of view in the teaching of all subjects laid down in the curriculum.
5. The development and culture of Christian character as the supreme end of all academic influence.[29]

The Southern Baptist Education Commission was equally specific in 1927 in its qualifications for church-relatedness. Baptist colleges

> . . . must be genuinely and actively Christian in spirit, control, faculty,

curriculum and objectives; otherwise there is no reason for their existence and no permanent place for their work. Especially do we believe that each of our schools should have a department of Christian Education, including good courses in Christian ethics and in the English Bible, and that this department should rank with the strongest departments in the school, and that the required courses for a college degree from a Christian college should include work in this department.[30]

While requirements for affiliation or federation have shifted in recent years, these denominational board statements illustrate the tendency toward consolidation of these educational efforts and the attempt to set standards for a Christian college or university.

Along with this denominational consolidation, with its mixed results, Protestant bodies began to explore ways of greater cooperation.

Under the Federal Council of Churches (1908), the Council of Church Boards of Education was organized in 1911 and held its first meeting in 1912. Through a periodical, *Christian Education,* and other means, it carried out its responsibilities of gathering and disseminating useful information, of stimulating the work of church colleges, of promoting and unifying church work in non-church-related institutions, and of recruiting for church vocations.[31] In the same period, scholars began to organize professional societies—the Society of Biblical Literature (1880) and the American Society of Church History (1888), to mention two prominent ones.

The character of church-relatedness shifted with the growth of the modern university and the development of philanthropic foundations, and the church's approaches to higher education took on new forms. The modern American university, public and private, began to take shape with the founding of Cornell University in 1865 and Johns Hopkins University in 1876. It was characterized by a more open cafeteria-style system and concentrated research faculties and facilities for graduate education.[32] The older liberal arts colleges which had set the pace for much of church-related education— Harvard, Yale, and Princeton—followed suit.

The modern American foundation also took shape with the fabulous increase of private fortunes and philanthropy. The policies of the General Education Board (1903), The Carnegie Foundation for the Advancement of Teaching (1913), the Carnegie Corporation

(1911), and the Rockefeller Foundation (1913), began to alter the relations between churches and their schools. More and more church-related institutions found themselves increasingly dependent financially upon philanthropists. In the case of the Carnegie "pension plan," institutions under sectarian control were specifically barred from participation. This plan, it should be noted, stimulated the accrediting process which denominational boards had begun several years earlier. Now some denominational schools redefined their relations to churches in order to take advantage of the pension fund. They became private colleges and universities or independent Protestant institutions, in the latter case often attempting to preserve some continuity with their roots.[33]

The new challenges called for new responses by Christians and their churches, directed not just toward church-related institutions but to the church's mission in public and private colleges and universities as well. In his volume entitled *Two Centuries of Student Christian Movements* (1934), Clarence Shedd showed the importance of peer relationships in higher education and the valuable contributions made in the organization of student work by the Young Men's Christian Association, the Young Women's Christian Association, the Student Volunteer Movement, and the World Student Christian Federation. He showed here that Christian higher education went on in places other than in the formal classroom. In his later study, *The Church Follows Its Students* (1938), Shedd showed how denominational and interdenominational boards and agencies tried to follow students in a variety of ways, not only to church-related and independent Protestant institutions, but to the fast-growing, state-supported and private colleges and universities.[34]

Cuninggim in *The College Seeks Religion* (1947), a history of the first forty years of the twentieth century, showed how institutions of higher learning which may have distanced themselves from denominational sponsorship and support began to take seriously the religious needs of students. Yale, Princeton, Duke, Northwestern, Denison, among the schools and "significant programs" studied by Cuninggim, provided some official institutional guidance for students with religious concerns, support for chapel services, and greater instruction in religion in the curriculum. Cuninggim indicated broad ecumenical Protestant support of this movement. He concluded that universities and colleges were seeking religion "not merely as mental discipline or as activity but as spirit for the whole campus life," so fragmented had academic life become by this state of our journey.[35]

The last portion of this road from the "GI Bill" of 1944 to the present has been marked by massive federal involvement in higher education through the National Defense Act of 1958, the Higher Education Act of 1965, and the Education Amendments of 1972. During these past decades, the United States emerged as one of the world's superpowers. New world responsibilities and the Russian leap into space goaded the government into the field of higher learning.

At the beginning of this period, however, there was an important signal from the Harvard Committee in its report, *General Education in a Free Society* (1945), about uncertainty in the educational field. What the educational policy paper did was to call attention to the difficulties which the committee had in defining the purpose of education in a free society. Perhaps the major finding of importance to the churches in their concern for higher education was that, according to the committee, "whatever one's views, religion was not now for most colleges a practicable source of intellectual unity." The committee went further, however, and suggested that unity was not being provided by the study of the great traditions in the literature of our culture, or in the scientific outlook or in science, or in organizing knowledge around the actual problems and questions which people expect to meet in mature life. The committee concluded that what was important was "belief in the worth and meaning of the human spirit."[36] Harvard had traveled a long distance from the affirmation of *veritas* in its early years.

While American higher education was burgeoning in size, both in enrollment and numbers of institutions, its purposes were becoming increasingly diffuse. Church-related institutions suffered the same development; and at the end of this part of the road, the future of these institutions had become uncertain. Indeed, the National Commission on United Methodist Higher Education sounded an alarm in 1976 for an "endangered service."[37]

In 1951, worried about what essentials were important to a Christian college, a number of denominations and their colleges joined in an ecumenical self-study. Forty-six church-related institutions—Protestant–Catholic, rich–poor, large–small, men's–women's–coeducational, located in various portions of the United States—engaged in the study. The self-study came to the conclusion that Christian colleges were different from tax-supported institutions and private schools having no Christian commitment. A college becomes "progressively and distinctly Christian as confidence is rested in the transforming love of God as manifested in Jesus Christ," a transforming love which sees the college organization and administration as analogous with the family and which allows this commitment to vitalize the curriculum and community life. The self-study placed an emphasis on the need for Christian colleges to deal with the needs of students and to include all without racial, religious, or political discrimination, an important note to recall.[38] In order to encourage Christians in the field of education, the newly formed National Council of Churches organized its work in the field under the Commission on Christian Higher Education with these purposes:

> To awaken the entire public to a realization that religious values may be achieved through all fields of study and through all phases of college life, that religion is essential in a complete education and that educational growth is prerequisite to the good life in the modern world.

> To foster a vital Christian life in the colleges and universities of the United States of America (tax-supported and independent as well as church-related and in the communities within which the institutions are located).

> To strengthen the Christian colleges, to promote religious instruction in them and to emphasize the permanent necessity of higher education under distinctly Christian auspices. To help the Christian institutions of higher learning in the United States of America fit the world-wide size of modern life and relate themselves effectively on student, faculty and administrative levels to the world movements toward Christian education.[39]

The commission sponsored or cosponsored numerous conferences, organized the Faculty Christian Fellowship, and supported the *Faculty Forum* and *The Christian Scholar*. Over the years it helped focus attention on the problems of church-related institutions of higher learning.[40] The self-study done in the early years of this period and the purposes set down by the commission expressed the concerns of many denominational agencies.

While church-related institutions found themselves still a vital part of higher learning and participants in the expanding growth business of higher education, they were educating proportionately fewer and fewer of the nation's youths. In their study, *Church-Sponsored Higher Education in the United States* (1966), Pattillo and Mackenzie found that there were still 817 colleges and universities associated in some way with 64 religious bodies, representing one-third of the 2,238 institutions of higher education in the nation at the time but with only one-fifth to one-sixth of the student population. The authors found church-related institutions still wrestling with the nature and extent of the church-relatedness; and they urged institutions to clarify purposes and policies, especially having to do with the relation between religious commitment and academic freedom. They appealed to denominations to increase substantially their financial support of church-related institutions. In considering what church-related colleges might contribute to higher education, they suggested a greater experimentation in educational theory and practice; greater commitment to teaching, to the humanities and public affairs, and to the common core experience of what makes an educated person; and greater commitment to help students—especially average students attending church-related institutions in large numbers—to arrive at a satisfactory Christian world view.[41]

The road we have taken so far has been a main-line—and independent—Protestant road. C. Robert Pace took a look at the conservative-evangelical institutions of higher learning in *Education and Evangelism* (1972). These institutions were more likely to produce better community than did main-line or independent Protestant schools, according to his study, and to encourage a firmer commitment to Protestantism among graduates, a result due partially to the more homogeneous student population. These schools were less experimental in instructional methods and produced a less critical prophetic attitude among students. But they enjoyed enthusiastic support from constituencies, Pace found, and it was his judgment that they had a better chance of survival than did some of the main-line and independent schools.[42]

These past years have been marked by competition of church-related institutions with tax-supported federal institutions and state-community colleges and by uncertainty because of the rising costs of educational services. Whereas in the early part of the nineteenth century, state-supported institutions were on the defensive, now church-related institutions have been placed in the position of justifying their existence. The debate over the meaning of the First Amendment to the Constitution has become crucial for church-related schools. So far the courts have held that aid is permissible to schools if "the sectarian functions of an institution can be separated from the secular and if enforcement of the secular use restriction does not entangle the state in religious activity."[43] So far the courts have not measured sectarian by questioning some kind of formal denominational control, limited church support, required courses in religion as a part of a liberal arts education, or the presence of a substantial number of students, faculty, and board members who are from sponsoring denominations—all marks which have been used to define church-relatedness throughout our history. It remains to be seen, as the recent Methodist study concludes, what course future litigation will take, but this debate over the constitutionality of government aid has emerged as a major factor in planning.[44]

Neglected Scenes: Higher Education for Women, Blacks, and Catholics

Those in church-related institutions sometimes attacked those in state-supported institutions because they believed the latter institutions were not really public. Rather they were established to instruct the children of the well-to-do and privileged at public expense. Protestants in the private sector thought of their purpose as that of providing for all an education for responsible citizenry as well as for leadership in the nation. Passing over well-traveled roads in higher education, we tend to think, because of our partial perspectives, in terms of the education of male, white Protestants, and we neglect the church's contribution to the education of women, blacks, and Catholic immigrants. Higher education for these groups of people has been shaped by attitudes toward sex, race, and education itself in the service of the church, as in the case of Catholic involvement in this field. The black and women's movements and recent Catholic scholarship have raised our consciousness about these elements.

During the colonial period, a number of highly capable women were running families and farms and businesses without the benefit of formal education for their tasks. They picked up most of their education in the larger schoolrooms which were the communities in which they lived. They read and listened, and according to the record some of them have left, they were a remarkably intelligent group. While numerous suggestions were made to advance the formal education of women by such vocal do-gooders as Benjamin Rush, the suggestions did not come to much. John Trumbull, one of Connecticut's wits, attacked those who discouraged and dismissed the higher education of women. He bemoaned in his poem, "The Progress of Dulness" (1773), the fate of Harriet Simper:

> But why should girls be learn'd or wise
> Books only serve to spoil their eyes.
> The studious eye but faintly twinkles,
> And reading paves the way for wrinkles.
> In vain may learning fill the head full:
> 'Tis Beauty that's the one thing needful. . . .

Harriet, according to Trumbull, was robbed of a rightful education because of this shortsightedness. She was doomed to be an addict of fashion, foolishness, and gossip.[45]

As the new nation grew, so did its appetite for operatives in industry and also for instructors to run the new school systems for children below the college level throughout the whole country. Women were therefore needed. The establishment of schools for higher education for women was based not simply out of a desire to provide an education belonging to all people in a republic so that women might live by choice and not simply by chance. Women were needed not only to be helpmates but to help train the nation's children—to fit into a society in which women could not participate fully in either the councils of the church or the commonwealth. According to the nineteenth-century scheme of things, shaped by evangelical Protestantism, women were spiritually equipped to train the minds and the morals of children.[46]

Women's institutions of higher learning were established slowly at first. In 1839, the Methodist Episcopal Church gave its sponsorship to the Georgia Female College, which was founded in 1830 and was the first such institution chartered to confer degrees on women similar to those of other liberal arts colleges. In 1837, Oberlin College opened its doors to women. Following Oberlin's lead, other institutions began to accept women applicants, but many of them refused to let women work for degrees. In 1839, the first state-supported normal training school was opened in Massachusetts for the education of female teachers. And in succeeding years, pioneer Catherine Beecher, daughter of Lyman Beecher, the New School Presbyterian preacher and educator and sire of Beechers, attempted to organize interest in teacher training through the newly organized National Board of Popular Education (1847) and the American Women's Educational Association (1852) to encourage professional education as well as the education of the mind.

Because many of the women's colleges were started after the Civil War at a time when denominational ties did not seem as important as they had been, these schools might be listed as independent Protestant colleges, and these turned out to be some of the better, more progressive institutions. Thomas Woody found in his study, *A History of Women's Education in the United States* (1929), still the most comprehensive treatment of the subject, that of the 126 women's schools in existence at the time of his survey, 80 of them were listed as "sectarian," underscoring the large role the church played in sponsoring and supporting female education. Moreover, as Woody points out, those schools not listed as "sectarian" in origin were established by pious Christians, often laywomen and laymen, and with strong, if not always orthodox Protestant, religious orientation. Henry Durant explained that Wellesley was "founded for the glory of God and the service of the Lord Jesus Christ in and by the education of women." Vassar, Bryn Mawr, and Smith, for example, expressed similar evangelical purposes. Rockford, Randolph-Macon, Hood, Goucher, Agnes Scott, several other institutions of high rank, were more directly under the sponsorship and support of Methodists, Episcopalians, and Presbyterians.[47]

The character of higher education for women was shaped by attitudes toward females during the nineteenth and twentieth centuries. Women were meant by God to be homemakers first of all, and higher education was intended to fulfill this divine function in a better way. This divine domestic purpose in the training of women led to the start of a new specialty in home economics. It was in the home that the training of the mind and the morals began under the beneficial spiritual influences of mothers. Women were meant by God to be teachers, and because of this they were treated to the same kind of courses as were men in the classics and biblical learning along with other courses which would make them more useful in the nation's classrooms.[48] Although women were denied roles in church and commonwealth, the attitude which made them spiritually superior to males and therefore persons to whom the minds and morals of the young could be trusted, granted to them great authority.[49]

At the end of the nineteenth century, alarm was expressed over the absence of many college-trained women from the home. Higher education made women discontented with their God-given roles, according to studies of college graduates. Many women suffered ill health and lower rate of fecundity than did non-college-educated women. These studies did not deter women, and they began to use their education in more and more ways. More and more women became professors and instructors in women's colleges, the number being considerably higher, according to Woody's study, in denominational schools than in the privately supported institutions. Moreover, since the church would not allow women to be ordained as ministers, many of them became missionary educators and doctors. Since the commonwealth would not allow them to hold political office, they invented social work; and through such experiments as the settlement houses, they raised the consciousness of the church and commonwealth to the problems of the poor in an increasingly industrialized and urbanized society.[50]

Denominationally sponsored and supported women's institutions have had the same difficulties in defining church-relatedness as have had other denominational schools. In addition, these women's schools have had to struggle with the attitudinal changes in the church and larger society. As more and more male institutions, public and private, have become coeducational and since more and more women seem to be attending these schools, churches and church-related colleges for women are rethinking the particular mission of these institutions in the society today.[51]

Churches have been deeply involved in the education of blacks. Education was not available for slaves nor for freedmen, except on a very limited scale before the Civil War. The first recorded attendance of blacks at an American college was in 1774. Bristol Yamma and John Quamine were sent by Samuel Hopkins of Newport, Rhode Island, to Princeton to prepare for missionary service in Africa under

John Witherspoon. Prior to the Civil War, Berea, Oberlin, and Antioch—not strictly church-controlled institutions—experimented with integrated education. In 1854, Presbyterians sponsored and supported Ashmun Institute, later to become Lincoln University, and in 1856 the Methodists organized Wilberforce College in Ohio.

After the Civil War, black higher education began in earnest under government and church auspices.[52] In 1865, "A Bureau for the Relief of Freedmen and Refugees" was organized under General O. O. Howard as a government commission, and in cooperation with various denominational agencies, it established numerous black colleges. Contrary to the judgment of W. E. B. DuBois, who paid tribute to the work of this bureau, historian Horace Mann Bond argues that it is almost impossible to make distinctions between state-related and church-related institutions, so closely did the bureau and the denominational agencies cooperate.[53] It should be noted also that most of America's blacks were in the South after the Civil War, and the church in this area was in no condition financially or psychologically to undertake the responsibility of developing educational institutions for those who were once slaves and servants.

White denominational agencies—the American Missionary Association (recognized by the Congregational Church as its agency), the Methodist Freedman's Aid Society, the American Baptist Home Mission Society, the Presbyterian Board of Missions for Freedmen, the American Church Institute of the Protestant Episcopal Church—founded schools. Black denominations—the African Methodist Episcopal Church, the African Methodist Episcopal Zion Church, the Christian Methodist Episcopal Church, and black Baptist associations—also provided the stimulus, the sponsorship, and support of the schooling of blacks. The institutions were further aided by the new philanthropists and foundations. For example, the George P. Peabody Fund for the Advancement of Negro Education in the South, organized in 1869, and John D. Rockefeller's General Education Board (1903), gave millions of dollars for black education. The Second Morrill Act of 1890 was another landmark in the history of black education. It provided for the establishment and maintenance of separate land-grant colleges for blacks, with the provision that funds were to be equitably distributed, although a fair distribution did not take place until recently. The Second Morrill Act preceded the Atlanta Compromise and *Plessy* v. *Ferguson* and helped to perpetuate a system of separate but unequal institutions for blacks.

Church-related institutions gave to many blacks what choice they had to participate as responsible citizens in their nation within a nation and in the republic. The chief purpose of these institutions was much like that of white church-related schools—the "glorification of God" in America. In 1868, the Freedmen's Aid Society put the purpose this way: "We must aid them in establishing good schools for the training of teachers and preachers and then as soon as possible deliver these institutions over to them for permanent support."[54] Blacks received training for the ministry, missionary service, teaching, and whatever other professional education was offered at these schools. The Methodists, for example, established Meharry Medical School in Nashville and Flint Medical College in New Orleans for the training of black doctors. But the Freedmen's Aid Society did not turn over institutions of higher learning to blacks themselves as quickly as it intended. Presbyterians pioneered in 1891 with a predominantly black faculty at Biddle University. Most schools of the white denominations, however, committed the educational enterprise in the black schools to white leadership and staffs. It is important to note that, as the predominantly black denominations established churches, they went on to establish schools and colleges; and though their resources were limited, these denominations gave sacrificially to the support and nurture of these institutions. Even today about 40 percent of the national budget of certain of the predominantly black denominations goes to their colleges.

In 1944, the black colleges and universities began to cooperate in raising financial support for their own institutions through the United Negro College Fund. Many black colleges still are marginal institutions because of lack of resources, having suffered throughout their history from proliferation and poverty, the former aggravating the latter. They have provided training of the mind and morals, however, to many blacks who would have received no such education, and still today they graduate almost as many black students with B.A. degrees as do the other institutions in the country. Benjamin E. Mays, preacher-president of Morehouse College for many years and the president of the United Negro College Fund in 1960, claimed that Negro church-related as well as independent colleges allowed blacks

> their freedom to experiment, to explore, to inquire unrestricted, to develop a leadership of spiritual power, to overcome the dangers that permeate a secular society, and to become centers of interracial, inter-cultural, inter-faith, and international living.[55]

The development of Catholic-sponsored higher education offers an interesting comparison with the history of Protestant-related institutions. With the establishment of St. Mary's Seminary and Georgetown Academy in 1791, American Catholics began their adventure in higher education in the new nation, several centuries after the early beginnings in Peru and Mexico. John Carroll had just been consecrated the first bishop of Baltimore in 1790. Protestant institutions were designed—as Lyman Beecher's *Plea for the West* (1835) vividly puts it—to counter infidelity and barbarism and to help transform the influences of Roman Catholics, whom evangelical Protestants thoroughly distrusted. Catholics faced an enormous problem in the nineteenth century with the flood of immigrants arriving in wave after wave from Ireland, Germany, and southern and eastern Europe, impoverished and often suspicious of education. Catholics perceived the danger to their own identity in the Protestant ethos, and they established their own schools for the training of leadership and to keep Catholics from leaving the fold.

American Catholics had to sponsor and support a parochial system for Catholic children in addition to institutions of higher learning. While they began to sponsor colleges, they did not always support them. Overbuilding and undersupport led to the early demise of many Catholic institutions. Church-relatedness of Catholic institutions is hard to describe. They were organized by about as many Catholic orders as Protestants had denominations and under almost as many conditions. Many graduates entered the service of the church as priests and as teachers in the Catholic parochial school system. Indeed, Catholics had difficulty in sorting out an educational approach which would be appropriate for those entering church vocations and yet would best fit men and women for a life of responsible Christian citizenship. The Catholic system grew. The Catholic University of America was founded in 1892. By 1904, the

Catholic enterprise was so large that the National Catholic Educational Association, with a College and University Department, was organized to bring some common purpose and order into Catholic education in its various forms. This development paralleled the Protestant bureaucratization process at the turn of the century.[56]

John Tracy Ellis, specialist in the history of education and American Catholicism, dropped a bombshell on the road of Catholic higher education in 1955, a date to be remembered, with an essay entitled "Catholics and the Intellectual Life." In this essay he analyzed and criticized the Catholic educational system. As an historian, Ellis remembered sympathetically the difficulties Catholics had faced in a hostile Protestant ethos and with a host of ethnics swarming to America in the nineteenth and early twentieth centuries. Still, he said, Catholics had not produced first-rate institutions—no Harvard or Yale or Princeton. No Catholic school had been admitted to the prestigious Phi Beta Kappa until 1938, and few Catholics had made it into *Who's Who,* an indication of achievement in America. In proportion to the number of Catholics in the population, Catholics had not made much of a contribution to the intellectual life of the nation.[57]

Discussion of Ellis's essay brought out some of the defensiveness of the Catholic educational enterprise in the past and the way in which the system had been governed by ecclesiastics for ecclesiastical purposes. John Ireland underscored this point when he warned the first rector of the Catholic University of America in 1892: "You must educate your professors, and then hold on to them—making bishops only of those who are not worth keeping as professors."[58] Defensiveness even led to the organization of separate professional institutions for Catholic scholars, which further separated them from the growing community of scholarship in America. "Assimilant" Catholics have argued that the church has for too long a time dominated the educational system. It has fostered a kind of "Mr. Chips" attitude toward those in higher education. While doing so much for so many, Catholic scholars have received little recognition and even less remuneration.[59]

Catholic educators have gone through the process of defining church-relatedness, trying to find the proper formula by which church-related institutions will survive and thrive. While recognizing the dangers of greater independence of schools—Harvard, Yale, Princeton, for example, which started out with close relationships to religious bodies before their secularization—Catholics have been trying to insure greater freedom of schools from the church's interference. In recent statements, "The Idea of the Catholic University" and "The Restless Christian College," they have attempted to state their purposes. Catholic institutions are those in which "Catholicism is perceptibly present and effectively operative" and yet in which a genuinely ecumenical rather than sectarian spirit should prevail. Truly Catholic institutions are those that will also foster critical and reforming attitudes within the American Catholic Church. Theological faculties within Catholic universities are expected to provide active and creative dialogue with other disciplines within the university and to guide administration, faculty, and student bodies in living by Christian ideals and ideas.[60] Catholics and Protestants, facing the same problems of the "endangered service"—the United Methodist description of the challenge facing church-related institutions—have been cooperating more and more in recent years in the field of higher education. They jointly sponsored a summer conference in 1970 through the Council of Protestant Colleges and Universities and the National Catholic Educational Association.[61]

Catholic ecclesiastical paternalism reminds one of the paternalism in the history of higher education for women and blacks, education dominated often by males and whites. Men know what is good for women. Whites know what is good for blacks. Ecclesiastics know what is good for the laity. So the story has been in the past. Some of this paternalism has given way to independence, partnership, and shared power in education. But some women, blacks, and American Catholics hold the churches responsible for fostering sexism, racism, and anti-intellectualism not only in higher education but also in the larger society. While there have been attempts at liberation, alienation from the church persists among those groups whose educational journey we have just surveyed.

This paternalism in education reminds one also of aspects of exploitation in all of American education. In the first half of the nineteenth century, higher education was dominated by Protestant clergy—the old-time college president and professor—and the debates over the curricula of institutions of higher education had in them something of the paternalism of those who thought they knew best what type of education was good for the republic. Thorstein Veblen noted the great shift which came to all higher education in *The Higher Learning in America* (1918) in the latter half of the century. The control of education passed from the hands of the church and men of the cloth into the hands of men of business and mammon. Fear of the trustee had replaced the fear of God, not simply in black education, but in all forms of higher education. In more recent years, higher learning has been sponsored and supported by the government in the name and for the sake of national defense. Fear of the board of trustees is being replaced by the fear of the federal and state governments, thus raising further questions about education dedicated to "the worth and meaning of the human spirit," to use the words of the Harvard *Report* of 1945.

Catholic Substance, Christian Commitment, and Prophetic Inquiry

What has been and is the purpose of church-related higher education, and what is it that such education offers that other institutions cannot, or do not, offer or that Christians involved in other institutions of higher learning cannot offer? Now that church-related institutions are an "endangered service," this problem of purpose has become a crucial one. The United Church of Christ has recently affirmed that church-related institutions have a "unique role in a unique time." What is that unique role? Discussions of this question have sometimes focused in recent years on the responsibility of church-related institutions to deal with catholic substance, Christian commitment, and prophetic inquiry and vision. These recent discussions are illuminated by reference to our past.

The first focus is on the responsibility of church-related institutions for "catholic substance," based upon Christian assumptions about the nature and destiny of creation, human life, and human community. During the conference on *Campus '70,* sponsored by the Council of Protestant Colleges and Universities and the National Catholic Educational Association, Martin E. Marty suggested that church-related institutions had a "mandate" to survive and also to champion "catholic substance" in higher education. Marty had in mind Tillich's emphasis upon the Christian's concern for the whole of existence. This Tillichian concern had to do with the embodiment of the Spirit, in a sacramental sense, as a constitutive and culture-forming activity in the lives of individuals and institutions. To fulfill this responsibility, church-related institutions must champion rationality in the face of the cult of irrationality and must use the mind to embrace the whole of creation and human culture as over against "counter-cultural rationalists."

Marty argued that the concern is based on the Christian confession, using biblical language, that all things are "created in and for Christ," with "all things cohering in him, the Logos taking form in him, and from this impetus Christians have legitimately taken up a concern to build, preserve, and care for the human world."[62] Church-related colleges have a mandate to be so involved in the mind's adventure that out of this concern for catholic substance a new culture may emerge. In the nineteenth century, President Walker of Harvard expressed this concern, although he made a distinction between Christianity, on the one hand, and its impact as a civilizing process, on the other. As church-related education helped to shape the culture in the past, it may be called to do so in a new way today.

It has been suggested that church-related institutions have a particular responsibility in an age of increasing religious illiteracy and that is simply to undertake effective teaching about Christian sources and traditions. Lloyd J. Averill has called attention to the widespread lack of knowledge about the Bible and of Christian tradition in recent times in his development of *A Strategy for the Protestant College,* a problem also faced by Catholic institutions. He maintained that the church-related institution of higher education had the responsibility, the special if not unique "responsibility to increase, among Christians and non-Christians alike, an intelligent understanding and appreciation of the Christian tradition in its work, its worship, and its intellectual heritage."[63] Averill maintained that in order to meet this challenge, trustees, administrators, and faculty in church-related institutions of higher learning had to bear the responsibility and to show a much greater Christian maturity than they have in recent years. John B. Cobb, Jr., is concerned that the church begin to "think again." Moving somewhat beyond Averill, Cobb suggests that the church-related institution, in helping the church begin to think again, must cease taking all norms for reflection from the scientific community and develop norms out of its own traditions and approach to knowing and knowledge.[46]

Albert Outler addressed the problem of knowing in an essay published in *Colleges and Commitments,* a volume edited by Lloyd J. Averill and William W. Jellema in 1971. Outler made the distinction between "discursive truth" and "evangelical truth." The first truth is that which is knowable and known about the world and human experience by means of "intelligible patterns and structures and values in the world and in our experience." The latter is the truth of "God in and through the event of Jesus Christ" as "pure unbounded love." The Perkins professor did not suggest that Christians champion a "double truth" in church-related higher education but maintained that the two aspects of truth should be correlated in the educational process.[65] Outler, as did Marty the year before, raised the question of the priority of Christian faith and focused on the ancient problem concerning *fides quaerens intellectum,* faith seeking understanding. How should faith seek understanding in our time in such a way that Christians may help contemporary culture to embody in some way a catholic substance?

Throughout the history of church-related higher education, colleges and universities have taken responsibility for defining the faith by which the church of Jesus Christ, as a community of believers, lived. This has been intimated here already with the emphasis upon teaching the Bible in these institutions. Will Herberg argued in the Averill and Jellema volume that this is one thing church-related institutions must be responsible for—the providing of an education based on biblical realism and a biblical world view and founded upon a knowledge of the Scriptures.[66]

Those engaged in higher education have often participated in debates about the way in which God's "pure unbounded love" and the "event of Jesus Christ" should be put in confessional terms and defended. In this process, Christians have challenged a number of isms. Deism was the subject for debate in higher education in the eighteenth century. Socinianism and Darwinism were subjects for debate in the nineteenth and early twentieth centuries. Humanism has been the subject for debate in the twentieth century. These struggles over aspects of Christian confession may have been carried on in a narrow sectarian manner at times. But the debates over these isms have involved questions about what Christians should confess about the nature and destiny of the creation and of human existence. When we look back to these struggles, we tend to be embarrassed when we recall how clergy and laity, often associated with church-related institutions, vulgarized the conflicts. William Jennings Bryan, for example, we remember as H. L. Mencken branded him, the "Fundamentalist Pope," the prime example of *homo boobiens,* after whom some of the sovereign people of Tennessee named a college. But if some clergy and laity vulgarized these debates, so others from Jefferson to Mencken tended to trivialize them. Educational historians, not particularly concerned about Christian theology, have tended to place these debates in the context of a Christian anti-intellectualism associated with denominational schools and in the context of the struggle for freedom in education.

Another focus in recent discussions of the purpose of church-related institutions has been the development of Christian commitment and consciousness. Charles Y. Glock and Robert N. Bellah have charted a "new religious consciousness" in colleges and universities.[67] While we were discussing "secularism" and "secularization," the campus "got religion," though the new religious consciousness is not necessarily sympathetic to the Christian consciousness and is not particularly concerned about corporate life and responsibilities. Many parents have sent their children off to church-related colleges with the expectation that they might be converted and challenged to some larger Christian commitment. Results have not always been what parents have expected. In the latter part of the eighteenth century, Episcopalian Charles Pettigrew counted the risk when he sent his son to Presbyterian Joseph Caldwell for study at the University of North Carolina. He was afraid because of "the danger of having all fear of the Almighty eradicated from his mind." In the early years of the twentieth century, a delegate to a Methodist General Conference complained that a parent could not "send a boy to Vanderbilt University to be educated without having his mind poisoned against the Methodist Church." At the end of the century, American Catholics were concerned about the Christian commitment of their students in higher education.[68] Now a parent may send a child off to a church-sponsored institution as well as a state or private institution and that student may come home only to announce that he or she is into some syncretistic cult, Eastern mysticism, sensitivity training, or Transcendental Meditation. The student may even come home a Protestant or Catholic charismatic.

The "new religious consciousness" today reminds one of the religious consciousness in church-related institutions of the past. Conversion was considered in many institutions an essential rite of passage and, to put it into contemporary language, a way of wedding the affective and cognitive in the learning process. Moreover, church-related institutions were considered proper recruiting places not only for Christians but also for Christian vocations. This was so in the First Great Awakening when there was a close relationship between religious affections and learning. This was so also at Yale and Hampden-Sydney colleges where the Second Great Awakening started. In laying the cornerstone of the first building at Amherst, Noah Webster exclaimed that one of the chief purposes of American colleges was "to reclaim and evangelize the miserable children of Adam."[69] Charles Grandison Finney, president and professor of Oberlin, was the chief revivalist of his time and, as Timothy Smith reminds us, was one of the intellectuals in his day.

It is instructive at this point to recall the purpose of the World Student Christian Federation, organized in 1895 and one of those instruments through which Christian students attempted to minister to one another. This voluntary society was directed by some of the most respected persons on the university and college circuit—Luther D. Wishard, Robert D. Speer, and John R. Mott. The WSCF was dedicated:

> To lead students to become disciples of Jesus Christ
>   as only Savior and as God.
> To deepen the spiritual life of students.
> To enlist students in the work of extending the
>   Kingdom of Christ throughout the whole world.[70]

So impressed was G. Stanley Hall with the importance of conversion to the process of growing up in America that he suggested in his famous study on *Adolescence* (1904) that conversion should be the "germ of all educational systems." Hall's colleagues questioned his apology for religion as well as his genetic psychology, but Hall, acquainted with the work of Dwight L. Moody among several generations of students, was up on the religious consciousness of that time.[71] The unfortunate thing is that revivalists who have attempted to burn over college and university campuses have not always helped the mind's adventure. Billy Sunday spoke with disdain about "higher critics"—"highbrows" who dreamed out their theories about the historicity of Jesus and the existence of two Isaiahs "over a pipe of tobacco and a mug of beer at Leipzig or Heidelberg." He gave his unadulterated opinion: "When the word of God says one thing and scholarship says another, scholarship can go to hell."[72] That was not very helpful. Probably for every college student Billy Sunday touched, several others just as thoughtful turned away. Since Sunday, our general reaction to conversion experiences has been, but for the grace of Horace Bushnell and Reinhold Neibuhr, there we go. But in the meantime, we have a "new religious consciousness," and we have turned over both evangelical and apologetic encounter with the faith to such voluntary groups as Inter-Varsity, Campus Crusade, or some charismatic cell.

Given this early history, church-related institutions have a special responsibility for dealing with the "new religious consciousness" on the campus in a Christian context and for helping students reach a higher level of maturity in their Christian commitment. Wesley A. Hotchkiss, breaking a taboo of nearly a century in colleges of the United Church of Christ in speaking about conversion, claimed recently that if properly understood it could be seen as a "liberating experience."[73] Over the past few years some theologians have been focusing attention on this matter in terms of both commitment and life-style. George W. Forell wrote about "The Nature of Religious Commitment" for *Faculty Forum,* describing it at three levels. At the first level we can have a commitment to religion as an historical-cultural tradition. At the second level, we can have a social-moral commitment to religion. At the third level, we can have a Christian or ultimate commitment to "Jesus the Christ as the disclosure of the meaning, purpose, and ultimate destiny of each human life in the plan of God." Such an ultimate commitment is, in the end, Forell argued, a gift of the Spirit, but it is a commitment about which church-related institutions should be concerned.[74]

Hugh T. Kerr, editor of *Theology Today,* went further and suggested that attention should be given to challenging people to commit themselves to Christ and to a Christ-life in the mythic sense.[75] It may be that church-related colleges have a unique responsibility for the nurture of the "new religious consciousness" and to help students develop a deeper style of Christian life, as well as commitment. Dean Hoge adds another consideration in his study of *Commitment on Campus* (1974) when he observes that there has been a tendency toward the privatization of religion among college students.[76] While this has been a danger in the past, it has not always been so. It may be that church-related institutions can move students from their present privatization toward a life of greater responsibility.

This brings us to a third focus. It has to do with the prophetic responsibilities of church-related higher education, the responsibility, as Kenneth Underwood put it in *The Church, The University, and Social Policy,* to engage in self-criticism, in criticism of the society, a questioning of all human pretensions.[77] This prophetic responsibility is an essential correlate to concern for catholic substance and Christian commitment. Since Underwood, there have been calls for Christians in higher education to fulfill this role in the society. Myron B. Bloy, Jr., in an article on "Academic Values and Prophetic Discernment" in *The Christian Century* has argued that Christians should challenge the rationalist ideology and hubris of the academic world—such as that expressed by Barnes in *The University as the New Church*—and to call it to account for simply training people to fit into a bourgeois, capitalist, and competitive society of individuals, rather than as persons prepared for responsible community life.

Kent E. Eklund, applying this argument more closely to the church-related institutions, has suggested that there must be a creative tension between churches and institutions of higher education in order not only to help the church deal with matters of catholic substance more intelligently but also to raise questions from Christian assumptions about social, political, and economic affairs.[78] The United Church of Christ, drawing upon this kind of approach, has described the best in its past and its hopes for the future of the church-related college as a prophetic institution encouraging prophetic inquiry and prophetic challenges to the nation.

Upton Sinclair put the problem for much of higher education in general and church-related education in particular in *The Goose-Step, a Study of American Education* in 1923 in a vivid way, bringing into question the route taken by Harvard educators in the early part of this century. Addressing himself to employees in American industrial and commercial society, he attacked the genteel, specialized business that academic life had become:

> Slaves in Boston's great department store, in which Harvard University owns twenty-five hundred shares of stock, be reconciled to your long hours and low wages and sentenced to die of tuberculosis—because upon the wealth which you produce some learned person has prepared for mankind full data on "The Strong Verb in Chaucer,"... Men who slave twelve hours a day in front of blazing white furnaces of Bethlehem, Midvale and Illinois Steel, cheer up and take a fresh grip on your shovels—you are making it possible for mankind to acquire exact knowledge concerning "The Beginnings of the Epistolary Novel in the Romance Languages,"...[79]

The same wealth which helped to sponsor and support Harvard in becoming a great modern university was also making possible church-related, male and female, black and white, Protestant and Catholic institutions.

Church-related institutions have not been altogether successful in transcending their partial perspectives without help either, and they have not been able to develop that Christian life-style and concern for others which would mark them as prophetic institutions. A journey through our past suggests this caution about their uniqueness. Take the case of slavery and racism. There were very few institutions able to transcend white attitudes toward blacks. Church and commonwealth were all too often joined by college and university to justify both slavery and the segregated life. In the South, for example, such church-related institutions as Wake Forest, Davidson, Duke, Southern Methodist, Baylor—just to mention a few—did not open undergraduate programs to black applicants until the early 1960s. Even then some boards were reassuring constituencies that their institutions would not enroll blacks.[80]

Neither have most church-related institutions shown any marked self-transcendence in terms of economic injustice or national self-interest. As a matter of fact, church-related institutions of higher education have had to rely upon outside voluntary societies for the protecting of the freedom of prophetic inquiry within and for the stimulus of prophetic vision. The American Association of University Professors was organized for the purpose of defending members in state-supported, private, and church-related schools whose professional lives were threatened because of stands they had taken on the basis of their academic research, speaking, and writing. In the same manner, Christian-sponsored voluntary societies prodded faculties and students on church-related campuses no less than on campuses not related to denominations toward a larger vision of justice. The YMCA and YWCA, for example, did this through student work departments. W. D. Weatherford helped to raise the consciousness of thousands of college students with his small study volume on *Negro Life in the South* (1909), and Walter Rauschenbusch prepared his *The Social Principles of Jesus* (1916) for a voluntary college study course. The Student Volunteer Movement and the World Student Christian Federation helped to give students a vision of Christian service throughout the whole world, a vision perhaps smacking too much of evangelical Protestant imperialism, but nevertheless providing a challenge to service for others they might not have had otherwise.

Behind the search for ways and means to insure the survival of church-related and private institutions of higher learning lies the idea that somehow these institutions might provide in a postindustrial age an alternative to materialistic, mechanistic, positivistic, and hedonistic approaches to life—an education, personal and humane, of genuine prophetic inquiry. But a trip through our history suggests that it takes a great deal of courage to transcend the system which sponsors, supports, and protects us. There has been a good deal of tension between church and college in recent years, and colleges, faculty, and students have reacted adversely to the "noise of solemn assemblies." It has been so in the past. Finney, the chief revivalist of his day and a supporter of many reform movements, held that there was a jubilee in hell whenever the General Assembly of the Presbyterian Church (US) met. How may institutions of higher learning and the churches which sponsor and support them understand one another better and cooperate in fulfilling the prophetic task?

Conclusion

The historian who travels down the various roads taken in Christian higher education is impressed with the large number of dedicated clergy and laity—Christians, men and women, white and black, Protestant and Catholic—who have believed that the church and they, as Christians, have a responsibility in the field of higher learning, for the sake of the commonwealth as well as the church. The dedication of these faithful has determined the quality and extent of the church's faithfulness in this field of endeavor. In his lectures at the University of Virginia in 1933, entitled *After Strange Gods,* T. S. Eliot made a comment about writers which may be appropriate here. He suggested that the chief clue to the understanding of most contemporary Anglo-Saxon literature at the time was to be found in the "decay of Protestantism." Individual writers, he maintained, could be "understood and classified according to the type of Protestantism which surrounded their infancy, and the precise state of decay which it had reached." Eliot included in his classification not only Protestantism of the more conservative type, but also "of an 'advanced' or agnostic atmosphere, because even agnosticism—*Protestant* agnosticism—has decayed in the last two generations."[81] Eliot's remarks may be adapted to suit Christian educators, Catholic as well as Protestant. It may be that church-relatedness depends in the end on the concern for catholic substance, Christian commitment, and the prophetic courage of those most involved in higher education.

As we have seen, Christians have developed numerous strategies to help the church carry its responsibilities. Some have been involved in state-sponsored and state-supported institutions. Some have been involved in private independent institutions. Some have been involved in the life of church-related institutions. The church's relation to colleges and universities has been varied. The church cooperated with the commonwealth in sponsoring and supporting schools in the eighteenth century. The church took the initiative in spreading and developing liberal arts institutions across the nation during the first half of the nineteenth century. Then denominationally and ecumenically, the church began the search for common directions and to coordinate work in the field of church-related higher education. In addition, the church shaped numerous strategies to help administrators, faculties, and students in fulfilling the mind's adventure.

The roads to our present have not been easy. The road ahead does not look easy. As we enter onto a new stretch, perhaps the best thing that we can do is to keep experimenting with a wide variety of options in the field, to close some schools and to consolidate others, to offer to some institutions that support which is necessary for them to stay open, and to help all those involved in this field to set new directions and to cooperate in the common cause in a new age. Moreover, we should keep our eyes open to discover just where the church is needed most in the field, to develop the kind of Christian and humane education needed in the society, to develop support systems for those engaged in higher education at every level, and to help enrich their vocations by building up the church as a living, vital community of believers and doers.

NOTES—Chapter 5

¹John Barth, *Giles Goat-Boy or, The Revised New Syllabus* (Garden City: Doubleday & Co., Inc., 1966), p. 363. Copyright © 1966 by John Barth. Used by permission of Doubleday & Co., Inc.

²The author is grateful to Douglas Sloan for his very helpful pamphlet, *Historiography and the History of Education* (New York: Teachers College Press, Occasional Paper No. 3, n.d.) for a brief survey of new directions in institutional history. See pp. 14-21 for references to authors such as Bernard Bailyn and L. A. Cremin who have called attention to an array of institutions other than universities and colleges engaging in education at all levels.

³Hazel E. Barnes, *The University as the New Church* (London: C. A. Watts, 1970), pp. 190-191.

⁴See John E. Cantelon, *College Education and the Campus Revolution* (Philadelphia: The Westminster Press, 1969), p. 119.

⁵Harry E. Smith, *Secularization and the University* (Atlanta: John Knox Press, 1968); for analysis of importance of departments of religions in universities see Robert A. Spivey, "Modest Messiahs: The Study of Religion in State Universities," *Religious Education,* vol. 63 (January–February, 1968), pp. 5-11.

⁶Julian N. Hartt, *Theology and the Church in the University* (Philadelphia: The Westminster Press, 1969), p. 133.

⁷F. Thomas Trotter, "One of Our Colleges Is Missing," *The Christian Century,* (September 25, 1974), pp. 873-877.

⁸See reference to Sloan above; also Donald G. Tewksbury, *The Founding of American Colleges and Universities Before the Civil War* (New York: Teachers College Press, 1932); Paul M. Limbert, *Denominational Policies in the Support and*

Supervision of Higher Education (New York: Teachers College Press, 1929); Clarence P. Shedd, *The Church Follows Its Students* (New Haven: Yale University Press, 1938); Merrimon Cuninggim, *The College Seeks Religion* (New Haven: Yale University Press, 1947); Manning M. Pattillo, Jr., and Donald M. Mackenzie, *Church-Sponsored Higher Education in the United States* (Washington, D.C.: American Council on Education, 1966); Kenneth Underwood, *The Church, The University, and Social Policy: The Danforth Study of Campus Ministries,* 2 vols. (Middletown, Conn.: Wesleyan University Press, 1969).

⁹ See fascinating study of George Williams, *Wilderness and Paradise in Christian Thought, The Biblical Experience of the Desert in the History of Christianity & the Paradise Theme in the Theological Idea of the University* (New York: Harper & Row, Publishers, Inc., 1962), especially pp. 201-210.

¹⁰ See Douglas Sloan, *The Scottish Enlightenment and the American College Ideal* (New York: Teachers College Press, 1971).

¹¹ See Frederick Rudolph, ed., *Essays on Education in the Early Republic* (Cambridge: Harvard University Press, 1965).

¹² "Charter of the University of Georgia, 1785," cited in Richard Hofstadter and Wilson Smith, *Documentary History of American Higher Education,* 2 vols. (Chicago: University of Chicago Press, 1961), vol. 1, p. 150.

¹³ Albea Godbold, *The Church College of the Old South* (Durham, N.C.: Duke University Press, 1944), pp. 150-151.

¹⁴ Jerald C. Brauer, "The Christian College in American Education," *The Christian Scholar,* vol. 41 (Autumn, 1958, Special Issue), p. 235.

¹⁵ Limbert is extremely helpful in dealing with early denominational attempts to define church-relatedness in this early period. See also David Potts, "American Colleges in the Nineteenth Century: From Localism to Denominationalism," *History of Education Quarterly* (Winter, 1971), pp. 369-373.

¹⁶ See helpful analysis by Douglas Sloan, "Harmony, Chaos, and Consensus: The American College Curriculum," *Teachers College Record,* vol. 73 (September, 1971), pp. 221-251; Hofstadter and Smith, *op. cit.,* vol. 1, p. 378.

¹⁷ George P. Schmidt, *The Liberal Arts College: A Chapter in American Cultural History* (New Brunswick: Rutgers University Press, 1957), p. 39; Limbert, *op. cit.,* pp. 11 f.

¹⁸ See Sidney Mead, "The Rise of the Evangelical Conception of the Ministry in America: 1607-1850," in H. Richard Niebuhr and Daniel D. Williams, eds., *The Ministry in Historical Perspectives* (New York: Harper & Row, Publishers Inc., 1956), pp. 207-249.

¹⁹ Williams, *op. cit.,* p. 205.

²⁰ Cited in Schmidt, *op. cit.,* p. 32.

²¹ Natalie A. Naylor, "The Ante-Bellum College Movement: A Re-Appraisal of Tewksbury's Founding of American Colleges and Universities," *History of Education Quarterly,* vol. 13 (Fall, 1973), pp. 261-274.

[22] See James Axtell's challenge in "The Death of the Liberal Arts College," *History of Education Quarterly*, vol. 11 (Spring, 1971), pp. 339-352.

[23] Robert H. Wiebe, *The Search for Order: 1877-1920* (New York: Hill & Wang, 1968); Sloan, "Harmony, Chaos, and Consensus," *op. cit.*, p. 225.

[24] Once again Limbert is very helpful in tracing this early development.

[25] For quotation see Thomas J. Wertenbaker, *Princeton, 1746-1896* (Princeton: Princeton University Press, 1946); and *Church Colleges, Their History, Position and Importance* (Philadelphia: H. Buchanan Co., 1895), p. 13.

[26] *Church Colleges*, p. 7.

[27] *Annual Report*, Board of Education of the Northern Baptist Convention, 1920, p. 22.

[28] *Minutes*, Biennial Convention of the United Lutheran Church, 1920, p. 260.

[29] *Annual Report*, Board of Christian Education of the Presbyterian Church, U.S.A., 1925, pp. 7, 8, as cited in Limbert, *op. cit.*, pp. 72, 75, 78.

[30] As quoted in Limbert, *op. cit.*, pp. 77-79; and Edith C. Magruder, *A Historical Study of the Educational Agencies of the Southern Baptist Convention, 1845-1945* (New York: Teachers College Press, 1951), p. 119.

[31] "Council of Church Boards on Education," *Christian Education*, vol. 7 (April, 1924), pp. 312-321.

[32] For overviews of these developments, see Schmidt, *op. cit.*, and Frederick Rudolph, *The American College and University* (New York: Alfred A. Knopf, Inc., 1962).

[33] Limbert traces these developments and the crises which the foundations caused church-related universities and boards. See *op. cit.*, pp. 224-225, 115 ff.

[34] Clarence P. Shedd, *Two Centuries of Student Christian Movements* (New York: Association Press, 1934), and *The Church Follows Its Students*, pp. 281-305.

[35] Cuninggim, *op. cit.*, p. 263.

[36] Harvard Committee, *General Education in a Free Society* (Cambridge: Harvard University Press, 1945), pp. 39-41.

[37] *Endangered Service: Independent Colleges, Public Policy and the First Amendment* (Nashville: National Commission on United Methodist Higher Education, 1976).

[38] "What Is a Christian College?" *Christian Education*, vol. 34 (December, 1951), pp. 257-340.

[39] "The Commission on Christian Higher Education," *Christian Education*, vol. 35 (March, 1952), pp. 3-15.

[40] See, e.g., *The Christian Scholar*, vol. 37 (Supplement, Autumn, 1954), pp. 175-349; vol. 41 (Special Issue, Autumn, 1958), pp. 183-340; and other reports of conferences under the auspices of the Council of Protestant Colleges and Universities:

The Mission of the Christian College in the Modern World (Washington, D.C.: Council of Protestant Colleges and Universities, 1962); *Challenges of Change to the Christian College* (Washington, D.C.: Council of Protestant Colleges and Universities, 1966); *The Contribution of the Church-Related College to the Public Good* (Washington, D.C.: Association of American Colleges, 1970). See also "Religion and Higher Education—A Symposium," *Religious Education,* vol. 48, no. 4 (July-August, 1953), pp. 215-283.

[41] Pattillo and Mackenzie, *op. cit.,* pp. 198-214.

[42] C. Robert Pace, *Education and Evangelism* (New York: McGraw-Hill Book Company, 1972), pp. 74, 105. The study shows ferment in the evangelical house. See also Marvin K. Mayers, Lawrence O. Richards, Robert Webber, *Reshaping Evangelical Higher Education* (Grand Rapids: The Zondervan Corporation, 1972).

[43] *Endangered Service, op. cit.,* p. 125.

[44] *Ibid.*

[45] John Trumbull, "The Progress of Dulness," cited in Kenneth Silverman, *A Cultural History of the American Revolution* (New York: Thomas Y. Crowell Company, Inc., 1976), p. 225.

[46] See Phillida Dunkle, "Sentimental Womanhood and Domestic Education, 1830-1870," *History of Education Quarterly,* vol. 14 (Spring, 1974), pp. 13-30; Jill K. Conway, "Perspectives on the History of Women's Education in the United States," *History of Education Quarterly,* vol. 14 (Spring, 1974), pp. 1-12. See also Ann Douglas. *The Feminization of American Culture* (New York: Alfred A. Knopf, Inc., 1977)

[47] Thomas Woody, *A History of Women's Education in the United States,* 2 vols. (New York: Science Press, 1929), vol. 2, pp. 186-187, 198; Schmidt, *op. cit.,* p. 143.

[48] See Mabel Newcomer, *A Century of Higher Education for American Women* (New York: Harper & Row, Publishers, Inc., 1959), pp. 72 f.

[49] See interesting treatment of this power in Dunkle, *op. cit.,* p. 20.

[50] See *The College Settlement Association* (n.p., n.d.) and *Bibliography of College, Social University, and Church Settlements,* 5th ed., rev. and enlarged (Chicago, 1905).

[51] For a recent brief survey see Pamela Roby, "Women and Higher Education," *The Annals of the American Academy of Political and Social Science,* vol. 404 (November, 1972), pp. 118-139.

[52] See Horace Mann Bond, *The Education of the Negro in the American Social Order,* rev. ed. (New York: Octagon Books, 1966); Henry Allen Bullock, *A History of Negro Education in the South* (Cambridge: Harvard University Press, 1967); and "The Negro Private and Church-Related College," *The Journal of Negro Education,* vol. 29 no. 3 (Summer, 1960), pp. 211-407; "Studies in the Higher Education of Negro Americans," *The Journal of Negro Education,* vol. 35, no. 4 (Fall, 1966), pp. 293-513.

[53] Bond in "The Negro Private and Church-Related College," *op. cit.,* p. 222.

[54] *Ibid.,* p. 254.

55 Mays in "The Negro Private and Church-Related College," *op. cit.*, p. 251. See also Richard I. McKinney, *Religion in Higher Education Among Negroes* (New Haven: Yale University Press, 1945).

56 See Edward J. Power, *Catholic Higher Education in America* (New York: Appleton-Century-Crofts, 1972); Neil J. McCluskey, ed., *Catholic Education in America: A Documentary History* (New York: Teachers College Press, 1964); see also Andrew M. Greeley, *The Changing Catholic College* (Chicago: Aldine Publishing Company, 1967); Andrew M. Greeley and Peter H. Rossi, *The Education of Catholic Americans* (Chicago: Aldine Publishing Company, 1966); and Robert Hassenger, ed., *The Shape of Catholic Higher Education* (Chicago: University of Chicago Press, 1967).

57 John Tracy Ellis, "American Catholics and the Intellectual Life," in Philip Gleason, ed., *Catholicism in America* (New York: Harper & Row, Publishers, Inc., 1970), pp. 115-132.

58 Cited in John Tracy Ellis, "To Lead, To Follow, or To Drift? American Catholic Higher Education in 1976: A Personal View," *Delta Epsilon Sigma Bulletin*, vol. 21, no. 2 (May, 1976), p. 45. This essay is an interesting sequel to Ellis's earlier piece.

59 See unpublished paper by R. L. Schnell and Patricia T. Rooke, "Identity Crisis in American Catholic Intellectualism, 1945–1975: Reaffirmation or Disintegration," pp. 1-26. This essay contains a valuable bibliography of this debate.

60 *The Idea of the Catholic University*, a statement issuing from two conferences held under the auspices of the North American region of the International Federation of Catholic Universities, 1967; Neil G. McCluskey, S.J., secretary. *The Restless Christian College*, a statement issuing from a conference held under the auspices of the University of Notre Dame, 1968, James Burtchaell, C.S.C., chairman. Also see "The Catholic University in the Modern World," *College Newsletter*, vol. 35, no. 3 (March, 1973), pp. 1-10; and "Relations of American Catholic Colleges and Universities with the Church," *Occasional Papers on Catholic Higher Education*, vol. 2, no. 1 (April, 1976), pp. 3-11.

61 See publication of jointly sponsored conference, *Campus '70: The New Feel of Things* (Washington, D.C., 1970); see for discussion of ecumenical education, "Symposium: The Ecumenical Revolution and Religious Education," *Religious Education*, vol. 61, no. 5 (September-October, 1966), pp. 331-397.

62 Martin E. Marty, "A New Christian Mandate for Higher Education," *Campus '70*, *op. cit.*, p. 8.

63 Lloyd J. Averill, *A Strategy for the Protestant College* (Philadelphia: The Westminster Press, 1966), p. 62.

64 John B. Cobb, Jr., "Can the Church Think Again?" *Occasional Papers*, vol. 1, no. 12 (Nashville: The United Methodist Board of Higher Education and Ministry, August 9, 1976), p. 4.

65 Albert C. Outler, "Discursive Truth and Evangelical Truth," in Lloyd J. Averill and William W. Jellema, eds., *Colleges and Commitments* (Philadelphia: The Westminster Press, 1971), pp. 102-106.

[66] Will Herberg, "Biblical Realism as a Norm," in Averill and Jellema, *op. cit.,* p. 150.

[67] Charles Y. Glock and Robert N. Bellah, eds., *The New Religious Consciousness* (Berkeley: University of California Press, 1976).

[68] See Godbold, *op. cit.,* p. 150: Kenneth K. Bailey, *Southern White Protestantism in the Twentieth Century* (New York: Harper & Row, Publishers, Inc., 1964), p. 32; James W. Trent with Jeanette Golds, *Catholics in College: Religious Commitment and the Intellectual Life* (Chicago: University of Chicago Press, 1967).

[69] Schmidt, *op. cit.,* p. 35.

[70] Shedd, *Two Centuries of Student Christian Movements,* p. 361.

[71] G. Stanley Hall, *Adolescence,* 2 vols. (New York: Appleton-Century-Crofts, 1904), vol. 1, p. 351.

[72] William G. McLoughlin, Jr., *Billy Sunday Was His Real Name* (Chicago: University of Chicago Press, 1955), p. 132.

[73] Wesley A. Hotchkiss, "The Prophetic Academy," *Journal of Current Social Issues,* vol. 14, no. 2 (Spring, 1977), p. 71.

[74] George W. Forell, "The Nature of Religious Commitment," *Faculty Forum,* United Methodist Board of Higher Education and Ministry, vol. 43 (January, 1968), pp. 1-2.

[75] Hugh T. Kerr, "The Christ-Life as Mythic and Psychic Symbol," *Princeton Seminary Bulletin,* vol. 55 (April, 1962), pp. 32-33.

[76] Dean R. Hoge, *Commitment on Campus* (Philadelphia, The Westminster Press, 1974), pp. 190-192.

[77] Underwood, *op. cit.,* vol. 1, p. 490.

[78] See Myron B. Bloy, Jr., "Academic Values and Prophetic Discernment," and Kent E. Eklund, "Conflict and the Christian Church: The Role of the Church College," *The Christian Century* (October 20, 1976), pp. 889-897.

[79] Rudolph, *The American College and University,* pp. 402-403. Used by permission of Alfred A. Knopf, Inc.

[80] Bailey, *op. cit.,* pp. 147-148.

[81] T. S. Eliot, *After Strange Gods* (New York: Harcourt Brace Jovanovich, 1934), p. 41.

RESPONSE

Douglas Sloan

It is a pleasure to be able to comment on James Smylie's excellent, comprehensive account of the church's involvement in higher education during the past couple of centuries. I want to underscore a few aspects of Professor Smylie's paper that, to my mind, particularly deserve being highlighted and then to explore some issues that he raises and that seem to be worth further reflection.

One of the things that a historian of education finds particularly interesting in the paper is Professor Smylie's portrayal of the strengths, dynamism, and pervasiveness of the cultural vision that motivated the Christian churches in the nineteenth century and that lay behind their impressive involvement in higher education during that period. Both the achievements and the problems, weaknesses, and shortcomings of that involvement are set forth in the paper. Three aspects of that involvement as they emerge in the paper merit some initial comment.

First of all, Professor Smylie brings out very clearly the breadth of the mission and social service functions of the early nineteenth-century college. On the one hand, we are becoming more and more aware of the extent to which the antebellum college was a community project. Although the colleges may have borne the name of one religious body or another, it is becoming increasingly apparent in recent scholarship, as the paper indicates, that the colleges were usually supported by the entire local community, were responsive to community needs, and were essentially community colleges. At the same time, as the paper also makes clear, the early college had a national orientation. The college was seen as a larger movement to shape the wider society and to provide unifying national goals and values. Most educational leaders at every level were consciously concerned with the promotion of common social values as the central core of what Robert Bellah, Sidney E. Mead, and others have called an "American civil religion." These educational spokespersons viewed higher education as part of the total national strategy which was to be carried out in various ways.

The second aspect of the cultural vision that is very clear in Professor Smylie's discussion is the extent to which these colleges were not narrow sectarian institutions but seem to have been interdenominational in orientation. As Professor Smylie points out, it is much more accurate to describe the early nineteenth century not as the era of the denominational church college but as "the era of the Christian college."

Third, Professor Smylie has opened up some promising lines for further investigation in understanding the total picture of the church's involvement in higher education in the nineteenth century. I am referring here to his argument—and I find it convincing—that a strong ecumenical interdenominational spirit persisted in higher education throughout the nineteenth century and may have even increased in scope and intensity. This in many ways suggests that an earlier picture, presented by some historians, which depicted church-related colleges in the late nineteenth century as being hopelessly caught in intense sectarian denominational rivalry is wrong and that we need to take a whole new look at the forms of cooperation and ecumenical commitment of college leaders during this period. Since I have upon occasion helped to perpetuate this earlier picture, I gladly take this opportunity to accept Professor Smylie's correction of it.

I am left with a question, however—one that I would like to have seen developed further. Professor Smylie notes some of the distinctive denominational perspectives regarding church-related colleges, but it would be interesting to see how these developed during the nineteenth and twentieth centuries. In the midst of the burgeoning ecumenical awareness, which Professor Smylie pointed out and which has often been underestimated, how significant were the differences in the denominational perceptions of what constituted a Methodist or a Presbyterian or a Lutheran college, and so on? Did the various churches' perceptions change over time in significant ways? What factors were most important at different times in shaping these perceptions of church-relatedness? Were they primarily theological, social, institutional, or curricular, and in what combination?

There is some evidence, for example, although it is not all in yet, that even very early in the nineteenth century perceptions of church-relatedness may have differed markedly among the denominations. For instance, David Potts' account of early nineteenth century Baptist colleges as ecumenical and community oriented[1] seems to present a conception of church-relatedness much different from that portrayed by Howard Miller's recent study of Presbyterian colleges during roughly the same period in which the colleges are described as militant and aggressively denominational.[2] It is a question that we as yet know too little about and, if pursued in relation to the last century and a half, might shed much needed light on our current situation.

However, in keeping with this larger cultural vision, Professor Smylie not only presents achievements of the churches in higher education but also underscores the problems that they encountered— many of which continue to plague us today. I realize that, in quickly and rather schematically listing the major problems he deals with, I am simplifying and leaving out much of the full texture of his account; but I think it would be useful to at least note them briefly.

First, there is the problem that became quite serious in the nineteenth century, namely, that of cultural diversity and the cultural conflict that went with it. The cultural vision of the churches was often deeply marred by various parochialisms and prejudices in matters of race, sex, and religion, for which we continue to pay a high price.

Second, there was the opposite problem that became more acute as the century wore on and that we now find extremely pressing, and that is the difficulty of maintaining the richness of cultural diversity in the face of increasing bureaucratization, organizational rationalization, and cultural homogenization.

Third, there is ambiguity in the churches' twofold commitment to serve, on the one hand, by helping people move up in the world and by contributing to sociological and technological progress and, on the other hand and at the same time, by trying to help people maintain their Christian commitments and develop a lively Christian cultural criticism of the world. These two goals are obviously not altogether compatible. And this question of the meaning of social service is a vexing one. I will return to it again in a moment. Suffice it here to note that service is one of these umbrella terms that cover many different things, many of them frequently conflicting. It lends itself nicely to rhetorical purposes; but unless its meaning is precisely specified, its careless use can be more obfuscating than clarifying, ultimately more harmful than beneficial.

It would be very interesting and useful for some historian to take a close and critical look at different ways denominations have perceived the meaning of the notion that the Christian mission of the church-related college is to serve society. Who in particular have been thought to be the recipients of this service? And what has been done, what have been the actual outcomes, what have been the latent as well as the manifest consequences of different perceptions and deeds of Christian service by church-related colleges? This strikes me as an interesting set of questions that it might be well to have some answers.

Finally, there is what we might call the problem of knowledge. What constitutes knowledge? Professor Smylie alludes to the problem in the latter part of his paper, and I would like to suggest that it is a key to understanding many of the problems of the church in higher education historically and that in a way it is a primary problem, much more important than any I have mentioned to this point. One area for which Professor Smylie's paper lays the foundation, and that now invites further investigation, is the whole topic of the curriculum and the concept of knowledge in higher education. Surely the substance of the knowledge enterprise has something to do with the church and Christian involvement in higher education. One thing that stood out as I read the paper was the contrast on just this point between the first and the second half of the nineteenth century. The church's conception of its cultural vision during the first half of the century was integrated into the whole of higher education and embraced student life, worship, and the curriculum—including moral philosophy and the teaching of the scientific method. All were seen as needing to be pervaded by the Christian faith and outlook. What becomes clear from Professor Smylie's account is that during the second half of the century, in spite of the expansion of the churches' activity on the campus and in association with the campus, one notices that this church activity seems to have been separated more and more from what really lay at the heart of higher education: the curriculum and the pursuit of knowledge. I think this is a key problem that reflects an underlying problem that was beginning to affect not only the church's mission in higher education but that of the humanities and liberal arts as well.

There has always been a close relationship between the church and the liberal arts, and in many respects these two have been fighting rear-guard actions in the university and in American higher education for the last century at least. What might be called an epistemological narrowing took place in the conception of the sources of knowledge. It was a momentous development and devastating for the churches and the liberal arts alike. It can be simply, and to a degree simplistically, expressed in this way. One of the branches of learning, science, began to be regarded as the one and only valid mode of knowledge. Recall that up until about the middle of the nineteenth century, although tensions were developing, it was common to think of the whole of higher learning as constituting one unified culture. There were different branches—literature, philosophy, the arts, and sciences—but they were regarded very much as equal branches on one single tree of learning. By the late nineteenth century, however, they were no longer equals, and science began to be regarded as the one and only valid mode of knowledge. As this conception became increasingly dominant, it began to make extremely difficult any discussion of values other than those embedded in a scientific and technological view of things. Art, literature, religion—all subjects, in fact, having to do with values and meaning—no longer enjoyed the status of being regarded as sources of genuine knowledge. Science alone was thought to be the only source for the ultimate objective world of knowledge. Art, literature, philosophy, religion were consigned increasingly to the sidelines. These nonscientific subjects were more and more regarded as expressions of the inner world of subjective feeling or of folk customs and established traditions or of habitual and benighted attitudes and prejudices and not, though, as modes of knowing. They began to have difficulty even finding a self-respecting place in the university, except insofar as they, too, made claims to being scientific, in which case they ceased being themselves.

By and large this situation still pertains. In fact, the computer scientist, Joseph Weizenbaum, has recently argued that this epistemological narrowing continues today—with a vengeance and with the most dire results. Weizenbaum speaks of the "imperialism of instrumental reason" in describing the strong current tendency to identify reason with the narrowest kind of instrumental logic, to exclude the emotions, the will, and intuitive insight from the domain of rationality, and to reduce all human problems to their lowest elements in order that this narrow view of reason can be applied to them, whatever the consequences to human wholeness might entail.[3]

Here we come once again to the problem of service. As long as the conception of knowledge in higher education is predominantly that of instrumental and technical reason, higher education will overwhelmingly serve a technological view of the world and the values embodied in that view. However else we might assess them, the student dissidents of the 1960s made it unmistakably clear for all to see that there is no thing as value-free neutrality, either personal or institutional. Service, as a general and unspecified notion, would almost always favor the dominant interests of the society—those most capable of making their desires and needs known—and thus buttress the status quo. And more specifically, a technologically dominated higher education will, willy-nilly, tend to favor the technologically oriented elements in the society. To the extent that the church-related colleges have accepted the main-line university and modern view of rationality and knowledge as their standard—as their canon—they have been badly disadvantaged in their effort to espouse Christian and humanistic values and at the same time to aspire to intellectual respectability as determined by the dominant forces in higher education.

But the students also discovered, to their dismay, that any attempt to introduce questions of alternative meanings and values met with angry incomprehension from opponents and even helpless embarrassment from friends; for friends, enemies, and indeed the students themselves—all tended to accept the reigning view that such questions have only a tangential relation to knowing and knowledge and were not properly the concern of higher education. Attractive and appealing as their counter-values might be, the students were told that they should go pursue them someplace else other than on the university campus or in the classroom or in the curriculum. The liberal arts, and some church-related efforts in higher education, have endured a similar experience in the past one hundred years.

We have seen various reform movements on behalf of meaning and value come and go again and again in American higher education, and since the 1870s they have always remained somehow peripheral to the university because they have been unable to demonstrate that they provide knowledge in the full sense of the word about the world in which we live. And since the university maintains that knowledge is its main business—and big business it still is, despite all—any other justification for concerns and studies dealing with values fails in the end. To me this is one of the fundamental, wider questions that arises from a reading of the paper. Is it going to be possible to talk about the mission of the Christian church in higher education and about the mission of church-related colleges without addressing this all-important question of what constitutes knowledge and who sets the standards?

NOTES

[1] David B. Potts, "'College Enthusiasm!' As Public Response, 1800–1860," *Harvard Educational Review,* vol. 47 (February, 1977), pp. 28-42.

[2] Howard Miller, *The Revolutionary College: American Presbyterian Higher Education, 1707–1837* (New York: New York University Press, 1976).

[3] Joseph Weizenbaum, *Computer Power and Human Reason: From Judgement to Calculation* (San Francisco: W. H. Freeman & Company, Publishers, 1976).

RESPONSE

John F. Murphy

I read with pleasure Dr. Smylie's paper, principally because I feel my own knowledge is so sketchy of the Protestant communions' historical experience with higher education in the United States. I was more at home with the Catholic experience, but the paper handled this area much less extensively. (I might point out parenthetically that even the descriptive language of our experience has been quite different.) Allow me to make a few observations about the history of Catholic higher education in United States, and conclude with a recitation of some perceptions of the agenda currently before leaders of Catholic higher education.

1. I think it is undeniable that Catholic colleges and universities were spawned from a defensive posture. Catholic leaders (here, read bishops) observed quite accurately that the Protestant churches in effect dominated the colleges and universities. Founding a Catholic institution was a counter to what were seen as Protestant colleges. This defensiveness lingered long into the twentieth century, as there has been a real history of anti-Catholic bias in our land. I do not wish to equate "Protestant colleges" with an "anti-Catholic bias," but I think that kind of hostility was present in the past.

2. It should also be noted, however, that despite the siege mentality that afflicted the Catholic Church in the nineteenth century, there were still voices that called for Catholic colleges and universities as places where the historic traditions of the medieval universities could be continued and renewed. Readers of the various volumes on the early years of the Catholic University of America will easily detect this goal in the speeches of bishops and rectors.

3. The typical Catholic student for the college was an immigrant's son (less usually a daughter in those early days). College was the door

to upward social and career movement. The parents and parish priests wanted this achieved in a Catholic atmosphere which would not threaten the faith. It perhaps also accounts for the interest in the professional careers rather than in the gentleman's course of studies more common to the wealthy.

4. There has been an historic harmony between the liberal arts and theology in the United States Catholic colleges, attributable to the strong rational and conceptual history and framework of Catholic theology. That more was not accomplished in interfacing theology and secular learning is due to the relatively weakened condition of Catholic theology in the nineteenth and early twentieth centuries. "Manual theology" was a betrayal of a vigorous and lively tradition. Improvement began in the 1940s with the work of such groups as the American Dominican Fathers, and the whole movement accelerated with Vatican II.

5. While the strength of Catholic higher education has rested on the generous labors of the various sponsoring religious orders who founded and staffed the colleges, this has also been the source of some notable weaknesses.

a. Parochialism presumed elitism, competition, exclusivity among the orders, and it produced too many colleges and universities for the Catholic people to provide adequate financial support. This in turn contributed to academic mediocrity in many cases.

b. A spirit of separatism effectively precluded the development of faculty exchange which could have added a dimension of richness and variety. Until very recently, Catholic University of America was the principal notable exception to this practice.

c. Tension between church leadership and the exempt religious orders sponsoring the colleges and universities resulted in little financial support for Catholic colleges and little shared responsibility and cooperation for their health.

6. Catholic colleges and universities have probably been less adequately funded than other church-related institutions. They often survived by means of the deceptive "support" called contributed service, viz., the difference between the scale by which laity were paid and the stipend received by the religious. It is also pertinent to point to the large financial burden undertaken by the American church to

provide parochial schools for those in elementary and secondary schools.

7. The foregoing points help us to understand that there never has been a *system* of Catholic higher education. There is no central control or jurisdiction, no centralized financing, no naming of presidents or trustees by the church. To illustrate this complete decentralization, it could be pointed out that, until very recently, members of the same religious congregation often could not cross from one province (region) to another to join the faculty of a college operated under the auspices of the other province.

8. Several points could be made about the role of women religious:

a. Special recognition should be given to the unique role of women religious in founding and operating colleges for women. The largest group of professional women in higher education has been, I think, women religious in Catholic women's colleges. Their accomplishments have merited better recognition than they have received from the higher education community as a whole.

b. It has often not been to the credit of previously men's colleges that they became coeducational at their convenience and often with insufficient concern for the effects on the women's colleges which were established in the first place because the men would not admit women students.

c. The present and future role of the Catholic women's colleges deserves special treatment. Just as coeducation seemed to have taken over entirely, the growth of the women's movement has surfaced anew the question of whether there is a unique contribution to women's education that can be made by colleges for women.

9. The history of church relations with colleges and universities seems to show that it is difficult to maintain a balance between free and creative scholarship on the one hand and sound theological reflection and religious commitment on the other. Too easily the slide is toward anti-intellectualism in the name of religious orthodoxy or toward religious indifferentism or secular humanism in the name of academic purity. It gives strength to those who have claimed that there can be no such thing as a Catholic university. John Henry Newman does not rest peacefully with those charges.

10. A passing note should be made that, regrettably, Catholic

colleges and universities did not break out from their initial defensiveness and assume any significant leadership in matters ecumenical—a condition that seems now to be changing. There is much evidence now that real leadership is coming from Catholic colleges. Many Protestant theologians are on theological faculties; Protestant ministerial services are frequently provided on the Catholic campus, etc.

11. Dr. Smylie may not have known of some other studies and documents which would have enriched his report, particularly on recent developments in U.S. Catholic higher education. I would recommend that he review some materials which I have presented as a partial list for his consideration.

My other main concern has to do with some issues which have emerged from the recent history and direction of U.S. Catholic colleges and universities. Let me list some briefly.

1. The reexamination of mission of the Catholic college, and the restatement of that new articulation. There is a real pluralism among Catholic institutions. Within the overall designation as "Catholic," a variety of emphases has been stressed. Since some groups interpret the Catholicity of their institution in a less than traditional form, some critics are tempted to charge they are no longer "Catholic." I predict that there will be a growing acceptance of a variety of ways in which colleges see their religious mission and identity. Of help to those wishing to study changing perceptions of this identity would be the so-called "Rome '72 Document," the National Catholic Educational Association statement of 1976 on "Relations . . . , " and the various Delta Epsilon Sigma lectures given annually at the NCEA annual meetings since 1974.

2. The opening up of leadership roles in boards and administrations to include laity. This could be a process of "laicization" which, in my opinion, should not be confused with "secularization," which is a blurring of the mission.

3. Arms' length legal distance from the sponsoring religious body, and efforts to work out constitutional issues with respect to participation in federal/state aid programs.

4. Exploration of what the Catholic history or identity means at present to the colleges and universities. How is the Catholic character to be implemented? Catholic leaders are well aware that many

formerly Protestant-related colleges have lost their special character and relationship, a process of secularization. How can this be prevented among Catholic institutions?

5. The quality of theology and religious studies programs. What are the demands of ecumenism?

6. How can a college or university witness to a religious commitment in a way that establishes an inviting religious climate among students and faculty?

7. Concern about the extent to which the college can open up the students to questions and interest in social justice.

8. The manner in which the college can support those issues that are of concern to the sponsoring religious (church) community.

CHAPTER **6**

An Overview of
Current Denominational Policies
and Studies in Higher Education

Robert Rue Parsonage

Introduction

Of the nearly 1,600 independent colleges and universities in the United States, more than 700 of them currently acknowledge a church relationship (see Appendix A for this chapter). But the collegiate affirmation of a church relationship presents only one-half of the picture. As a recent publication of the National Commission on United Methodist Higher Education reminds its constituents, that denomination is "a college-related church."[1] So, indeed, are many other religious denominations and sects which sponsor, support, or in other ways contribute to the life of the colleges and universities with which they maintain continuing formal relationships.

As one indication of that fact, both colleges and churches which are partners in higher education have been reviewing and rethinking their relationships to one another to an increasing degree in recent years. To be sure, such reconsideration is an ongoing process between many churches and colleges; but there are a number of specific factors which have contributed to such a heightened interest in the nature of the relationship as well.

Some churches and their colleges are being moved to a review of the compacts between them because of broad, general changes which

189

are occurring within religious institutions and within higher education. Changes in missional priorities, in the availability of financial resources, in theological and social perspectives, and shifts in the locus of power and responsibility in ecclesiastical decision-making are either suggested by the churches or deduced from their actions to be current reasons for reviewing and, in some cases, altering the nature of the church-college relationship. Likewise, changes in the purposes and aims of education and in the economics, demographics, and politics of educational institutions are increasingly cited by church-related colleges, or perceived in their actions, to be necessary reasons for rethinking and, in some cases, for reordering of the church connection.

Most college-related churches and their colleges have felt impelled to review the impacts between them in recent years because of actual challenges or perceived threats to their distinctive relationships from private and public forces beyond the churches and colleges themselves. Of necessity, they have had to engage in such a review in response to the greatly increased scrutiny over and regulation of higher education by the legislative, administrative, and judicial branches of government; on the basis of their commitments and in light of their stake in higher education, they have chosen more and more to engage in such a review in order to provide a sound basis for defending the churches' role in higher education in the public arena.

Finally, many churches and their colleges are engaged in such rethinking because they sense new possibilities and opportunities both for contributing to each other's mission and for strengthening the ties between church and college. In this regard, some churches and colleges exhibit greater awareness of the success—others, of the failure—of their past collaboration. Some choose to emphasize the strengths—others, the weaknesses—of their present relationships. Some view their future partnership more in terms of the visions they hope to realize in church-related higher education; others, in terms of the dilemmas they believe must be overcome. Yet given their diverse perspectives, a great many churches and schools are involved in projecting plans and policies—some modest, others more ambitious—which they believe will make it possible for them to continue to be significant partners in serving one another and the larger society.

As a result of this intensive and extensive review of the church-college relationship, a number of denominations have reasserted their commitment to higher education and the church-related college. Some colleges have discovered more compelling reasons than they have recently known for continuing as institutions of the church, just as others have found sounder bases for beginning or completing the process of disaffiliation. The attention and interest of policy makers and students of higher education have been drawn increasingly to the issues and institutions represented in this sector of American education.

But the most tangible result of this process is found in the vast amount and variety of data that have been and are being generated and include: descriptive and interpretative information on the legal, financial, and ecclesiastical relationships of colleges and churches; studies of the history, perceptions, and viability of church-related colleges; theological and educational rationales for the churches' involvement in higher education; policy statements on the appropriate roles and relationships between churches, colleges, and the public; and proposals for the development of curricula, support, and future directions of church-related higher education. Vast and varied as these materials are, a further preliminary word about the nature of them and the attention which will be given to them in this discussion is necessary.

As the title suggests, the focus here is on recent policy statements which have been adopted and studies which have been conducted or sponsored by official religious bodies—denominations and their agencies, including religious orders, church boards of higher education, and associations of church-related institutions or officers. Thus, recent self-studies of colleges which deal in whole or in part with the church relationship and studies of church-related higher education undertaken by secular educational associations, independent research agencies and scholars pursuing their own interests are not reviewed in this paper (though some of them are commented upon elsewhere in this study).

As persons familiar with church-related higher education know, the relationships of churches and their colleges differ among—and even within—denominations. They may differ historically, culturally, theologically, philosophically, legally, financially, and in the matter of governance. For these reasons, and because of the particular contemporary problems which their colleges face, denominations and their educational agencies have been involved in differing aspects of the debate and discussion about church-relationships and educational policy. To put it another way, they have sought the kind of information and guidance which they have believed would best equip them to understand and fulfill their particular responsibilities in higher education.

So denominations and their educational agencies have tended to work alone on the problems of church-related higher education rather than in consort; they have defined for themselves those aspects of the problems and possibilities they would address, and they have devised their own strategies and timetables for research and action. It should be no surprise that this process has produced an amazingly varied body of written material, but one which lacks internal coherence and widespread accessibility. Nevertheless, the material which is emerging sheds new light on the rich history and diversity of church-related higher education, explicates the contemporary plight and promise of this segment of the educational system, sets out new models of church-college cooperation, and contributes to a much needed policy base for all of church-related higher education.

The material described above is already having an impact on the colleges and churches which have been engaged in the processes of study and action. Insofar as the many reports and policy statements can be summarized and to the extent that trends may be drawn from them, the material may prove to be useful in a general way to the diverse church-related colleges and college-related churches and to others who are concerned about and interested in this significant higher education enterprise. Toward that end, the following attempt is made to summarize current denominational efforts at reviewing and rethinking their role in higher education and to offer some generalizations about the significance of the results for church-related higher education.

Naturally, not all of the denominations referred to in other papers are represented in this summary. Some have not prepared documents or published statements in the last seven or eight years which reflect current thinking about their role in higher education; nor has the author been able to obtain the results of some studies still in progress.

Further, materials have not been sought from all college-related churches in the United States, particularly those denominations with fewer than five colleges and those which support "nondenominational" or "interdenominational" institutions of higher education. With this as background, let us turn to current denominational policies and studies of higher education.

Denominational Policies and Studies

African Methodist Episcopal Church

The policy governing the relationship of the African Methodist Episcopal (AME) Church with its colleges is set out in *The Book of Discipline of the African Methodist Episcopal Church,* as amended by the General Conference of the church in June, 1972. The *Discipline* states that the General Board of Education of the church has overall responsibility for the educational life of the denomination. However, two units which report to the board are the direct links between the denomination and its colleges and universities.

The Division of Educational Institutions—one of three functional units within the board—represents the AME Church "in all activities connected with higher, theological and ministerial education." Directed by a general secretary, the division has as its primary objectives the development of "an educational plan and purpose which shall definitely relate the educational institutions of the church to the church"; the fostering of "the highest educational standards" and the "soundest business practices" in the member colleges; and the creation and maintenance of an institutional atmosphere in the colleges "conducive to the development of a Christian Philosophy of life to the end that all members of the college and university communities may possess a knowledge and understanding of the Christian Faith, and that students may emerge from their educational experiences prepared to witness to the gospel in every area of life."[2]

To this end, the division is charged with formulating regulations necessary to its tasks, is given supervisory authority over the colleges, is available on request to advise the boards of trustees of the institutions, and, in cooperation with annual conferences of the church, is expected to assist the colleges and universities in providing religious activities and to promote religious training among AME students at both church and non-AME institutions of higher education. Further, the division is charged with recommending to the General Conference of the church—with prior approval of the Board of Education—ways and means for supporting the several related colleges and universities. In recent years, the direct financial support of related colleges and universities has amounted to nearly one-third of the approximately three-million-dollar annual budget of the national denomination.

The Executive Commission on Educational Institutions is the "accrediting and standardizing agency for educational institutions in the United States related to the African Methodist Episcopal Church." It is an elected body of nine persons—"6 elders and 3 laymen, not members of the General Board of Education and fitted by training and experience for the technical work of establishing standards and evaluating educational institutions in accordance with the standards. . . ."[3] Responsible to the board, the commission is available for educational consultation with the colleges and their boards of trustees, but its primary function is the investigation and accreditation of related colleges. The commission is authorized to investigate both the religious and educational fitness of member institutions, make recommendations for change and/or improvement, monitor progress toward compliance, and report yearly to the board which institutions should continue to receive the official recognition and financial support of the church. The general secretary of the Division of Educational Institutions serves as staff for the commission.

American Baptist Churches in the United States of America

A number of initiatives undertaken in recent years by boards and agencies of the American Baptist Churches in the U.S.A. (ABC) have led to considerable reflection about the denomination's role in higher education and resulted in significant changes in the pattern of the church's funding of its educational institutions.

In 1973 the mainly white ABC and the mainly black Progressive National Baptist Convention, Inc., initiated a four-year project known as the Fund of Renewal "to raise $4,440,000 for some 20 Baptist-related minority institutions of higher education, and $2,860,000 towards regional projects, validated locally, that will help minority persons toward self-development and self-determination."[4] Citing a number of conditions that have weakened minority educational institutions in recent years, the two denominations pledged that funds would be allocated to enable colleges to improve the quality of education, engage in experimental education, develop competent faculty, recruit more high-risk and low-income students, and provide seed money to test the viability of merging programs and services.

In keeping with the denominations' understandings of their educational commitments, it was determined that funds would go to institutions historically and actively related to the two denominations. Further, in order to receive grants, colleges had to be accredited (or actively engaged in the accreditation process), fiscally responsible, viable, committed to quality education, and genuinely interested in the self-determination and economic development of minorities. Finally, money from the special fund was to be awarded to those colleges ministering to the "total needs of the students: spiritual, moral, cultural, social, as well as intellectual" and to institutions affirming and committed to "the basic beliefs of the Judaeo-Christian heritage as manifested in the life, ministry, and teaching of Jesus Christ."[5] The special project of the two denominations employs a field staff charged with the responsibility of interpreting the need to and raising funds from the churches.

In another attempt to relate the denomination's funding of its colleges and universities to the educational priorities of the ABC, the Board of Educational Ministries was authorized in 1972 to replace its awarding of yearly block grants to related institutions with a program of "strategic funding." This change was initiated for two reasons. The primary locus for funding ABC-related colleges had shifted some years earlier from national to local and regional sources. While national dollars had diminished, local and regional funding had significantly increased (of the $636,000 received by colleges in 1972, $524,000 was from direct local church giving). The second factor was that the grants by and large were minuscule in relation to college budgets. Based on some long-forgotten formula, they ranged from $1,100 to $25,000, with the majority under $5,000.

ABC-related colleges were invited to submit strategic funding proposals for one- to three-year grants (in the range of $5,000–$15,000 per year) to underwrite educational programs in the following priority areas:

to assist the laity in achieving full personhood and to be equipped for ministry . . . ; to express the Gospel of Jesus Christ in terms of racial justice, equality of opportunity, and the elimination of racism . . . ; to strengthen and extend the life and ministries of the church as expressed through the local congregation . . . ; to identify the professional leadership needs of the ABC, interpret those needs to the churches, and provide adequate professional leadership for the American Baptist Churches . . . ; to extend the ministries of the church to other areas of public life . . . ; to enable the ABC to reflect upon contemporary issues and values from an informed theological perspective, and to examine its own history and heritage.[6]

A National Review Committee composed of persons from church and university was established to receive, review, and recommend the funding of grant proposals. At the end of the first three-year cycle, the program was extended for another three years. Grants totaling almost $300,000 have been made to fourteen colleges during the six-year period, 1973–1978.

In yet a third attempt to introduce greater responsibility into the denomination's funding of related institutions, the General Board of the ABC established a Commission on Institutional Funding in 1976. At the request of that commission, and on behalf of the Board of Educational Ministries, documents have been drafted in search of a philosophy of funding for each of the segments of higher education (seminaries, colleges, and campus ministries). The document related to the colleges presents current assumptions regarding trends in higher education, the denomination's rationale for support of higher education, the relationship between the denomination and its colleges, and the development of a strategy in higher education for the ABC.

This report assumes that higher education will continue to be a principal means of developing an educated citizenry and that a college education will continue to be a primary preparation for professions and careers. Regarding the denomination's rationale for support of higher education, the report assumes that, because the Christian enterprise has as one of its objectives the development of an educated citizenry where Christian values and life-style permeate all of life and where faith and learning are integrated, the church must be involved in education to accomplish these goals.

While adequate support of church-related colleges necessitates a new partnership of government, business, and the church, the report assumes that the church, for its part, must reassess the level of its support and the nature of its relationship in light of denominational goals and resources. It is also hoped that this endeavor will eventuate in a national strategy for denominational involvement in and support of higher education.

Church of the Brethren

The church-college relationship has received considerable attention within the Church of the Brethren during the past seven years.

In 1971 the Committee on Higher Education of the Church of the Brethren—an unofficial, voluntary association of the presidents of six Brethren-related colleges and the denominational seminary—engaged a consultant "to study the role of higher education in the Church of the Brethren and indeed to press the study to an evaluation of each of the colleges basically in relation to the local [church] districts to which each may be accountable in some degree." While commissioned by the presidents for the use of the colleges, a condensed version of the report entitled *The Colleges and the Church of the Brethren*[7] received wide distribution in the churches. Major recommendations were directed to the colleges. In keeping with their heritage, the colleges should provide every student with an exposure to the Christian faith, should clarify and state their purposes succinctly, should involve faculty and students more fully in collegiate governance, should cultivate the active support of the church, and should give more attention and funds to student recruitment. The church also received an admonition in the report. The national Church of the Brethren should have a concern for higher education—which would best be expressed by encouraging the understanding, commitment, and support of church-related colleges and by promoting interaction between liberal learning and the Christian faith.

A second call for a reconsideration of the relationship of church and college was issued in 1973—this time by the church. Confused and dissatisfied by the changes taking place in one of the colleges related to it, the Atlantic Northeast District of the church asked the General Board of the denomination to call a national conference on the Church of the Brethren and Higher Education. After due deliberation, the General Board agreed to such a conference. In preparation for the meeting, it commissioned a study of the history of higher education in the Church of the Brethren;[8] composed a syllabus of questions on goals, mission and philosophy, value issues, program issues, and structure and control issues it wished the conference to deal with; and held three regional preconference consultations. A cross section of more than 160 persons from church and college were invited to participate in the special national conference held in the summer of 1976.

As a part of its work, the conference in plenary session formulated a document entitled "Recommendations of the Conference on Higher Education and the Church of the Brethren." That report was received by the General Board of the church; the Executive Committee has evaluated it and drawn recommendations from it.

In the introduction to the report a number of assumptions and convictions about the Christian faith, higher education, and the church-college relationship are set out. Brethren colleges are understood to be "pluralistic communities in which a liberal education and career training are provided in an atmosphere that encourages Christian commitment and service." Thus, there should be open dialogue between church and college—neither one trying to dominate the other; both value academic freedom in their search for truth; both affirm certain general values—among them self-development, the responsibility of world citizenship, appreciation of personal relationships, freedom of inquiry—and traditional Brethren and Christian values—among them peace, service, simplicity, integrity, and no force in religion. While "Brethren colleges are unique in providing a witness to the ideals, goals, and way of life that have been informed and shaped by our heritage," they share a number of goals with other institutions of higher education—such as a desire to serve students and provide quality education. Finally, since a majority of Brethren students attend non-Brethren schools and because liberal arts colleges are a part of and are affected by the total higher education system, the church must realize its ministry in this broader spectrum of education as well.[9]

Following the introduction, recommendations are made in nine specific areas. Under the rubric of college program policies, it is recommended that church-related colleges be noncoercive forums for the examination of Christian and other faith-communal affirmations—including the Brethren peace witness; that these colleges continue to give attention to the issues of campus unity, cross-cultural and cross-generational education, intuitive and nonrational ways of knowing, and minority education; that the colleges support full-time campus ministry, Brethren Scholars-in-Residence, and the revival of the Brethren Student Christian Movement; and that the colleges remain alert to public policy issues and, in concert with the churches, resist intrusions of external control.

In terms of personnel, it is recommended that church districts and colleges devise common plans for the selection of church-related trustees, that arrangements be made for trustees to hear student and faculty views, that more women be selected for decision-making positions in Brethren colleges, and "that the colleges give highest priority to the selection of faculty and administration who not only excel as educators but are also committed persons of faith who integrate faith and knowledge in their own personhood and who support the Brethren thrust of the college." In the area of curriculum, it is recommended that Brethren colleges consider ethical and value questions; provide for the study of human sexuality, women's studies, biblical studies, and studies in Brethren traditions; provide for experiential education and cultural exchanges; and "make a special effort to prepare students for world citizenship by focusing on the interdependence of world cultures and on the limitations of western culture, with particular attention to the issues of war, hunger, justice, ecology, technology, materialism, and scientism." [10]

To increase church-college understanding, communication, and cooperation, the conference recommends a variety of regular and short-term exchanges between persons in church and college, regular higher education conferences in the church, and work opportunities for students in the churches. It is recommended that the colleges provide on- and off-campus religious instruction for the laity and professional in-service training for clergy. In terms of church support for colleges, it is recommended that a network of church and district persons be formed to assist in promoting Brethren colleges in the churches; that the churches and church members provide a variety of new and expanded scholarship and loan funds; and that information about financial aid available in Brethren colleges be shared more widely with potential students and their families.

Recommendations are also offered in the area of organization and structure. The church is encouraged to establish a new and broadly representative higher education advisory committee, accountable to the General Board of the church and generally supportive of its total mission in higher education. (However, by action of the June, 1977, General Board, it was decided that such a committee would not be brought together at this time.) The colleges and the church are encouraged to explore the establishment of covenants between them, expressing mutual expectations. The colleges are encouraged to explore mutual expectations with appropriate church committees. Concerned "that the church be supportive of the education of all its members, not only those in the liberal arts setting, but also in other kinds of post-secondary education," it is recommended that local congregations and families make special efforts to minister to Brethren students and provide for Brethren and ecumenical ministries on non-Brethren campuses. Finally, concerned with special group needs, it is recommended that qualified senior citizens be given access to courses at reduced tuition in Brethren-related colleges.[11]

Christian Methodist Episcopal Church

The colleges of the Christian Methodist Episcopal (CME) Church are connectional, receiving their support from the entire church and operating under the supervision of the General Board of Christian Education through its Division of Higher Education. As outlined in the constitution of the General Board of Christian Education (currently under review and slated for discussion at the 1978 General Conference of the church), the division is responsible for assuring the fiscal soundness of member institutions, safeguarding the property interests of the colleges, nominating one to three members to the boards of trustees of the schools, assisting the colleges in the hiring of faculty, determining entrance and graduation requirements, assisting in raising endowment funds, and working "in every way practicable to advance the cause of education for our Church."[12] In addition to overseeing these tasks, the general secretary of education is responsible for convening an annual meeting of the Educational Senate of the CME Church (a twenty-one-member group comprised of chief administrators of institutions of higher education, representatives of Episcopal Districts and boards of trustees, the College of

Bishops, and members of the General Board) to discuss educational standards and to plan for cooperation and coordination of CME colleges. He is also responsible for organizing "youth groups among the C.M.E. students attending state and other non-C.M.E. Colleges, in order to continue their contacts with and to hold them in the C.M.E. Church."[13]

Prior to the meeting of the General Conference of the CME Church in 1974, the College of Bishops requested that the Division of Higher Education "compile data and statistics on the accomplishments of the C.M.E. educational institutions for the 1970-74 quadrennium" for presentation and discussion at General Conference. In concert with the leadership of CME-related colleges (the President's Council), the division established an editorial committee which prepared a report describing the Christian Methodist Episcopal Church's investments in higher education.[14]

While facts and figures dominate the report, the interpretation of their meaning for the present and future role of the church is, at points, clearly set out. The total enrollment of the five colleges and one seminary related to the CME Church showed a decrease during the period of 1970-1974. Because declining enrollment, according to the report, is a major problem facing all predominantly black institutions of higher education, it is recommended that a more effective program of recruitment among the membership of the CME Church be undertaken jointly by the schools, Annual Conferences, and local congregations. Further, it is suggested that a staff person be employed by each school to direct this special recruitment effort.

Income of the colleges and seminary from the national church totaled $470,000 in 1973-1974—an increase of nearly 10 percent over the 1970-1971 level. Institutional income from Annual Conferences of the church totaled more than $228,000 in 1973-1974—an increase of more than 70 percent over the 1970-1971 level. The report commends the significant amount and increase in church support of higher education, but notes that Annual Conferences and Episcopal Districts in which the colleges are located "are called upon to bear too much of this [financial] burden." For this reason, the report commends to the denomination the establishment of "a program that can assure an equitable distribution of Annual contributions by Annual Conferences."[15]

Data on financial aid to students in the five church-related colleges and one seminary show that the average student was able to pay no more than one-third of the direct student cost in any of the four years from 1970–1974. Information on those persons graduating during the quadrennium suggests that CME colleges are successfully preparing persons for careers not traditionally pursued by blacks; the report also observes that many graduates are returning to "small cities and towns to become leaders in their communities, giving guidance to those persons and families who have not had the opportunity to go to college or send their children.[16] A summary of the annual operating budgets of the six institutions shows that approximately 5 percent is contributed by the CME Church. In explaining these and other facts, the report seeks to make clear that CME colleges are providing an indispensable service to the churches and society; that the contribution of the church to its colleges provides an important base and has a significant multiplier effect; and that increasing costs and needs demand new and expanded resources. The report concludes, finally, that the CME Church must increase its contribution of money and nonmaterial support to the church-related colleges, lest "more than 92 years of history go down the drain due to the lack of financial commitment."[17]

Christian Church (Disciples of Christ)

In 1975 the General Board of the Christian Church (Disciples of Christ) (hereafter referred to as the Christian Church) authorized the appointment of a special higher education evaluation task force of five persons and commissioned them

". . . 'to make an evaluation of colleges, universities, schools of religion and Bible chairs' that are member institutions of the Board of Higher Education, taking into account such factors as the depth of church relatedness and the contribution of the institution to the church; the fairness and equity of funding; the quality of the education experience provided; total financial support; and other matters relating to funding by the Christian Church (Disciples of Christ)."[18]

The task force set out immediately on a four-phase program of study and research and submitted the "Higher Education Evaluation Task Force Report" to the General Board in June, 1976.

According to the Task Force, it is essential that the church as a whole understand the "environmental crisis" and the "struggle against mediocrity, irrelevance and extinction" which the independent sector of higher education faces. While declining enrollments, burgeoning post-secondary educational opportunities, preoccupation with career-oriented education, and inflation could have debilitating effects on independent higher education, the more fundamental priorities about which church-related colleges must be concerned are "purpose, meaning and relevance." [19]

In its investigation, the Task Force discovered that Christian Church-related colleges have different understandings of what constitutes church-relatedness, different ways of supporting that understanding, and different ways of responding to the larger mission of the church. Though discovering no precise measure for gauging the degree of church-relatedness, the Task Force concludes:

First, a pivotal determinant [of church-relatedness] is the active involvement of committed leadership.

Second, a church-related institution is characterized by a critical mass of people who share a common tradition.

Third, a church-related institution provides an environment in which the campus community may clarify and reinforce its values.

Fourth, a church-related institution is characterized by the way in which people on a campus express their concern for other human beings [20]

Acknowledging that the church and the college most often understand their relatedness in terms of money, the report suggests that the present relationship must also be based on a clearer affirmation on the part of the colleges of their historical and current ties to the church, a more decisive expression on the part of the church about the vital role higher education plays in the fulfillment of the church's total mission, and a more thoroughly informed mutual understanding between church and college. Toward that end, the Task Force recommends that the General Board approve in principle a covenantal relationship between the Christian Church and the related colleges and that the following principles be considered in drawing up the covenant.

It is suggested that the church agree to assist in interpreting and advocating the cause of the colleges, aid in student recruitment, offer supportive services, be a testing ground for learning and research, stimulate the dialogue between faith and knowledge, interpret the church's mission in higher education to college and congregation, and provide a more adequate financial investment in the colleges "to the extent permitted by resources and priorities."[21]

It is suggested that the colleges agree to reflect the Judeo-Christian tradition in collegiate leadership, provide opportunity for the study of Judeo-Christian tradition and teachings, offer opportunity for worship and spiritual development, provide resources for cultivating the church-college relationship, state the present church relationship in interpretive literature, emphasize the total person in the learning experience, provide educational services to churches, and maintain academic accreditation. As part of this covenantal recommendation, the Task Force recommends that institutions seeking to be related to the Christian Church for purposes of funding should accept the covenantal relationship.

Turning to the subject of funding, the Task Force concludes that "value oriented inquiry and person-centered learning are crucial to an age so desperate for the joining of conscience with competence." Here, it claims, those church-related institutions which nurture the moral, spiritual, and intellectual development of the whole person are needed more than ever and must have the undergirding of the church. The church, however, must begin to understand its financial contribution as "an investment in the total mission of the church rather than as a response to financial need or as a means of saving institutions."[22] Therefore, the Task Force recommends a new pattern of funding for higher education in the Christian Church.

First, it is recommended that all covenanted colleges receive a basic grant of $30,000 as evidence of the church's commitment to undergraduate education as an important mission of the whole church; second, that each college receive $10 for every full-time student as recognition of the church's commitment to the education of all students; third, that each college receive $100 for every Christian Church full-time student as evidence of the church's concern for the education of their own youth in church-related colleges; and fourth, that each college receive $500 for each Christian Church graduating student who enrolls in seminary. This last criterion in funding is in response to the major priority on ministerial education set by the denomination.

The report offers additional recommendations which will clarify and strengthen the church's relationship with certain special purpose institutions and which will strengthen the research and fund-raising capabilities of the denomination's Board of Higher Education and the Christian Church Foundation.

In June, 1976, the General Board of the Christian Church endorsed the report of the Task Force. Subsequently, the "Covenant Between the Christian Church (Disciples of Christ) and Related Colleges/Universities" has been drafted and approved and includes nearly all of the provisions suggested in the Task Force report. More recently, the Christian Church-related institutions have considered the covenant, and individual copies have been signed by the general minister and president of the church and the presidents of all the colleges Also, figures based on the funding criteria outlined above have been collected from all of the related institutions and have been incorporated in the church budget for 1978.

The Episcopal Church

The Association of Episcopal Colleges (a voluntary association of nine colleges with varying relationships to the Episcopal Church) exists for the purpose of providing a liaison among the colleges and between them and the church; to conduct and encourage financial, historical, and scholarly research; and to expand constituencies beyond alumni/ae groups. Though not an official agency of the Episcopal Church, the association maintains offices in the church's national headquarters and receives moral support from the denomination.

In 1969 the association engaged the services of Booze, Allan, and Hamilton to study the effectiveness of its work. Evaluations of the academic and fiscal practices of member colleges were specifically excluded from the study. The study presented a "Summary of Existing College-Church Relationships" and offered "Considerations for Future College-Church Relationships," along with more specific discussion of the association.

Noting that all nine member colleges make formal acknowledgment of a relationship to the Episcopal Church in official documents, reflect some religious or ethical orientation in their statements of purpose, and demonstrate other indications of church-relatedness (i.e., church members on the board of trustees, chaplaincy and chapel programs, special scholarships, academic requirements), the report concludes that "other criteria of church-relatedness examined in the study show that, except for Sewanee and Voorhees [both owned by the church], the colleges do not have a strong formal relationship with the church."[23] (However, the presidents of Episcopal-related colleges and the deans of the church's seminaries are automatically granted seats in the House of Deputies by the General Convention, the church's highest governing body.)

Further, claiming that the church relationship is primarily traditional and historical in the more prestigious and well-endowed colleges, that "the Church relationship appears to have little impact on the everyday life of students on almost all of the campuses," and that some of the colleges appear to believe that a strong and clear relationship to the church will diminish their chances of attracting top students, faculty, administrators, trustees, and donors, the report also concludes that, "for most of the colleges, the Church relationship can be characterized as somewhat tenuous."[24]

At the same time, the report states that the church relationship has been a significant factor in the fund-raising efforts of the colleges. (Sewanee receives about $250,000 yearly from dioceses and parishes; the predominantly black colleges together receive $800,000 to $1,000,000 per year from the General Convention of the Episopal Church; and the colleges receive funding—sometimes in significant amounts—from individual Episcopalians, Episcopal foundations, and parishes.)

The tenuous nature of the church-relatedness of the colleges aside, the report states that "the colleges can benefit from a continuing relationship with the Church, provided the relationship is properly defined and contributes to the major purposes of the college."[25] A church relationship in which church and college cooperate to foster the study and exploration of religion, to provide for a chaplaincy, to seek and encourage competent Episcopalians to serve on boards of trustees, to seek and encourage individual Episcopalians to provide financial and moral support for the colleges can be beneficial, according to the report. And where a college is concerned that the church relationship might be debilitating, the report suggests that the official statement of the relationship be defined more accurately and completely and that the freedom of the college from church control and dogma be stressed.

In further pursuit of its research and development function, the association—with the cosponsorship of the National Association of

Episcopal Schools—initiated a colloquium on educational curriculum in 1974. Predicated on the conviction that "we are ... in need of a new theoretical foundation for our education," the project, Colloquium 20-20, seeks to develop a new epistemological base which will make possible the development of a human-centered education which is, at the same time, transcultural, multilingual, ecumenical and global—and necessary for survival in the twenty-first century.[26]

The task is being undertaken by the two Episcopal-related educational associations for the following reasons.

> Within the private sector, the community of [nine hundred] Episcopal schools and [nine] colleges offers advantages. First, there is a sizable interest in theoretical matters and a competency to pursue such an inquiry. Many of the schools are of national rank, with able administrations and faculty, genuine power of intellect and historic openness of mind. Second, the educational range-level of the Episcopal schools and colleges is inclusive, extending from nursery school to the graduate level. Third, the necessary global dimensions required for this theoretical inquiry are also present—the Episcopal schools and colleges are spread across the United States with related institutions in Liberia, the Philippines, Brazil, Japan, Central America and Puerto Rico. Further, the faith-foundations in the Christian doctrine of Man and of the Kingdom of God are inherently global. Fourth, these schools and colleges understand themselves to exist within a related educational community and within a related universe of discourse; yet at the same time, they are not ruled by any hierarchical system of central government that inhibits freedom, initiative or innovation.[27]

Since its beginning in 1974, members, consultants, and staff of the colloquium produced twenty papers exploring the need for a new curriculum, the purpose of education, education and epistemology, and the design of a new curriculum.

Lutheran Educational Conference of North America

The Lutheran Educational Conference of North America (LECNA), a tri-Lutheran agency providing research and information on higher—particularly Lutheran—education and serving as a forum for planning and strategy among Lutheran educators, traces its history back to 1910 when its predecessor organization, the National Lutheran Educational Conference, was formed.

In 1972, LECNA established a special, three-year research project called the Commission on the Future. The commission was charged with the task of studying the educational needs of the church constituency, the probabilities for cooperation among Lutheran institutions, the changing character and needs of the student population, the strengths and problems of Lutheran colleges as separate units in an international system, trends in the economic and political communities, and possible positions and strategies for influencing public policy. Progress reports were made to LECNA during the three years of the project, and a three-part final report was presented in 1975.

The first volume, *Church-Related Identity of Lutheran Colleges,* was written by Francis C. Gamelin for the commission. Noting that the commission has recognized church-related identity as one of the key problems of Lutheran colleges and citing similar testimony from other denominations, the author, on the basis of a study of college catalogs, suggests that there are five styles of church relationship among Lutheran schools. He characterizes these as the church vocations college, which essentially prepares church workers; the church college, committed primarily to the service of the church; the Bible-centered college, in which biblical studies are central; the Christian college, in which a Christian stance is explicitly affirmed; and the church-related college, related to the church by heritage, governance, and financing.

On the basis of his analysis, Gamelin concludes that all of the Lutheran Church—Missouri Synod (LCMS) and American Lutheran Church (ALC) colleges and many of the Lutheran Church in America (LCA) colleges fall in the first four styles of church-relatedness; all seven of the church-related colleges are related to the LCA. Gamelin writes:

> Within Missouri Synod and the American Lutheran Church, the style of relationship is much more homogeneous than in LCA and, ideologically, closer to the church. Only in LCA does one find catalog statements that would puzzle both pastors and laymen about the extent to which the college is committed to a Christian stance. It is important, therefore, to go beyond catalog statements.[28]

In order to find this additional information, the author turns to an official document, "The Mission of LCA Colleges and Universities," and the covenants between the 17 LCA colleges and their supporting synods. From these documents the author extracts a list of standards for recognition of colleges and statements of college commitments to the church and church commitments to the colleges. Further, interested in the expectations of church members for their colleges, he reviews three studies of Lutheran constituents on this subject.

While Gamelin acknowledges that there are differences of expectation among and between constituents of the three Lutheran bodies—just as there are differences in the degree of autonomy asserted by the colleges in relationship to their churches—he goes on to state that "a large majority of both Lutheran church members and college leaders expect Lutheran colleges to serve primarily the church's educational needs ('Church Colleges') or broader constituencies from an open Christian stance ('Christian Colleges')." Thus, according to Gamelin, "the fate of non-affirming 'Church Related Colleges' appears dim with respect to church support, financial or psychological."[29]

A second report was authored on behalf of the commission by Allan O. Pfnister. *Trends in Higher Education in the United States*[30] gives a detailed overview of recent literature dealing with the status of higher education in this country and gives particular attention to the implications of recent literature in the areas of enrollment, students, governance, instructional programs, and finances for independent higher education.

Pfnister reports that virtually every recent survey of higher education in the United States notes the importance of maintaining a dual, public-independent system. He cites arguments and evidence that independent higher education adds diversity in size, philosophy, curriculum, community, and the potential for experimentation in the educational process; further, that it avoids the bureaucratic problems and excessive governmental interference which characterize public institutions.

Pfnister does not assume that recent trends will affect all institutions in the same way. Rather, he leaves to the individual institution the task of drawing implications for its own situation from the issues his report presents as those most likely to confront higher education.

The third and final report of the Commission on the Future is entitled *Cooperation for the Future* and was edited by Arthur L. Olsen. In summary fashion, the report reviews the work of the three commission committees—on master planning, public policy, and liberal learning—and outlines the further actions recommended by the commission. An appendix includes study-papers written for the commission, "A Statement on Public Policy and Church-Related Higher Education," recommendations on specific public policy issues, and extensive institutional data for Lutheran colleges and universities.

One of the basic purposes of the commission was "to establish a context in which Lutheran institutions might plan together more effectively for carrying out their mission in the future.[31] Issues related to cooperative planning were assigned to the Committee on Master Planning. As a result of its work, the committee was able to ascertain the need for and to make available to the denominations and colleges the Pfnister and Gamelin reports, the systematic collection and collation of annual institutional data, and provisional arrangements for the establishment of a research and planning center. Further, it was able to obtain "evidence of a sense of institutional interdependence and a variety of modes of voluntary interinstitutional cooperation and coordination of effort." However, its major finding is this: Because many Lutheran colleges enjoy regional identities, loyal constituencies and support, and a good deal of institutional independence, "the possibility of increased voluntary collaboration and 'meshed planning,' as a dynamic process rather than as an imposed, static 'master plan,' holds considerable promise for Lutheran colleges and, at another level, for similar cooperative planning between the higher education coordinating agencies of the respective Lutheran church bodies."[32]

The Committee on Public Policy developed its task around the assumption that Lutheran colleges, for the sake of their very survival, must be concerned with the development of public policy and the adequate representation of their interests in seats of government. To insure an adequate flow—and, more importantly, interpretation—of information, the committee has drawn up a list of pressing issues to be monitored and has suggested ways to cooperate with other church and educational agencies in obtaining adequate interpretation of issues. In order to provide a more adequate representation of the Lutheran position in the public policy arena, the committee has recommended that Lutheran law school presidents and deans be requested to provide research on church-state issues and that an advisory committee be formed to assist government relations staff in formulating policy positions and strategies. Finally, the committee has agreed that public policy effectiveness will depend, in large measure, on "a relatively consistent and generally accepted Lutheran concept of desirable public policy. . . ."[33]

Toward this end, the committee and the commission have adopted a statement affirming the importance of involvement in higher education to the Lutheran church, its commitment to providing for quality education, its commitment to a dual system of higher education, and its resolve to oppose injustice in public and independent education. Further, the statement affirms the Lutheran churches' belief that church-related colleges may receive public funding "for services rendered for the public good . . . ," its pledge to be publicly accountable for public funds received, its conviction that government should give high priority to providing financial assistance to qualified and needy students which accounts for the cost-differential between public and independent higher education, and its hope that Christian citizens will exercise their judgment wisely and actively in public policy affecting education.[34]

The work of a third committee—the Committee on Liberal Learning—is also summarized in the report. Following the discontinuation of the commission, LECNA has maintained some programmatic involvement in the area which was of concern to the Committee on Liberal Learning. In 1976–1977 the successor Curriculum Consultation Project undertook three pilot curriculum consultations at Lutheran colleges. A fourth, conducted in spring, 1978, was intended to further refine the process of curriculum consultation by exploring an institution's own highest expectations about how it relates Christian faith, liberal learning, and professional learning in its curriculum and institutional life.

While all three Lutheran communions participate in and contribute to the work of LECNA, their interest in and nurture of the church-college relationship are not limited to their joint endeavors. We turn next to their individual efforts.

American Lutheran Church

In the summer of 1975, the Division for College and University Services of the American Lutheran Church (ALC) sponsored a workshop for selected representatives of church and college. The purpose of the workshop was to engage in disciplined thinking about the nature and mission of ALC colleges in the next decade. (A similar conference was held in 1961 and had a significant impact on the church's role in higher education, according to participants.) A number of speakers made formal presentations, but the focus of the consultation was on small group discussions. *"Toward 1985—":* *Report of the ALC Workshop on the Church College* contains the proceedings of the conference.

Affirming the interdependence of the ALC and its colleges, conferees focused their attention on the process for determining the mission of the college, the nature of the mission itself, and ways in which the mission of the church college can be communicated and strengthened. According to workshop participants, determination of the mission of the church college must reflect the needs, interests, and commitments of the whole constituency. But understood primarily as one manifestation of the church's mission in the world, the college has a particular responsibility to provide for consideration of the heritage, policy, and mission of the church in such deliberations.

The mission of the church college, according to the workshop participants, is one of helping the church to carry out its mission in the world. Some view the particular mission of the church college more in terms of the tasks of faith—to engage in proclamation, evangelization, celebration, social change, service. The majority of group reports emphasize the particular mission of the church college in terms of the relation of faith and learning, or the infusion of education with Christian meaning and purpose. Here the mission of the church college is described as one of emphasizing liberal learning in a Christian context; "infusing questions of value and meaning, especially from the perspective of the Christian tradition, into the pursuit of all knowledge"[35] to the end that students might become morally sensitive, theologically literate, service oriented, critically knowledgeable, aesthetically aware, emotionally mature, understanding of a Christian vocation; or fostering qualitative human relationships which will contribute to the growth of loving and caring communities. Further, the institutional mission is described here as one of providing an alternative to secular and public education and making visible the concern for value and meaning.

Finally, the workshop participants suggest that the mission of the church college can be strengthened by such measures as developing clear, concise statements of theological commitment; by cultivating and utilizing the diverse and useful human and material resources of the churches more fully; by discovering persons both highly qualified and strongly motivated to teach and administer in the church college; by communicating more information about institutional strengths and distinctiveness; and by providing quality education.

The workshop report has no official status within the denomination but has been widely distributed as a stimulus to discussion about the church-related college.

Lutheran Church in America

The relation of the Lutheran Church in America (LCA) to its colleges is principally through the synods, except for certain administrative, regulatory, and research functions which are delegated to the denomination's Division for Mission in North America. In pursuit of its function, the national church and its agencies have both conducted research and adopted policy on church-related higher education in the last few years.

In 1970 the Board of College Education and Church Vocations adopted an official interpretation of the church-college relationship in the LCA. The statement, *The Mission of LCA Colleges and Universities*, was prepared by a specially called committee of church and university persons. The document set out the mission of the colleges, standards for recognition of the college by the church, the responsibilities of the church, and the relationship of the colleges and synods.

It is the task of the church-related college to foster the intellectual growth of its students primarily through study in the arts and sciences. "By acknowledging that God alone is absolute, they may affirm that no institution or system of knowledge can be absolute and may thus provide a setting in which all issues, secular and religious, academic and personal, may be freely studied and discussed." For its part, the church affirms the importance of this task, the ability of the colleges to accomplish it, and the obligation of the church to support and protect freedom of inquiry and expression within the collegiate community. Further, it is the task of these institutions to "foster Christian life and learning as an integral part of their educational programs, recognizing that spiritual growth is an essential part of their total educational mission."[36] Maintaining their identity as church-related colleges, providing for the study of religion, for worship, service, and the up-building of Christian community are all ways that the college will show its concern for Christian life and learning.

The colleges serve the church in all of the aforementioned ways; but they can also serve the church by educating Christian workers and the laity, by providing advice and assistance to the church in fulfilling its mission, and by conducting scholarly research on the church. Finally, "the church recognizes that the colleges have a responsibility to society at large as a part of their responsibility to their students and to the church." The colleges have an obligation to make a creative contribution to the dual system of higher education in the nation, to seek opportunities to aid in the study and solution of major social problems, to continue "to enroll poor and other disadvantaged students through special recruiting methods, supplementary instruction, scholarship funds and other means,"[37] and to educate persons in the human serving professions.

Based on this understanding of the mission of the church-related college, the document states that in order for a college to be recognized by the LCA it must affirm a Christian commitment, affirm its relationship to the LCA, give evidence of academic quality through accreditation, maintain and uphold academic freedom consistent with the standards of the American Association of University Professors, and seek constantly to fulfill the mission requirements outlined above.

At the same time, the LCA—through its congregations, synods, and national agencies—promises to acknowledge the relationship it has with its colleges; to provide the colleges with regular financial support for operating expenses, student aid, and special programs, with technical support services, and with additional monies for "programs of particular relevance to the church on a church-wide basis"; to assist in the recruitment of qualified students and faculty; to share appropriately in the naming of governing board members; and to "foster understanding of and support for the mission and work of the colleges among their church constituency."[38]

Finally, recognizing that the most vital relationships between church and college are at the synodical level and that there is need to both formalize the relationship and regularize the contact, the document recommends that the colleges and affiliated synods formulate a covenant. It is stated that the covenants will include—at least—a statement of the purpose of the college, mutual acknowledgment of the relationship, a statement of the services and support to be provided by each, a plan for communication, and an agreement on the nature and frequency of reports from college to synod. Procedures for review are also included.

In order to strengthen these relationships further, the Council of the LCA Colleges joined with the LCA's Division for Mission in North America in 1976 in commissioning a major research project, to be conducted by the Youth Research Center, Inc., under the direction of Merton P. Strommen. In preparation for the research, Charles Bruning was asked to review current literature in the field. His findings were published by the LCA in a document entitled *Relationships Between Church-Related Colleges and Their Constituencies.*[39] As a part of the larger higher education community, church-related institutions are faced with many of the same social, economic, and political problems that threaten the whole system. And as a part of the independent sector, church-related colleges are confronted with the same problems of declining enrollment and increasing accountability to the state in return for public aid. But the literature suggests that church-related colleges have another problem, according to Bruning: they face an identity crisis.

Faced with the issue of identity, Bruning notes that some writers have turned their attention to delineating what is said to be distinctive about church-related colleges: their commitment to the human good; a moral seriousness in both living and learning; the freedom to pursue the relationship of faith and knowledge; the providing of leadership for church and world; a distinctive Christian world view; a concern for wholeness; a commitment to the liberal arts; and their small and residential character. Others have approached the problem by suggesting alternative directions for church-related colleges: either to become more a part of the mainstream of education or to redefine their mission more in terms of the church. Still a third group has sought to deal with the identity crisis by studying the problem of institutional image.

According to this group of researchers, while church-related colleges may claim or want to project a particular image—and attempt to do so through planned efforts, it is evident that they do not control all the variables in projecting an image. The expectations of the constituencies of a college are such an uncontrollable factor, and when those expectations are unmet, they can cause friction or create a lack of sympathy for a college and its program. On the basis of a further review of the literature dealing with image studies, Bruning concludes that the image dilemma church-related colleges experience today has a great deal to do with unmet expectations on the part of its constituencies. Thus, the college should engage in more extensive and intensive dialogue with the church in order to plan ways to meet expectations or in order to provide the kind of information which will help the church to gain a more accurate perception of the college. But more, the college needs to communicate its interest in having feedback from its several constituencies if they are to feel that they are involved in the mission of the college.

Following the Bruning review, the major research project of the LCA was carried out and was summarized and interpreted by Strommen in a comprehensive report entitled *A Survey of Images and Expectations of LCA Colleges.*[40] The purpose of the national survey was to identify what constituencies expect of the eighteen colleges and universities of the LCA and the degree to which they perceive their expectations are being achieved. Trustees, administrative leaders, faculty, seniors, freshmen, alumni/ae, parents of seniors, parents of freshmen, synod board members, pastors of LCA congregations, and laity made up the constituency groups represented in the 6,728 respondents. These constituency groups ranked the following six goal expectations of the LCA colleges above all others.

First, wholeness of persons. Four out of five respondents believe that one's college should give attention to those virtues which further personal integration and growth as well as to intellectual virtues. Church constituencies perceive this goal as being achieved by LCA colleges while college constituencies do not.

Second, preparation for life. Students expect their colleges to prepare them for a professional career; clergy, for contributing to society; faculty, for living. Except for seniors, there is general satisfaction about how well their college prepares students for life.

Third, liberal arts education. Laity, pastors, and synod leaders place less emphasis here and are not disappointed with the efforts of LCA colleges in education in the liberal arts. Faculty and administrative leaders are disappointed with what is achieved, largely because they give such high priority to it.

Fourth, the centrality of Christianity to a life perspective. Helping students adopt or sharpen a life perspective centered in Christianity is a significantly higher expectation of synod board members, LCA pastors, and older laity than it is for faculty and administrative leaders. Church constituencies are the most disappointed with what they perceive is achieved in campus religious life. Students and non-Lutheran faculty are not in sympathy with this critique because they do not favor a strong religious emphasis. Slightly more than half of the students want no moral standards or expectations imposed on them outside the classroom. The role of the college in orienting students toward a Christian perspective is a point of tension between church and college constituencies.

Fifth, social change. Half the respondents seek the involvement of their college in social change with its community. The majority agree that the college should not be viewed as the church's social tool for solving its own or society's problems but as an agent for preparing students for working toward constructive social change later in their lives.

Sixth, religious diversity within a Christian orientation. Six out of ten respondents want an atmosphere of intellectual freedom for the LCA college where Christianity is in dialogue with other beliefs. Seniors, freshmen, and non-Lutheran faculty and non-Lutheran alumni/ae are less enthusiastic here since they do not share the concern for a strong religious emphasis. Half the respondents want religious diversity among the faculty and students. Administrative leaders and faculty are somewhat dissatisfied with how well their college has achieved religious diversity. Younger laity, freshmen, and seniors believe that far less is being accomplished to assure a broader range of diversity than they expect should characterize their college. Religious diversity is another point of tension between the college and the church. Less than half the respondents give high importance to efforts which encourage religious diversity. The administration's accent on religious diversity concerns LCA pastors and laity who do not hold that greater diversity is an element to be desired.

Following his analysis of considerably more data, Strommen concludes:

> Good will characterizes the dominant attitude held by constituencies of LCA colleges. They view their schools as being superior educational institutions, Christian in life and character, and symbols of a coveted ideal. Key leaders in college and church feel uneasy, however, about future relationships between their two institutions and are ready to press for a more intentional identity with the other.[41]

The attempt to achieve a closer relationship will meet with difficulties, however. Strommen notes that some faculty oppose a religiously distinctive college on the grounds that greater attention to the church's agenda will interfere with achieving educational excellence. Congregational laity tend to be supportive of church-related colleges but vague about the ones with which they have some connection. Church persons have widely different notions of what a church-related college ought to be. And many young people, raised in a different ethos, expect from their colleges something quite different than do church and college leaders.

So, according to Strommen, a great deal more communication is needed between college and church. But, in addition, there also needs to be a great deal more theological clarity about "the primary task of the college as distinct from the church."[42]

At its Eighth Biennial Convention, held in July, 1976, the LCA adopted a statement outlining *The Basis for Partnership Between Church and College.* Going beyond the 1970 statement, the new document attempts to reaffirm the church's commitment to its colleges, to set out a theological base for higher education, to describe the common concerns and colleague relationships which ought to exist between church and college, and to encourage continuing dialogue and interaction between the two—subjects which the Bruning and Strommen studies suggest need more careful attention.

The document states that there has been an erosion of church-related colleges of late because of the declining proportion of Christians in church-related colleges, the increasing secularization of them, spiraling costs, pressures on these institutions to expand beyond the ability of churches to support them, and the commitment of the church's energies and resources to other social concerns. All of this has led many to question the wisdom of maintaining the church-college tie; but the document suggests there are compelling reasons to press for strengthening the relationship.

The statement proclaims that "the living triune God is the Lord of both church and college. Their tasks, though different, are both God-given. He rules over both through his Word, and both are important in the fulfilling of his Will for his creation."[43] God makes his will known through the church, as the Spirit leads us to Christ. Through response to Christ's claim on our lives in trust for obedience, we are bound together in the church. But more than for our own advantage, our vocation is to give glory to God by involving ourselves in his purposes, in tending to his unfolding creation, and by caring for one another. As we attend to this vocation, we begin to see that it is God's will that we ally ourselves with all persons and organizations which are moved by reason and conscience to improve and advance the human condition. The statement continues:

> This means that education in general, and the church-related college in particular, have an integrity and purpose grounded in the Creed's first Article, concerning Creation. The capacity to learn—to search into the secrets of nature and use its resources, to search into the mystery of the human and perceive our misery and grandeur, to search into the riddle of history and be stalkers of meaning—is possible because of God's goodness. The fact that sinners are not justified by knowledge or cultural refinement should not obscure the further fact that education is the gift of a loving Creator. Through it he would enhance and enrich people's lives. Through it he would inform, motivate and equip them to make human society what he intends it to be. Sound scholarship, careful research, and effective teaching do him honor and serve his cause.[44]

This understanding of education as grounded in Lutheran theology "establishes the freedom and significance of educational institutions. It affirms the college as a college, devoted to its primary task, blending together the differing talents and convictions of many persons."[45]

Given this understanding that church and college have differing but nonetheless God-given tasks, each is free and empowered to serve the other reciprocally. The college affords the church a potentially effective means to exercise its prophetic concern that the structures and forces of society become wiser, more just, and more compassionate; it serves the church's witness to the world as it fosters responsible citizenship (seen by many, hopefully, as an expression of their baptism identity); and it provides the church with a setting where theology and other academic disciplines probe and illuminate one another. From the church, the college gains financial support, potential students, faculty, administrators, trustees, and help in retaining a distinctive character and commitment.

In light of this rationale, synods and colleges are encouraged to review the covenants between them, asking whether there is clarity about the purposes of the college and about the relationship between college and church; whether there is freedom of inquiry, consideration of the values by which persons live, study and debate the goals of society, opportunities for worship, witness, service, development of a shared life of Christian faith; whether there is diversity of religious commitments and religious perspectives in the college community; and whether the church affirms the primary educational role of the college and provides adequate support.

Lutheran Church—Missouri Synod

The relationship between the Lutheran Church—Missouri Synod (LCMS) and its colleges—in terms of governance and operational procedures—is set down in the denomination's *Handbook*, last revised in 1975. The section on higher education outlines the responsibilities of the Board for Higher Education, the college Board of Control, teaching staff and faculty, college presidents, and the Commission on Lay Higher Education; further, it contains regulations on finances and the election of the president and specific regulations for educational institutions.

The Board for Higher Education is responsible for promoting and protecting—by taking corrective measures in the schools—the objectives prescribed by the synod. The board is also responsible for studying trends and philosophies of contemporary education and determining their relation to and implications for the synod's educational standards, policies, and objectives. Finally the board is responsible for recruiting students for the pastoral and teaching ministries and other synod-approved training programs.

The Boards of Control are responsible for promoting and supervising education for the preparation of ministers and teachers and for assisting and advising in the means to Christian higher education. The Boards of Control are responsible for facilitating the achievement of the purposes for which the synod operates and maintains its institutions and for promoting and protecting the synod's religious, academic, and financial interests. The Boards of Control are also responsible for adopting standards and regulations governing off-campus activities of the instructional staff and other employees and are responsible for the appropriateness of the nonacademic and off-campus interests, activities, and employment of students.

The teaching staff and faculty are responsible for developing curricula which implement the purposes of the institution and for attaining the synod's objectives for training professional church workers. The faculty is responsible for developing policies for the nonacademic life and activities of students "so that cocurricular and off-campus activities of the student contribute to the attainment of the educational objectives of the institution."[46] These policies are to be developed so as to be conducive to Christian deportment. The *Handbook* makes clear the relative responsibility of the faculties and the Boards of Control:

> a. Each faculty shall develop, formulate, promote, and foster ideals, standards, and criteria of personal conduct and of the community life of the campus worthy of the Christian calling and of ministers in training for the church.
> b. Each Board of Control, on recommendation of the faculty, shall adopt a comprehensive policy statement committing the school and its officers to the principles of Christian discipline, evangelical dealing, and good order governing the students individually and collectively.[47]

Theological as well as academic criteria guide hiring and advancement decisions concerning faculty. "Limitations of academic freedom because of the religious and confessional nature and aims of the institution shall be stated in writing at the time of the [faculty] appointment and conveyed to the person being appointed."[48]

The section on "Specific Regulations for Educational Institutions" outlines the eligibility and placement of students in the synod as church workers, ministers, and teachers. The Commission on Lay Higher Education is responsible for informing pastors and congregations about educational opportunities and for encouraging synod members to take advantage of opportunities for Lutheran lay higher education.

Mennonite Church

The relationship of the Mennonite Church and its educational institutions and programs is described in a document entitled "Mennonite Board of Education: Roles and Relationships," adopted in 1972 and reaffirmed in 1977. The statement describes the primary role of the Mennonite Board of Education, the differences in role at various levels of the educational system, and the specific functions exercised in relationships with higher educational institutions which are under the board.

The document states: "The primary role of the Mennonite Board of Education is to consider Mennonite Church educational objectives and to provide for the use of Mennonite personnel and financial resources in meeting these objectives in the best way." Unlike the denomination's elementary and secondary schools—which are regional and local in character, largely nonresidential, parallel in program offerings, and supported by local groups and patrons— Mennonite institutions of higher education are largely residential, increasingly less regional and more churchwide, challenged to provide special programs to meet special educational needs, and more costly to operate. Thus, the Mennonite church affirms that "churchwide governance and planning perspective" are particularly important for accomplishing the church's goals in higher education.[49]

At the college level, "the local institutional boards are responsible to consider the specific objectives of their institutions and to ask how their local traditions and history, their buildings and other facilities, their available income, and their personnel resources can be used to meet these objectives." The Board of Education has other, complementary functions which are to: appoint college presidents and board members; state and clarify general aims and objectives and approve insititutional statements of aims and objectives; provide for or approve long-range plans; review and approve new and continuing programs; establish basic board policies; make policy decisions regarding the relationship between the Mennonite educational institutions and between them and the church; act as the corporate body holding title to the assets of the schools; and participate "in the allocation of the church's financial resources through recommending per-member asking levels for congregational contributions to the several institutions."[50]

In addition to these more formal functions, the document gives examples of the coordinating and service roles which the board has developed to meet the particularly timely needs of church and college. These include such things as the development of a broad policy concerning qualifications of college faculty members and the undertaking of a two-year churchwide thrust on education to assist church and school people in a refocusing of educational goals and tasks. The document also suggests that the board, in developing its policy perspective and decisions, has found it especially useful to invite the regular counsel of college presidents and board chairpersons and the input of other board representatives and college administrators from time to time. These persons have been able to make valuable contributions.

In conclusion, the document notes that church bodies do not have a particularly impressive track record in making efficient use of their educational resources. "Mennonites have had a certain sense of identity and common churchwide purpose, but they live among denominations and private groups whose schools have been largely independent or regionally-based." Thus, the denomination has had to look elsewhere for models of effectiveness. "Creative efforts in some multi-campus public systems in recent decades have been more helpful to Mennonites as they have tried to work at the development and maintenance of structural relationships appropriate to their educational objectives."[51]

And in recent years, Mennonites have come to see their "peoplehood education" philosophy and models as different from the educational commitments and role of other denominations. (The executive of the Mennonite Board of Education has defined this notion of education in another context as "intergenerational conversation within the people of God" and has suggested that at least two models for facilitating it are the "believers' church college" and "a church-related academic subcommunity on a university campus.")[52] Given this understanding of the distinctiveness of the Mennonite ideal, the document concludes: "The Mennonite Board of Education senses in a special way its responsibility for being aware of Mennonite educational needs and objectives and discerning the means—including governance arrangements—that can best achieve church and school goals in peoplehood education."[53]

Church of the Nazarene

The relationship of the Church of the Nazarene (and specifically of the executive director of the Department of Education and the Ministry) to its colleges is contained in the church's *Manual*. Portions of the polity and practice relating to higher education were amended, and the entire section was adopted by the General Assembly of the church in 1976. The document defines the managerial, supervisory, regulatory, and advisory responsibilities of the Department of Education and the Ministry in relation to the educational institutions related to the church.

It is the duty of the Department of Education and the Ministry to promote education generally, to maintain an advisory relationship to schools and colleges in all aspects of their life, to encourage the attainment of higher standards and greater efficiency in educational institutions, and to determine both the number of schools which will receive financial support from the denomination and the supporting church territories for each. The department has managerial oversight over the colleges; it also is to determine the amount of money each school is to receive yearly from the denomination.

In terms of education, the department is to determine at least every four years the minimum requirements for admissions and graduation in each of the church-related schools and to insure that all schools provide for "the historical, literary, practical, and devotional study of the Bible." It is also to encourage all the schools of the denomination "to promote courses in moral education with instruction in the holiness ethic and life-style."[54] The document also sets out the responsibilities of the department for the recruitment, education, deployment, and continuing education of ministers. The *Manual* directs the Board of General Superintendents of the church to appoint an advisory committee to the department which shall meet at least once a year.

In pursuit of its task, the department assists the colleges in recruitment, maintains a file of prospective teachers, and maintains liaison with educational associations and the government on behalf of the related colleges. The executive director of the department also serves as executive director of the association of Nazarene college presidents, of the Nazarene College Consortium, of the national honor society of Nazarene colleges, and of the Nazarene Athletic

Association and as co-chairman of the annual Nazarene Student Leadership Conference.

Presbyterian Church in the United States

During the last several years the Presbyterian Church in the United States (PCUS) has engaged in an intense reevaluation of its commitment to higher education. One of the distinctive features of this examination has been a resolve to view ministries in higher education (campus ministry) and the church's mission in and through PCUS colleges as inseparable aspects of the church's whole commitment to higher education.

A significant step in this process was taken in the Higher Education Consultation held in January, 1976, after two years of preparation, which brought together church, campus ministry, and college leadership. The elimination of the staff position for Higher and Public Education from the church's national Mission Board just a few months earlier gave added impetus to the consultation and to the "Statement of Conscience and Consensus" which was forwarded to the church's General Assembly which met the following June.

One of the developments from the consultation was the subsequent forming of the Association of Presbyterian Colleges, whose presidents had long been related to each other informally but who now organized for the furtherance of closer communication, discussion of mutual concerns, and assistance to the church in the pursuit of its mission in higher education.

The General Assembly took seriously the higher education concern presented to it and appointed an Ad Interim Committee

"to study the rationale, the relationship, and the role of the Church in higher education in order to recommend to the 117th General Assembly what its future commitment to higher education may be; . . . and for 1978 the General Assembly instruct the Mission Board to give high priority to the restoration of the function of Higher and Public Education."[55]

The report and recommendations of the Ad Interim Committee, which were adopted one year later by the 1977 General Assembly, called for dramatic and urgent action to help the church catch up with new understandings of the issues at stake in higher education and to reaffirm the church's ministry in and with higher education. This action the General Assembly took in the light of the report's assertion that the church had given little attention to higher education for more than a decade, that there was need for repentance for not being "true to our mission and our heritage," and that major changes in society and in public policy had drastically altered the system and condition of higher education.[56]

The report was based on two major findings: one that noted the radically changing character of higher education, and the other that affirmed the church's need to recover or find anew the theological and biblical rationale for its responsibilities in higher education.

A number of "current, emerging and interconnecting trends" in higher education and in the church demand attention, according to the report, "if the Church's ministries in public and Church-related higher education are to avoid danger and respond to opportunity and challenge." These include: a new and much broader constituency for higher education than ever before; the unpredictability of future enrollments together with the increased percentage of high school graduates going on to college; the continuing entry and reentry of older persons; the expansion of higher education opportunities through community colleges, state institutions, and increased student financial support—all of these illustrating the new and challenging open-endedness in higher education.[57]

Further, the report puts these trends alongside the increasing financial pressures and problems in recruiting students on the part of church-related colleges; the reduced attention of the church to its role both in campus ministry and to church-related colleges; the lack of clarity in the church's purpose; the difficulties posed by denominational restructuring, inflation, new federal and state regulations; the respectable size of the church's past and present financial investment in higher education together with the critical need for much more. "The crisis, uncertainty, and in some instances, impending doom must be seen over against the foundation and framework of responsibility and faithfulness which our spiritual ancestors carefully laid and nurtured."[58]

In light of this, the report states:

> The crisis, then, is one in which the Church must decide *why* it is important to continue its ministry in and with its own institutions and public higher education. It is one in which strategies must be found to relate the Church's ministry to more than the few four-year colleges and universities upon whose campuses we have historically placed professional clergy. It is one in which relationships with its own colleges must be

clarified both conceptually and jurisdictionally. It is one in which new patterns for funding and recruitment must be developed if some of the Church's colleges are to continue to fulfill their ministry. And finally, it is one in which the Church must re-think, regain, and re-articulate its own mission to its risen Lord in a rapidly changing context and in a contemporary, refreshing and exciting manner.[59]

The rationale for the church's involvement in higher education begins with its existence as a covenanted community called upon to "claim the promises and undertake the demands of the gospel of Jesus Christ to proclaim, live and work for his kingdom of justice and love."[60] The church's concerns and values are thus sometimes congruent and sometimes in opposition to the values and concerns of higher education and other institutions in society.

The biblical and theological rationale for the church's mission in higher education lies, first of all, in its call to stewardship; stewardship for God's creation; for the developing of individual human potential; for all human knowledge—that it be used for the welfare of humanity and especially for the disadvantaged; and for the "knowledge of God's nature revealing in Jesus Christ, the Word of God, to whom the Scriptures and the people of God witness." The church must be present also in higher education "to contribute with others there to the community of learning in which people care for and support one another, experience both personal and academic interdependence, and develop appreciation for the variety of persons with whom God has given us to share the world."[61]

Since relationships in society are not simply personal but also institutional, the church's strategy for mission, according to the PCUS statement, is at least threefold: to commission and equip people to call others to faith and discipleship in the field of higher education, to work with these as they become a resource with the church in what is often a common mission, and to work "with institutions of higher education as *instruments* through which the Church may influence persons and society in behalf of the Gospel message."[62]

With this rationale as a guide, the PCUS report places an enlarged responsibility upon individual congregations for making ministry in higher education an integral part of their own ministry. Further, individual congregations are called upon to renew the ties of fellowship with an understanding of the distinctive educational experience offered at the PCUS-related colleges, to give guidance to parents and young people, and to provide scholarships and gifts to PCUS colleges, understanding their importance as alternatives to public education.

A call to provide leadership, understanding, and support for ministry in higher education is issued also to presbyteries and synods, together with the request that they make increased use of these ministries and the PCUS colleges in providing resources for the mission of the church. New patterns of relationship need to be negotiated in some cases between the colleges and the church, usually at the synod level. Middle judicatories are admonished to respect "the corporate responsibility and integrity of the colleges as they negotiate covenants and contracts for program services and financial support." Possible changes in funding patterns, it is suggested, "may include underwriting specific programs carried out by the colleges, minimal line-item budgeting to maintain the Church's symbolic connection with a college, and a judicatory's assistance to a college in securing outside funding to replace funding no longer supplied through budgeting." [63]

Congregations and judicatories are urged to give attention to the issues emerging from state and regional systems of public and independent higher education, calling attention especially to the need for advocacy in behalf of the poor and disenfranchised, the historically black institutions, and the independence of higher education from government interference.

The General Assembly was itself urged to give leadership to the churches in these areas. It accepted the report's rationale for the church's mission in and with higher education and reaffirmed its "heritage, leadership and commitment to higher education as a field of mission, a resource for ministry, and as an instrument of service." [64] The assembly authorized the establishing of higher education as a special churchwide emphasis for 1979–1981 and the establishment of an assembly Higher Education Task Force to guide this undertaking for a limited period of five years, 1978–1982. It defined the functions of the Task Force, authorized the employment of a staff person to guide the process, and guaranteed necessary funding to undergird it.

Among the functions defined for the Task Force are the developing of a variety of models for new strategies, the encouraging of institutions individually and cooperatively to address the question

"What is the unique contribution of each Church-related institution of higher education?," and the developing of guidelines and criteria for the relationships between institutions officially related to the church and its appropriate jurisdictions.[65]

Religious Society of Friends

The Friends Council on Education is an association of schools, colleges, and study centers in the United States and Canada which are under the care of Friends. Founded in 1931 and composed of representatives of all Friends schools and colleges, the council early adopted two aims which are "basic to the religious heritage of the Society of Friends: to develop the feeling of friendliness and mutual understanding among our institutions; to impress upon the schools and colleges the importance of reverence for the truth and respect for the divine element in each person, student and teacher alike."[66] In pursuit of these aims, the council provides a number of services to Quaker educators and institutions and seeks to interpret the philosophy and role of Friends schools and colleges to constituents and the public as well.

According to a brochure entitled *What Does a Friends School Have to Offer?* and published by the council, "Friends schools aspire to have their deepest roots in the Quaker religious experience." Thus, Friends schools attempt to create a setting in which students and faculty both "can continue to mature as companions in a wide range of experiences"—experiences which are both "outward" and "inward" in nature. These experiences may lead to "a deepening awareness of the presence of God," according to individual readiness and in forms appropriate to individual personality. But persons are free to respond or not; therefore, Friends schools cannot promise the outcome of a Quaker education.[67]

Promises aside:

> Friends see all education as inescapably religious regardless of age, subject matter, or setting. For while these Friends school communities are searching for understanding in sets and numbers, poems, animal reproduction, party platforms, situational ethics and racial tensions, they are also seeking to know more clearly the Truth which sets men free and gives them the more abundant life.[68]

Thus, Friends education is pervaded by a sense of social responsibility. "A man's training and heightened gifts belong to his neighbors as well. Peace and war, racism and brotherhood, ignorance and poverty, justice and law and violence, all these are both subjects for study and issues for commitment, now as students and soon as effective citizens."[69] Further, Friends schools seek to develop the skills, abilities, and sensitivities which will free their students from ignorance and incompetence and also enable them to deal with the "signals of meaning" that men and women employ. Finally, Friends educational institutions hope to be both communities that care about their members and incorporate certain aspirations:

> A Friends school hopes to offer a community that cares very deeply about what kinds of persons its members, young and old, are becoming, what goals and motives are effective in their lives, what their response is to the high calling of being human. They hope to be communities of those who have not only techniques and knowledge but also a vivid relationship to reality, a hunger for worship, a passion for truth, and the experience of growth, both in the Light and toward the Light.[70]

In support of these objectives, the Friends Council on Education, through its constituent committees and the work of its executive director, runs a teacher placement service for Friends and graduates of Quaker colleges; provides consultative services to Friends institutions, administrators, and boards of trustees; conducts a variety of personal and professional enrichment seminars and programs for teachers and administrators; provides funds for scholarships, equipment, and programs; maintains a computerized roster of Quaker scholars—used for placement and in locating scholars with mutual research interests; and sends representatives to educational meetings and to various Friends Yearly Meetings.

Roman Catholic Church

Responsibility for Roman Catholic colleges and universities rests with the sponsoring religious bodies. In most cases these are religious orders; in about a dozen cases the sponsor is a diocese; in only one case (Catholic University of America), the bishops of the country. There are voluntary associations of Catholic colleges and universities which seek to serve their memberships by assistance and encouragement with their Catholic mission and character (nationally, the National Catholic Educational Association and, internationally, the International Federation of Catholic Universities). The hierarchy of the church (nationally, the National Conference of Catholic Bishops;

internationally, the Sacred Congregation for Catholic Education) provides encouragement and counsel in matters pertaining to doctrine and church discipline. In recent years, all of the above have been engaged in serious attempts to study and interpret the roles and relationships of church and college.

"The Catholic University in the Modern World" is a statement of the Second International Congress of Delegates of the Catholic Universities of the World, which met in Rome in November, 1972. The document was written over a three-year period and represents the collaborative efforts of the Sacred Congregation for Catholic Education, the International Federation of Catholic Universities, and participants in four regional conferences. The document was issued, however, in the name of the Second Congress.

The statement identifies the following as essential characteristics of the Catholic university: a Christian inspiration of individuals and the university community, a continuing reflection on knowledge from the perspective of the Catholic faith, fidelity to the Christian message as it comes through the church, and commitment to serve the people of God and the human family. "In a word, being both a university and Catholic, it must be both a community of scholars representing the various branches of human knowledge, and an academic institution in which Catholicism is vitally present and operative."[71]

According to the document, the Catholic university has as its objectives: to be a place where disparate disciplines confront each other for mutual enrichment; to make theology relevant to all human knowledge and vice versa; to witness to Christ; to make scholarly discoveries available to the people of God; to contribute to the solution of the major problems confronting humanity. Further, it is to examine the values and norms predominant in modern society from the Christian point of view; to prepare professionally competent, ethically sensitive leaders for society and the church; to offer students a milieu conducive to their integral development; to contribute to ecumenism by preparing persons qualified to participate in serious interfaith dialogue; to encourage continuing education and to show profound respect for culture.

The statement acknowledges that Catholic colleges differ greatly in their nature and in relation to the governments and regulatory agencies of the countries in which they are located. Thus, their internal government must be adaptive to local conditions, laws, and the great diversity among them. But all Catholic universities should provide in some way for the participation of the whole university community in the decision-making process, should respect the rights and insure due process for all, and should facilitate sincere dialogue among the whole university community.

"To perform its teaching and research functions effectively a Catholic university must have true autonomy and academic freedom."[72] This is understood to include freedom to establish programs of study and confer degrees; freedom in admissions, appointments, and research; administrative autonomy; and financial autonomy or viability. In addition, the Catholic university should understand the importance of and be involved in long-range planning.

As any authentic university, the Catholic university engages in teaching, research, continuing education, and other services for which it is equipped. But in order to meet its special, aforementioned objectives, it strives to impart a Catholic character to all its activities, seeks to provide an authentic human community for those who participate in its life, and has an important task of promoting human and social development. The document offers myriad suggestions for accomplishing these goals, all the while reminding its readers that all the activities of the university have as their ultimate goal the forming of persons capable of effectively undertaking their responsibilities in the church and in the world.

Recognizing that the Catholic universities render an indispensable service to the communities which sustain them, religious authorities will, according to the document, accept a particular responsibility for sustaining the Catholic universities in their region. Thus:

> Catholic universities can rightly expect inspiration, encouragement and support from the Hierarchy in carrying out their difficult task. For their part, the universities will seek to promote a frank and confident collaboration with Church authorities, knowing that it is only in the context of the Church that they can accomplish their specifically Catholic mission.[73]

The Catholic university is autonomous; but it must recognize the authority of the church in doctrinal matters. This recognition does not imply that the hierarchy has the right to intervene in matters of university government or administration. It will intervene only when the authentic Christian message is at stake.

At almost the same time that the statement on "The Catholic University in the Modern World" was being circulated, the National Conference of Catholic Bishops published *To Teach as Jesus Did: A Pastoral Message on Catholic Education*. The primary focus of the document is with the lower schools; but higher education and campus ministry receive specific, if less extensive, attention.

While the pastoral message represents the views of the American bishops, it reflects their attempts "to obtain the views of persons from a variety of backgrounds and interests priests, religious men and women, lay people, professional educators at all levels of education, parents, students." The bishops also note that the pastoral was written in light of the Second Vatican Council's *Declaration on Christian Education* which called for national statements on educational ministry. Not to be regarded as the final practical or theoretical word on the subject, the bishops offer their pastoral in the conviction that "it will serve a useful purpose if it proves a catalyst for efforts to deal realistically with problems of polarization and of confusion now confronting the educational ministry."[74] The bishops affirm that:

> Catholic education is an expression of the mission entrusted by Jesus to the Church he founded. Through education the Church seeks to prepare its members to proclaim the Good News and to translate this proclamation into action. Since the Christian vocation is a call to transform oneself and society with God's help, the educational efforts of the Church must encompass the twin purposes of personal sanctification and social reform in light of Christian values.[75]

In order to provide meaningful education which will serve these twin purposes, it is most useful, according to the pastoral letter, to understand the educational mission of the church in terms of an integrated ministry with three interlocking dimensions: "the message revealed by God (*didache*) which the Church proclaims; fellowship in the life of the Holy Spirit (*koinonia*); service to the Christian community and the entire human community (*diakonia*)." Proclamation of the revelation of God in Jesus and teaching of right doctrine are central tasks of the teaching church. But these are understood to involve more than intellectual assent; that is, persons are to act on the new vision of God, the world, and the self which they experience in faith with their whole being. Through baptism, persons are joined to others in the Christian community in faith, hope, and love. The teaching church nourishes that community through all its forms of education and especially through the celebration of the Eucharist, "which is at once sign of community and cause of its growth."[76]

But experience in Christian community is not an end in itself; it is to equip persons to be better able to build community "in their families, their places of work, their neighborhoods, their nation, their world."[77] Experience in Christian community leads naturally to service. The teaching church helps persons to discover, acknowledge, and use their God-given gifts. But service is not limited to the Christian community alone; Christians render service by prayer and worship and direct participation in social reform.

Faced with the paradoxes of the technological age, the church must proclaim the gospel of Christ in our time in a way that is faithful to the past and open to the future. One of the ways in which the church fulfills this educational mission is through higher education. The bishops' statement acknowledges the importance of higher education in our society, states that the cooperation between church and university is essential to the health of the society, affirms "the critically important contribution made by Catholic institutions through their commitment to the spiritual, intellectual, and moral values of the Christian tradition," invites the practical support of the Catholic community to ensure the continuing viability of these colleges, and suggests that the same support and concern should be extended to all of higher education in the hope that every college and university will be committed to "the full and free pursuit and study of truth, including the place of religion in the lives of individuals and society."[78]

Noting that the Second Vatican Council urged all pastors to seek the spiritual welfare of students at Catholic and non-Catholic institutions of higher education alike, the pastoral letter first turns its attention to campus ministry. The goals of campus ministry are to promote theological study and reflection and encourage holistic thinking, provide pastoral care and sustenance for the Christian community on campus, work for the integration of this ministry with other ministries in the community, and help the Christian community on campus to serve its own members and others. Campus ministry is pastoral, educational, and prophetic and is the work of priests, religious, lay faculty and administrators, students, and community members. Campus ministry is to be given high priority, "not only for its own sake but for the sake of increased dialogue between the Church and the university."[79]

The bishops state that "the Catholic college or university seeks to give the authentic Christian message an institutional presence in the academic world." It follows from this that

> Christian commitment will characterize this academic community. While fully maintaining the autonomy concomitant to its being a college or university, the institution will manifest fidelity to the teaching of Jesus Christ as transmitted by His Church. The advancement of Christian thought will be the object of institutional commitment. The human sciences will be examined in light of Catholic faith. The best of the Christian intellectual and spiritual tradition will be blended with the special dynamism of contemporary higher education in a way that enriches both.[80]

Of course, the Catholic college, according to contemporary criteria, will be committed to academic excellence and academic freedom; but there is a special aspect to academic freedom in such an institution. While natural truth is directly accessible through reason, the datum from which theological reflection arises is not fully accessible in the same manner. "The authentic Christian message is entrusted by Jesus Christ to His community, the Church." Theological research and speculation deal with divine revelation as their source; therefore, the results of such investigation are "subject to the judgment of the magisterium."[81]

The statement on higher education concludes with a discussion of theology and the Catholic university. "As an institution committed to examination of the full range of human existence, the university should probe the religious dimensions of life."[82] Thus, scholars in religion and theology should be a part of the academic community; theologians should be engaged in dialogue with scholars in other fields for mutual enrichment; theologians should encourage students to confront religious questions and explore the religious dimensions of life; and college departments of theology—a vital resource to the Catholic community outside the university—should provide support to the pastoral ministry of the church.

As a contribution to the dialogue on church-related higher education taking place within the Catholic Church, the College and University Department of the National Catholic Educational Association (NCEA)—representing 220 of the 250 Catholic colleges and universities in the United States—publishes *Occasional Papers on Catholic Higher Education* twice a year, invites scholars to address each annual meeting of the association on some issue related to the nature and purpose of Catholic higher education,[83] and engages in a host of other related activities. In 1976 the College and University Department of the NCEA prepared and published a position paper entitled "Relations of American Catholic Colleges and Universities with the Church."

Cognizant of the variety of Catholic institutions, the paper suggests that they have five characteristics in common: they are chartered by the state as public trusts and enjoy tax-free status; they are independently supported and controlled; they profess a Catholic identity; they maintain a Catholic presence through personnel, theology departments, campus ministry, in official policy and institutional concerns, and in the "impact of theological and philosophical reflection on the various disciplines"; and they affirm the goal stated in "The Catholic University in the Modern World": "to form persons who are capable of effectively undertaking their responsibilities in the Church and in the world."[84] The paper points out, however, that even these general characteristics do not apply uniformly to all Catholic institutions of higher education.

Central to this document is the description of the Catholic identity of the colleges. The paper affirms the bishops' statement concerning the indispensable service which Catholic institutions perform for the church and the society. Further, it suggests that the Catholic identity of the colleges is evidenced in the provision that is made for theological and religious studies, in the support of ecumenical scholarship and dialogue, in the importance placed on a strong program of campus ministry, and in the interdisciplinary programs which seek to relate the insights of theology and ethics to those of other disciplines. Also, Catholic identity is found in the nurturing of the worshiping community as an integral part of the living/learning experience, in the attention which is given to utilizing the college as a forum for dialogue in the church, and in the work of the NCEA which is "explicitly concerned with the issue of Catholic identity and service."[85]

The paper points to some particular, timely concerns of the Catholic colleges as well. The rapid expansion of low-cost public education, inflation, and the limitations of modest endowments contribute to the problem of survival of independent colleges. Thus, if they are to remain competitive and provide an affordable option to public higher education, Catholic "colleges and universities are obliged to seek funds from sources other than constantly escalating tuitions. Because of our public service, we feel government has an obligation to help." But, as the paper indicates, constitutional constraints and continual legal challenges of public aid to church-related higher education make the situation tenuous at best. In light of this, any indication of interference by the official church in an institution's proper autonomy could have disastrous effects. The problem is not without solution, however. The paper states: "A cooperative relationship of people who are recognized as having genuine responsibilities—Bishops, Trustees, Presidents—maintains a Catholic identity within the limitations imposed by American law, and thus fosters the noble purpose of Catholic higher education."[86]

The paper goes on to provide examples of how, in light of these constraints, the Catholic colleges in this country are attempting to maintain and strengthen the Catholicity of their institutions. Further, it commends the American bishops for their understanding, support, and recognition of "the existence of a new stage in the relationships between Catholic higher education and the American Church." Finally, the document points to the inappropriateness of juridical, canonical, statutory relationships between the church and university in the United States and suggests:

> In the spirit of Vatican Council II and with the long history we have had in providing a genuine Catholic educational experience in an American framework, we believe the word "cooperation" or the phrase "mutual respect and support" best characterizes the kind of relationship that should exist between institution and Church.[87]

Society of Jesus

As stated previously, most Roman Catholic colleges and universities in the United States are sponsored by religious orders. While a number of orders have been or are engaged in studying their involvement in higher education, the most extensive current study by a religious order is that which has been conducted by the Society of Jesus (Jesuits). What follows is a discussion of that one study.

In 1972, following a two-year period of self-study, American Jesuits proposed and the Father General of the Society approved the formation of the Jesuit Conference—a national process to enable Jesuits in the ten U.S. provinces "to communicate with one another, work together, meet common problems, and make the very best of their resources in their service of the Church."[88] As the first project to be conducted under the auspices of the conference, the order chose to examine its principal and, in many ways, most rapidly and profoundly changing apostolate—the Jesuit apostolate of education in the United States.

As a first phase of the project, the provincials of the order and the staff of the Jesuit Conference devised a consultation and publication process which engaged members and institutions of the order in discussion and reflection on their educational mission and eventuated in the publication of six study books, each of which in turn invited further discussion and response from Jesuits and their institutions.

The first volume of *Project 1: The Jesuit Apostolate of Education in the United States, An Introduction,* outlines the nature of the project, describes the process to be followed in carrying it out, and summarizes the themes to be dealt with in subsequent publications. Additionally, the introductory volume contains a digest of the responses which members of the Society made to an initial inquiry asking them to state what questions ought to be addressed in such a study, what information needs to be gathered, what problems should be approached on a national basis, and how the Jesuit Conference can best serve the educational apostolate. Responses are wide ranging and varied, raising such basic issues as why Jesuits should be engaged in education and whether or not "theology and philosophy hold a place of distinction" in Jesuit institutions and posing such practical questions as how Jesuits can continue to finance their educational apostolate and continue to staff eighty institutions.[89]

The second volume, *An Overview,* describes in detail what Jesuits are doing in education and the resources they have for the task. While Jesuits are engaged in a great number and variety of educational endeavors (as well as other forms of ministry), 1,283 members of the Society—or 19 percent of all Jesuits in the U.S.—are actively engaged in the teaching and administration of some twenty-eight Jesuit colleges and universities.

The report goes on to discuss the location of the institutions (most are in urban centers in northeast and north central United States); faculty (Jesuit institutions of higher education employ 6,979 teachers; "the percentage of full-time faculty Jesuits ranged from a high of 41.3 percent to a low of 6 per cent"[90]); student body (the average full-time and part-time total enrollment in the twenty-eight schools in 1972–1973 was 5,558); and degrees conferred. Further, the document presents information on programs (the average number of under-graduate majors at the twenty-eight schools is 21.8; within the twenty-eight schools there are thirteen professional schools of law, five schools of dentistry, four of medicine, three of social service, and one divinity school); governance (there are non-Jesuits on all but two of the twenty-eight boards of trustees; the number of Jesuit administrators in the schools range from 72.9 percent to 8.1 percent); and finance (while tuition and fees are the central resource, gifts and contributed services from Jesuits to their institutions average 29.2 percent of individual compensation, or a total yearly average gift to each of the twenty-eight schools of $189,582).

The report also provides data on available Jesuit personnel ("during the next fifteen years, there will be fewer Jesuits in the educational apostolate in our institutions, and they will be older") and on the expansion of the educational apostolate ("the Jesuit apostolate in education expanded more swiftly than the Assistancy itself during the past thirty years").[91]

The final section of the overview outlines provincial and national supporting structures and organizations for the educational apostolate.

The third publication in the series, *The Issues,* presents "the best efforts to date on the part of the Jesuit Conference staff to identify the issues which deserve attention in the apostolate of education"[92] and is offered for the specific reaction of Jesuits.

Some issues, it is noted, cut across all forms of Jesuit education. They include the Jesuit role in the formulation of a "new humanism" and in the concomitant educational reform; the Jesuit responsibility for "placing the attainment of social justice and peace, national and international, as a high priority"[93] of the apostolate; the need to evaluate the advantages and liabilities of Jesuit institutional commitments; and the necessity of clarifying and coordinating Jesuit personnel assignments. There are also specific issues related to higher education (as there are to secondary and other educational efforts as well).

Diverse as Jesuit colleges and universities are, the document states that similar, substantive changes have taken place in all twenty-eight institutions in the last decade. These include changes in relation to traditional religious life and practice (the "abolition of obligatory religious practices" and "the provision for personal opportunities for spiritual growth"); changes in Jesuit authority and influence (including "autonomy from provincial jurisdiction," "new structures of governance, and "displacement of the systematic series of scholastic philosophy and theology courses which characterized Jesuit higher education"); and changes in institutional character ("increased professionalism and specialization," increasing involvement of lay people in institutions, changing economic realities, and more). Further, "the cultural and religious currents which produced and, in many instances, were affirmed by Vatican II have had enormous influence upon Jesuit higher education."[94] According to the document, these include the emphasis on community over structure, the recognition of religious pluralism, the stress on the freedom and dignity of the individual, the legitimation given to the secular, the importance placed on liturgical renewal.

Beyond changes rooted in religious tradition and belief, the report states that those forces which influence all of higher education—changing expectations of constituents, government regulations, accreditation pressures, changing mores and life-styles—have deeply affected Jesuit higher education as well. As a result, "Jesuit universities and colleges today are not exempt from but, rather, very much a part of the complex pattern of American institutional life."[95]

These changes, taken together, "have had a profound impact upon Jesuits and Jesuit communities," according to the document.

> Some have accepted and adapted to these changes with thoughtful flexibility, seeing in this new situation newly-revealed opportunities for preaching the Gospel Truth with deeper integrity to our contemporary

world. But even among the more optimistic, whose individual performance is noteworthy, the *corporate* apostolic posture and purpose of the Society are not clear—or at least not publicly articulated.

Many individuals and communities, on the other hand, are groping in their efforts to understand and come to grips with these changes and their own radically modified relationship to the academic institutions. . . . Confidence in the *religious* character of their work, and therefore Jesuit self-confidence, have come into question. Consequently, academic productivity, pastoral concern for students, and general apostolic satisfaction seem to have suffered.[96]

It is in light of these realities that certain issues stand out as worthy of immediate attention—for the good of the Society's educational apostolate and for the help their responses might be to all of Catholic higher education.

The first issue is this: "Does the Assistancy think that it is possible and preferable—the better thing—to pursue a *corporate* Jesuit apostolate in these Jesuit institutions which have changed so radically?"[97] If the answer is yes, then the order must deal with some further, complex questions. What would a "corporate apostolate" mean in such radically changed institutions? What would it take to develop a new conception and rationale for such a corporate apostolate? What would be included in such a formulation in regard to the relationships of Jesuits to one another, to others within the institutions, and to the institution itself?

The second issue is this: "Does the Assistancy think that other options should be pursued in the apostolate of higher education, on the grounds that the Society either cannot or should not—it is not the *better* thing—have a corporate apostolate within these radically changed institutions?"[98] And if the answer is yes, what are the options and how would they be developed and implemented?

Whichever path is followed, it is stated that there is a third set of interrelated issues: How can the level of scholarship among Jesuit educators be raised? Should priorities for the placement of Jesuits be established? What can be done to insure the hiring and retention of Jesuit scholars in Jesuit schools? What structures and procedures are needed to facilitate continuing dialogue among and between Jesuits and their colleagues in higher education?

Following the review of Jesuit responses—from both individuals and some communities—and their own deliberations, the provincials "chose to focus the efforts of Project 1 in the immediate future on four basic issues"—one each relating to secondary education, higher education, other educational efforts, and the whole apostolate. A fourth document, *Options*, sets out the four issues and offers a series of options for dealing with each of the issues.[99] The preferred option of the staff of the Jesuit Conference is indicated in each case; again, the responses of individual Jesuits, communities, agencies, and institutions are requested; and a decision-making process stated.

The higher education issue is this: "Does the Assistancy think that it is possible and preferable—the better thing—to pursue a corporate Jesuit apostolate in these institutions which have changed so radically?" Nine options "which might prove adequate responses to the issue" are described and discussed.[100] They include options for corporate national, individual, and local community apostolates; selection of particular institutions or particular segments of institutions as a focus of apostolates; development of a Jesuit system of institutions; a continuing adaptation model; development of Jesuit residential colleges within universities; and the combining of secondary and higher education into one experience. Some options provide a positive response to the issue in that they affirm that a corporate apostolate is possible and preferable; others imply a negative response.

The staff of the Jesuit Conference prefers the pursuit of a corporate national apostolate, a positive response to the issue.

> By corporate apostolate is meant an apostolate undertaken by a group of Jesuits through the mandate of the Society, and with the intention on the part of the Society that these Jesuits take common action in a particular endeavor, for which they pool their resources of talent and will toward a common end.[101]

However, to continue a corporate apostolate "in institutions which are clearly recognized to be independent" will necessitate more clearly articulated relationships between and among the institutions and the local, regional, and national Jesuit agencies engaged in and responsible for the higher education apostolate; "greater and more active involvement of more Jesuits"; and "a rationale . . . which makes intellectually comprehensible and psychologically satisfying the purposes, mission, and goal of the Society in the apostolate of higher education."[102]

According to the document, the development of *collaborative colleagueship* is the key to the facilitation of this option and central to the success of the educational endeavor. As outlined in the option, the development of rationales by institutions and within Jesuit communities will go on concurrently under the direction of the two national bodies most generally responsible for the educational apostolate—the Association of Jesuit Colleges and Universities and the Jesuit Conference. While there may be differences between the rationales, they must be consistent if the institutions are to maintain their status as Jesuit institutions and if "Jesuits and Jesuit communities are to fulfill the apostolic goals of their religious vocations."[103] Furthermore, the involvement of the whole Jesuit establishment in the development of rationales for a corporate national apostolate and the simultaneous restructuring of relationships should serve to clarify the goals of each community and the entire apostolate, facilitate a planned, shared utilization of human and material resources, and increase the long-term ability of the Society to make a constructive contribution to higher education.

Other options, of course, are discussed in similar detail.

Following distribution of the volume on *Options*, the ten Jesuit provinces and a number of Jesuit committees and associations discussed the material and came to their own conclusions about the best course of action. These deliberations are reported in a fifth volume, *National Consultation*.

The majority opinion expressed in all ten provinces is that:

> The Society should pursue an apostolate in Jesuit institutions of higher education which is a corporate apostolate. Its attempt to clarify, redefine, and better realize this corporate apostolate ought to follow Option #1, modified by elements of Option #3 and Option #7.[104]

Reasons given for choosing Option #1 are that it accurately assesses the present and foreseeable situation in Jesuit higher education, utilizes present human resources and structures, accounts for institutional diversity, blends local autonomy with national planning, stresses the corporateness of the apostolate, calls for the development of rationales, presents the roles of local rectors and provincials appropriately, invites cooperation and provides a better structure for it between the institutions and the Society, and "leaves room for the principle of subsidiarity to function, which is most important." Elements from the corporate local community apostolate option and from the continuing adaptation model are offered as modifications. Local Jesuit communities, say the respondents, are "the locus of our corporate apostolate and should be the focus of planning for it." In suggesting elements from the continuing adaptation model, some contend that it is necessary to resist basic change in order to discourage "outside meddling with the institutions of higher education"; others state that the difficulty in interpreting changes in higher education in the past decade makes apostolic planning impossible or unreasonable.[105]

Some ten months after the publication of the *National Consultation* document, the provincials of the Society of Jesus published their *Agreements and Decisions* on the issues under consideration. These, too, were submitted to the Jesuit community for study and reaction before publication.

Some decisions about the higher education apostolate are possible, according to the provincials, but not in as much detail as those agreements for secondary education. Noting the widespread endorsement of Option #1—with modifications, "the provincials now decide to make this direction their own in the name of the Assistancy, namely, a corporate Jesuit apostolate in higher education if it can be realized and in as many of the twenty-eight AJCU institutions in which it can be realized." [106]

In order to facilitate this major direction, the provincials call for the development of rationale statements by local Jesuit communities. They anticipate that the rationales will differ from one community to another, given differing local circumstances; but they state that all of them should include "a concrete plan of action" as well as a theoretical statement and that central to them should be a "focus on the promotion of faith and justice as decreed by the 32nd General Congregation" of the Society. As the community develops its statement, "it should invite the institution to join in designing and establishing mutually collaborative relationships on various levels." It is recognized in the document that a Jesuit corporate apostolate will be able to continue in the institution only insofar as there is a "mutual responsiveness" to each other's central values.[107]

The document also sets out specific tasks for the provincials in facilitating the major direction. They are to coordinate the work of higher education communities in their provinces; review, approve, and insure regular community evaluation of rationale statements; develop relationships with both communities and institutions; and together convene meetings of Jesuit presidents (who make up the board of the Association of Jesuit Colleges and Universities) "in order to clarify further their mutual aims in the apostolate of higher education." Finally, "after local community rationales have been developed, distributed broadly, and compared, the provincials will develop a process for the draft of a national statement of Jesuit aims in higher education to assist common identity and cooperation." [108]

Additionally, the volume sets out a process and a timetable for achieving these objectives and gives a brief progress report on work already begun.

In April, 1978, the ten Jesuit provincials in the United States issued their national statement, entitled *The Jesuit Mission in Higher Education: Letter from the American Provincials*. The statement marked the completion of the first phase of Project 1, the ongoing study begun four years earlier.

In their letter, the provincials express their corporate commitment to the higher education apostolate, state their intention to speak frankly about Jesuit aims, and note that the purpose of the letter is to "direct and stimulate the implementation of contemporary Jesuit ideals within local communities," not to impose a "national rationale" on each higher education community. [109]

Focusing first on Jesuit identity and motivation in higher education, the letter addresses two questions raised frequently and seriously within Jesuit circles today: "Why will we continue to give Jesuits a mission to the apostolate of higher education at Jesuit colleges and universities?" and "Why do we feel it is a realization of *'Our Mission Today'* to maintain a significant corporate presence in these institutions?" The provincials point to the "vigorous tradition" of Jesuit involvement in higher education. But they also point to pressing, current reasons to continue and strengthen this apostolate as well. Today the academic disciplines contribute in significant ways to definitions of meaning and purpose and to the solution of the world's practical ills. "We must be 'ready to give ourselves to the demanding and serious study of theology, philosophy, and the human sciences which are ever more necessary if we are to understand

and try to resolve the problems of the world.'"[110]

The reasons for continuing in higher education thus stated, the letter goes on to suggest the particular way in which the Jesuit presence ought to be embodied in academic institutions. The provincials write, "We are *religious of the Society of Jesus,* given a mission, by the Church and through our superiors, to live poorly, chastely, and obediently in a community with a corporate work at a particular institution." Thus, not just individual Jesuits, but their community must be a witness to the professed Christian values.

> Such aspects include: our union of minds and hearts both in prayer and in faith, hope, and love; the frugality of our love; corporate plans and accountability for our mission; a loyal and affectionate support of differing viewpoints among brothers; the fraternal encouragement of creativity in developing one another's gifts for fuller service; generous financial contributions to the university or college[111]

While Jesuits in the higher education apostolate are to be, in every way, "'professional academics,'" their academic role and labor are to be characterized by their primary identification as *ambassadors and apostles of Christ.* As *communities of priestly service,* Jesuits share Christ's presence in word and sacrament. All Jesuits are *teachers—* some more formally than others. But, the provincials write, "beyond our concern for ideas and structures and the value they have in themselves, there is our basic interest in and love for the people we serve." With a renewed sense of urgency—in light of the mandates of the 32nd General Congregation—"Jesuits are to be identified as *agents of change,* through a corporate mission of the service of faith and the promotion of justice." Finally, the traditional perception of Jesuits as *men of ethical concern* must be closely linked to the Society's concern for justice.

> Surely this concern must now go beyond our being sensitive confessors and competent moral counselors. The mission to justice requires, particularly of Jesuits in higher education, the development of new concepts and analyses that will contribute to the solution of socio-economic inequities and other moral problems of our day. If indeed our identity as men of ethical concern is to influence the culture of these times with professional and apostolic efficacy, we need Jesuits in higher education.[112]

Focusing second on Jesuit response to change and new challenges, the letter states that the main question confronting the order is how to work out its mission in an irrevocably changed social, cultural, and educational context. Noting particularly that "a transition from the position of institutional 'control' to one of full collaboration has been challenging for a number of Jesuits," the provincials write that Jesuits ought to respond to changed situations *with faith* ("our faith in the providential guidance of God must now be accompanied by an attitude of mutual dependence and deep trust in others"), *in the spirit of the spiritual exercises,* and *in obedience* ("no Jesuit merely 'happens' to be serving in a Jesuit institution of higher education; he is there because he has been sent on this mission by the Society").[113]

The provincials also offer specific suggestions to Jesuits and their communities for consideration in achieving their purposes. Communities should continue to plan for their mission, reflecting in that process a sensitivity to the apostolic leadership roles of both rectors and presidents and a consideration of overall institutional planning. Jesuits should seek to share the Ignatian heritage with the whole academic community. "Jesuit communities on our campuses should be living, accessible symbols of Christian harmony, prayer, simplicity of life, and zeal for justice." Jesuits should bring all the resources of Catholic tradition and learning to bear at both the undergraduate and graduate professional levels in their attempt "to train men and women of both competence and conscience."[114]

In collaboration with campus ministers, the Jesuit community should seek to use the diverse and abundant resources of the university "to serve students, faculty, and staff in 'inculturating' the sacramental and paraliturgical expression of contemporary Catholic faith in the United States." Through participation in social and spiritual ministries, Jesuits can gain firsthand experience and sharpen their academic understanding of the ways in which injustice and unbelief affect the life of people and nations. Committed to the liberal arts, Jesuits can offer the kind of intellectual experiences that will challenge the values of career-minded students.

> We endorse the high priority being given to carefully designed programs of liberal studies that integrate human and ethical values, because we all share the conviction that through them students gain freedom from undue preoccupation with security, from insensitivity to the plight of the morally deprived and the socially oppressed, and from paralysis before seemingly unchangeable political, economic, and social mores.[115]

Finally, through writing, research, consultation, and public advocacy, Jesuits bring their influence to bear on the nation and world. The provincials remind their confreres that the Society is an international resource and that "Jesuits from other nations, alive to realities different from our own, can help us become sensitive to the claims of an international common good and world order."[116]

In conclusion, the provincials note with satisfaction the serious consideration of mission that has gone on in most communities, concur with the general conviction "that the primary responsibility of the Jesuit community lies in service to the university and college" and "also welcome a growing recognition that the communities have wider responsibilities to the Church and civic community and, in particular, to the poor."[117]

Seventh-day Adventists

In 1971 the General Conference of Seventh-day Adventists (SDA), North American Division, established a Board of Higher Education and adopted a working policy which describes the duties and obligations of that board.[118] One year later, the church formulated a companion document, the *Seventh-day Adventist Philosophy of Higher Education.* These two statements, as amended, provide the basis for the denomination's involvement in higher education.

According to the SDA philosophy, "belief in God's creating, sustaining, enlightening and redeeming activities through the Son is fundamental to this church's world view. Acceptance of the Gospel Commission supplies the motive for its world-wide teaching ministry." Colleges and universities are understood to be essential to the church in the fulfillment of its mission, and the value of a church-operated system of higher education "must be judged by the contributions it makes directly and through its alumni toward: (a) fulfillment of the mission of the sponsoring church, (b) the pluralism of the larger society, and (c) solutions of human problems by means not appropriate to totally secular agencies."[119] Acknowledging that the similarities between SDA and other higher education institutions are both obvious and numerous, the statement attempts to set out the very basic differences which, nevertheless, may not be so apparent.

First, SDA higher education is informed by some basic assumptions about the nature of reality ("the universe is the expression of an intelligent Personal Being"), about creation and natural process ("the Creator . . . is infinitely wise, infinitely powerful, and is the Source of all positive and benevolent forces and qualities to be found in the world"), and about revelation (God has spoken and continues to speak; the Bible is "the criterion of truth for teaching and doctrine, the norm by which the continuing revelation may be identified and understood"; Jesus Christ is "the Supreme Revelation of God to man, the perfect example of life, and the focal point of hope for the human race").[120] The rigorous pursuit of knowledge in the disciplines in SDA colleges and universities is motivated by humane and intellectual concerns, but it is grounded in, and is an expression of, religious motivation as well.

Second, SDA higher education is informed by some basic assumptions about original human nature ("according to the Scriptural record man was created in the image of God, a personality dependent on his Creator but still a free acting self"), about the change which occurred in human nature (in the attempt to achieve "God-likeness through independence," humankind "lost control over the natural world and in many respects became subject to it"), and about restoration of the original nature ("the way of return begins with the point of departure; the creature must acknowledge his dependence on the Creator. The dictum is unequivocal. 'You must be born anew.'").[121] It is this belief about the nature of humankind—about the nature and potential of the student—that informs the theory, aims, and methods of SDA higher education.

Third, the SDA document explicates the denomination's understanding of knowledge as well. Like other institutions of higher education, SDA colleges and universities are organized and operated so that students may acquire knowledge through direct personal experience and the recorded experiences of others and by logical reasoning. In SDA schools these learning processes are viewed, additionally, "as avenues toward contact with the work and will of the Creator," in which a deeper dimension of knowledge can be apprehended. But the statement emphasizes that learning, approached from the perspective of the "science of redemption," results in the discovery of new dimensions of greater magnitudes, not new sources, of knowledge.

> Although human discovery is pursued by the usual means of investigation the true meanings of facts are probed within the perspective of

revealed reality. This wholeness of view is indispensable to Adventist educational theory, for it holds that all spheres of human life are interrelated and that God is at the center of and determines the purpose of all. To omit God's revelation from the study of things is to omit that which makes them fully understandable and meaningful. In no sense is this a mixture of theology with secular studies. Rather, it is an elevation of secular studies to their highest level as avenues toward an understanding of truth the totality of which, if it could be comprehended, would reveal God fully.[122]

Fourth, the statement of philosophy also comments upon values, declaring that "Seventh-day Adventists reject all forms of egocentric relativism," believe some human actions are intrinsically good and others, by nature, evil, and that "the norm which distinguishes good from evil is rooted in the absolute good of the divine nature as revealed in Holy Scripture." Because the highest good is redemption, "helping human beings find God's solutions to their problems is a calling for which Adventist higher education seeks to prepare students."[123] Other ancillary values are affirmed by Adventists as well and are dealt with in a fifth section on the aims of higher education.

As stated in the document, SDA higher education has two overall aims: "to actualize with the student all that he is intended to become—a child of God, and to prepare him for the joy of humane service in the world that now is in anticipation of even wider fulfillment in the world that is to come."[124] Recognizing that the goals or philosophy of an institution cannot successfully be imposed on a student, the statement delineates six specific aims of SDA higher education.

It is the religious aim of the SDA college to develop Christian character, nurture spiritual sensitivity, teach the church's doctrine, foster understanding of and respect for other faith traditions, "make religion—worship, faith, participation—an integrating and unifying force in learning," provide an environment in which modest and moral behavior is practiced and taught, and "inspire commitment to the Christian mission."[125]

The intellectual aim of SDA institutions is "to provide God-centered liberal, professional, and vocational education with teaching and learning of the highest quality."[126] While the document insists that teaching and research in all subjects be conducted according to the methodology appropriate to each discipline, it also recognizes that all teaching and learning are informed by some world view concerning the nature of knowledge, truth, values, and humanity and affirms that Christian faith and commitment provide such a perspective for SDA higher education. Not merely one among many perspectives, a Christian world view provides unique intellectual advantages. The paper states:

> When research is done by Christian scholars a deeper realization of the harmony between faith and empirical inquiry develops. . . . The Adventist scholar who searches for or disseminates truth recognizes an area of reality largely ignored by the secular scholar of today. He should be at a definite advantage in his pursuit of such truths as deepen the understanding of and give meaning to human life as well as alleviate its material shortcomings.[127]

In addition to offering a liberal education, SDA colleges and universities emphasize work-study and provide opportunities for the development of various manual skills, to the end that all students may develop "competence by which they may become economically independent." Students are also encouraged to cultivate their abilities in art appreciation and creation. Through artistic creation of high quality, students may develop their God-given abilities and come to a fuller understanding "of natural beauty as a portrayal of God's activity in the world."[128]

SDA colleges and universities also aim to develop in their students an understanding of the human body, the cultivation of its health and well-being, and an appreciation of its nature as a temple of the Holy Spirit. Physical fitness, careful grooming, simplicity in dress and adornment "are upheld in the denomination's schools as appropriate expressions of Christian character."[129] The social aim of SDA schools is rooted in Jesus' commandment, "You shall love your neighbor as yourself." Accepting the infinite worth of each person is understood to foster self-pride, respect for others, an active concern for justice, respect for legitimate authority, and a concern that the highest values of Adventist faith be shared, examined, and maintained in SDA schools.

It is the expectation of the denomination that the colleges of the church will seek to achieve Adventist aims in the following ways:

> . . . first by the persuasiveness of knowledge, insight, reason, and understanding that are the expected outcomes of serious involvement in

the school program; secondly, through the influence of example in the lives of the faculty and the majority of students; and thirdly, by rules and regulations which require at least minimal conformity by all students.[130]

Citing the once church-related colleges in the United States which have "turned away from their original vision" as faculties have "lost their unity of spiritual purpose," the statement affirms the church's right and obligation to control the election of trustees and the hiring of faculty (employing "only those who willingly support the religious concepts and philosophy of the church"). Further, it declares that the church is committed to equal human rights and that "selectivity on the basis of religious conviction in a church college" should never be confused with this basic doctrine. Finally, stating that "religious persuasion is not an admissions qualification for students," students are urged to acquaint themselves with Adventist belief and practice and warned that "deep antagonism" for the tradition and program of the colleges is not condoned. All of these measures are understood to contribute to the building of a vital community and to the vision of Christian colleges serving in the role of contemporary "schools of the prophets."[131]

The "Working Policy" states that the Board of Higher Education is responsible for establishing guidelines for governance in each of the SDA colleges and universities, for coordinating the work of the institutions, and for initiating and developing long-range planning for the whole system of SDA higher education. Specific duties of the board include responsibility for the establishment or discontinuance of institutions; setting of minimum standards for admissions and graduation; conducting periodic reviews of programs of instruction, research, and training for service to the church; allocation of special funds; and reporting to the board and the church on the life and work of the colleges and universities.[132] The policies and directives of the board are facilitated by an executive secretary.

The system of SDA higher education is comprised of one junior college and nine senior colleges—supported, operated, and governed by the constituents of the ten union conferences of the church—and two universities—operated and financed by the General Conference and governed by churchwide boards of trustees. Annual church support to the colleges and universities averages about $1,000 per student.

Southern Baptist Convention

Some eight hundred persons from church and college gathered in June, 1976, for a National Colloquium on Christian Education, sponsored by the Education Commission of the Southern Baptist Convention. The program featured a series of addresses by Southern Baptist leaders and public figures together with workshops on central issues facing Southern Baptist higher education.

There were several consequences from the colloquium. A series of workshops was held on different campuses on such concerns as trustee orientation, faculty development, and the search for values and the contribution of Southern Baptist colleges to that search. A series of reaffirmations about Christian education was adopted, and the decision was made to engage in a major study of Southern Baptist colleges and universities, to be conducted by Earl J. McGrath.

The ten reaffirmations were adopted as "guidelines for individuals and institutions who wish to reexamine seriously the Christian basis for education and who wish to engage in a renewed commitment to the great Biblical and doctrinal themes which have guided in centuries past." The first reaffirms allegiance to the covenant relationship between the Southern Baptist churches and schools. It declares that it is a "covenant which finds its unity in the purpose of God, the mind of Christ, the work of the Spirit, and the authority of the Scriptures, and which causes the churches and the schools to work together in freedom and faithfulness." For Baptists, providing Christian education is not an optional activity but "our response to our Lord to know and to teach the truth."[133]

The second reaffirms unity in diversity—"that has enabled Baptists to witness in faithfulness and creativity"—and pledges faith to and support of the local church and denominational programs. The third reaffirmation speaks to Christian witness in a secular culture. The recurring crises in human affairs result from the unwillingness to recognize the nature and extent of sin; but believing that Christ has intervened in the world to save his people, "our schools and our churches confront the secular views of materialism and nihilism with the Christian message of faith, hope, and love, and with the Christian principle of the individual's infinite worth."[134]

The fourth reaffirmation deals with the Christian idea of a liberal education. It states that Christian education is based on the presupposition that all truth is created, ordered, and sustained by God and that liberal arts studies provide the context in which the Christian view of education can best make its impact. It notes, however, that "the earthen vessel of liberal arts education, unless also used to transmit the Biblical and theological content of the Christian faith, cannot effectively serve the church or its institutions." [135]

The fifth reaffirms the biblical view of stewardship that all persons and all things belong to God and are to act and to be used for his honor and glory. The sixth speaks to Christian absolutes. "We reaffirm our belief that there are Christian absolutes which history does not change nor time erode." The Bible is reaffirmed as the self-sufficient guide of faith and practice; the Ten Commandments are reaffirmed as God given and cannot be modified or amended— "through the mind of Christ, they are not burdensome legal obligations but become guidelines for a joyous and fruitful way of life that has eternal significance." Church and school have a responsibility for transmitting ethical and moral values by precept and example and for guiding the student in the development of Christian character. The seventh points to the Great Commission. "We reaffirm our responsibility for carrying out the mandate of the Great Commission, at home and abroad, . . . to work with our mission boards in recruiting and training missionaries, . . . to develop in the laity a Christian world view that will be supportive of missions." [136]

The eighth reaffirmation speaks of student-teacher relationships. Church and school reaffirm their commitment "to seek and employ the Christian teacher." They also reaffirm their responsibility to treat students as persons of worth, to instill the thirst for knowledge, to enable the development of life goals, to assist in the search for values, and to encourage students to achieve a fuller Christian life—through a deeper commitment to Christ, church participation, sense of vocational mission, and responsible Christian citizenship. The ninth reaffirms responsibility for the stewardship of institutional management. The tenth speaks of Christian citizenship. "We reaffirm our commitment to bring the word of God, the mind of Christ, and the power of the Spirit to bear in developing moral courage, social sensitivity, and ethical responsibility as an inseparable part of Christian citizenship." [137]

The study conducted by Earl J. McGrath for the Education

Commission of the Southern Baptist Convention and the Association of Southern Baptist Colleges and Schools had the participation of forty-nine of the fifty-three Southern Baptist junior and senior colleges and universities. It was a comprehensive study and was presented at the annual meeting of the association in June, 1977. A printed report summarizing the major aspects of the study is available for general interest.[138] A lengthier version which includes the supporting data was shared in confidence with the presidents of the participating institutions, and it is expected that much of the study's value will lie in each institution's self-examination in light of the findings.

Commenting in general on the study, McGrath reports that "the SBC institutions are in remarkably good shape, comparing them with other private institutions around the country. No other denomination, as a whole, can compare with Southern Baptists as a group." He argues, "One major factor in this growth among Southern Baptist schools is directly related to the clarity of their purpose and mission."[139] McGrath points to another index of the health of Southern Baptist institutions: "In the past 10 years, private institutions have increased their enrollments about 10 percent, on the average. Several denominations have actually lost enrollment. But Southern Baptist institutions have increased their enrollment by 31 percent in the past 10 years."[140]

McGrath's study undertakes four basic inquiries. One is to explore the character of the church-college relationship. For this purpose a questionnaire was devised to assess the statements of religious purpose and how these reflect themselves in the activities of the institution. The institutions rank high in the inquiry, with forty-seven of the forty-eight responding institutions indicating clear statements of Christian purpose and/or service to the denomination, and most of them (thirty-seven) responding positively that they have programs relating to the churches and denomination. Nevertheless, McGrath recommends that most of the institutions could evaluate the effectiveness of their religious activities more systematically.

Another major inquiry is undertaken to identify strengths and weaknesses of the Southern Baptist colleges and universities as these are perceived by trustees, administrators, faculty, and students. For this purpose the Institutional Functioning Inventory (IFI), used for ten years in a variety of institutions across the country, was employed.

Among the findings: concern for undergraduate learning in Southern Baptist institutions ranks higher in the judgment of trustees, administrators, and faculty than similar groups perceive it among comparable institutions nationally. Students, however, have a noticeably lower perception, leading McGrath to flag this discrepancy as a matter of concern. On the concern for innovation, trustees have a higher estimate for their institutions than trustees among a broader, comparable group, but then it falls to a considerably lower perception on the part of faculty. Also regarding innovation, perceptions among faculties of Southern Baptist junior colleges are more positive than those among faculties of senior colleges.

When it comes to governance, trustees have a positive view of the democratic governance in Southern Baptist institutions, with administrators less favorable and faculty less positive than faculty at other comparable institutions. Students clearly show the lowest of the four groups' perception of democratic governance among Southern Baptist institutions.

Concern for advancing knowledge takes a generally low ranking among Southern Baptist colleges—as it does in comparable colleges that are also strongly committed to quality undergraduate teaching; but among Southern Baptist complex universities, a higher ranking than among comparable institutions is indicated.

On the human diversity scale, Southern Baptist colleges generally rate below the average of other institutions which have used the IFI. McGrath observes that this might be expected when so many of the students are Southern Baptists with similar attitudes and values but suggests in his report that in the diverse culture of the times the colleges might be concerned to provide a more heterogeneous and varied experience. Commenting on this matter, however, in an appendix to the report, Daniel R. Grant, president of Ouachita Baptist University, writes:

> Most would agree that there is simply an inevitable conflict between the accomplishment of certain institutional purposes in Christian commitment and service to the denomination, and the existence of too great a degree of diversity in faculty and student attitudes toward those stated purposes of the institution.[141]

Attention has already been drawn to the institutional esprit report where Southern Baptist institutions rank high. Trustee groups at all forty-nine responding institutions rank morale higher than it is perceived by trustees at other comparable institutions, while the ratings of administrators and faculty (except for a few marked exceptions) compare favorably with other schools.

On the freedom scale—pertaining both to academic and personal freedom—members of Southern Baptist communities give their institutions their lowest scores. The ratings of only four of forty-six responding faculty groups are as high or higher than the average of other independent or church-related schools, and no student group of the forty-six scores its institution as high as the average. McGrath comments that this might be in line with the strength of Southern Baptist institutions with their distinct set of moral values, but he suggests that this area of concern needs discussion within the institutions. Daniel Grant, quoted above, comments that "there are certain kinds of diminished freedom that simply are inevitable at a college that takes its Christian commitment seriously, and we should be proud of it."[142] Further, Grant suggests that there is a freedom in Christian colleges not measured by the IFI instrument; namely, the freedom from the unsympathetic pressures of a secular society.

The other scales that are ranked have to do with self-study and planning, concern for the improvement of society, intellectual-aesthetic extracurriculum, and meeting local needs.

Another major inquiry in the study makes use of a goals inventory to assess the presently perceived goals and objectives of an institution (according to faculty members and administrators) and the preferred goals. Faculty groups perceive that high priority is given to support and institutional goals, church-college goals, and moral and general education goals, with the exclusion of most of the academic and educational goals included in the inventory. Research goals stand near the bottom. With a few exceptions, administrators generally state the same perceptions. When it comes to preferences, however, there is a marked rise among faculty in favor of educational goals, together with academic position goals like "maintaining top quality" and "keeping up to date," while at the same time a high preference continues for moral and general education goals. Church-college and denominational service goals disappear from the list of high preference. Deepening theological understanding drops significantly as a preferred goal among those faculty reporting from comprehensive institutions and junior colleges, and an emphasis on liberal arts also drops, perhaps out of preference, McGrath suggests, for disciplinary and preprofessional programs.

The fourth area of McGrath's study consists of a financial trend analysis which was conducted in association with W. John Minter. The general conclusion is that Southern Baptist colleges and universities as a group show "evidence of real financial growth and sound financial management. Their overall performance is as good as and slightly superior to the aggregate performance of the 100 colleges in the national sample."[142a] Southern Baptist institutions have a high rate of giving for current operations and own a generally larger proportion of their assets than their national counterparts; their assets are growing at the rate of 7 percent for the last two years, compared to the national average of 5 percent per year for private institutions. This favorable report should not obscure the fact, however, that a few institutions are experiencing financial stress.

In concluding his report to the convention, McGrath states:

> Professional and lay members of the Southern Baptist Convention, which is enjoying such vigorous growth, will want to consider the steps that can be taken to engender in *all* their institutions the same level of high morale and commitment now exhibited in *some* of them. . . . This group of Southern Baptist institutions is in about the best condition of any denominational group we have examined.[143]

"The most glaring need revealed by the study," McGrath continues, "is the urgent necessity for trustees, administration, and faculty—and in some cases students—to fully understand the institution's basic purposes and for all to come to a meeting of the minds as to how to meet those purposes."[144]

United Church of Christ

In 1969 the Seventh General Synod of the United Church of Christ (UCC) adopted "A Statement of Relationship" between the church and its related colleges. The statement was recommended to the synod by the Council for Higher Education, a voluntary organization of colleges, universities, academies, and seminaries related to the UCC and staffed by the Board for Homeland Ministries.

According to the statement, the concern for higher education is one which grows out of the nature and purpose of the church itself. Chief among its reasons for involvement in higher education are these:

> 1. Man, created in the image of God, has intellectual capacities, potentialities and responsibilities given to no other creatures, and the fullest possible development of man's intelligence is a major dimension of the work of the church; 2. A prime tenet of the Christian faith is that God is the source of all wisdom and truth.[145]

Therefore, the free pursuit of knowledge is essential if men and women are to perceive God and understand his will for their lives, and providing for the development of the intellectual resources of young people is a means by which the church can glorify God.

The United Church of Christ shows its concern for higher education by supporting in various ways the colleges that historically and traditionally have been related to it. The statement notes that the church's support of higher education is not for any special ecclesiastical advantage but for the reasons stated above. The church-related colleges, for their part, "have a humanistically and theologically important task of maintaining an interaction between Christian faith and higher learning." That interaction, it is noted, is important to both partners.[146]

The statement acknowledges that there is sufficient freedom within American higher education for the encounter between Christian faith and higher learning to occur in both public and independent institutions. Applauding that development, it also suggests that it is important the encounter be built into the structures.

> It is important to the church and to higher education . . . that somewhere entire faculties at least occasionally ask the important questions, that somewhere every department of learning have a responsibility to keep the questions from being pushed aside. The church-related colleges have such a reason for being. This is their peculiar opportunity and responsibility. There is in such a purpose no inhibition upon freedom of inquiry—rather an enhanced freedom, although sometimes a burdensome freedom—to break out of the routine restrictions which haunt much of education.[147]

But the statement also suggests that it is not essential that there be many such colleges—the notion of church-related higher education being predominant was given up a long time ago. Rather, it is important that there be a variety of such "pilot centers" within higher education and enriching the whole system.

In attempting to define further the place of the church-related college within the whole of higher education, it is suggested that three questions be kept in mind: "What are the historical origins of such colleges?" "What purposes are presently being served by these colleges?" "What will be their function in the future, not forgetting their own institutional responsibilities and their relationship to the church?"[148]

Historically, church-related colleges were founded to provide people in a given geographical area with a college sympathetic to their religious aims; but since the 1920s those colleges related to the UCC have met the challenges of the accrediting associations and of localism by "reasserting their concern for academic excellence and by enrolling more and more students with diverse religious backgrounds." Recognizing that we live in a pluralistic society, these colleges have been formulating academic and extracurricular programs to meet the intellectual and religious needs of their diverse students. The statement suggests that the function of these church-related colleges in the future is to continue to be adaptive to the needs of a changing society; and the responsibility of the church is to "understand the importance to society of a church-college relationship that exists for the enrichment of both institutions and for the broader enlightenment of our young people."[149]

Key to the understanding of the church-college relationship in the UCC is the concept of equality in partnership.

> The colleges and the church are in a real sense cooperating institutions, which have decided to consult and work together for their mutual advantage and for the ultimate welfare of society. The colleges do not regard the church as the only source of truth or the necessary seat of authority; the church, by its policy of non-control and non-interference, acknowledges these facts. The colleges and the church are indeed independent, equal partners.[150]

Early in 1976, the Council for Higher Education of the UCC commissioned Miller Upton, former president of UCC-related Beloit College, to identify and articulate the underlying educational philosophy of the UCC-related colleges. Upton examined literature and documents from all thirty colleges and made visits to ten of the schools which were believed to be a "reliable cross-section of the membership." In his summary report to the members of the Council for Higher Education of the United Church of Christ, Upton outlined points of commonality and difference in educational mission, caveats about his report, and "implications to the colleges in their relation to the church." [151]

About the commonality of mission, Upton wrote:

> The end result of all my study is that our thirty institutions, despite their many structural, locational and operational differences, represent a much more common educational mission than I had even imagined possible. With only slight variation, regardless of where I visited, the responses were the same. [152]

According to the report, commitments held in common include the conviction that learning is an individualized process and, consequently, that education must be greatly personalized; the belief that personalized education occurs best in a caring community where the welfare of individual students is a prime concern of faculty and administrators; the belief that "the ultimate purpose of all education is to upgrade the moral standards of society"—even though there is little confidence about how this is best accomplished; the opinion that "smallness of size" is essential for attaining these other goals; the commitment to the liberal arts as the "requisite curricular vehicle" for achieving these other goals; and the conviction that private support is indispensable to the continuing institutional autonomy that makes this particular educational mission possible. [153]

Upton also finds that, while there are many great differences among these institutions, they are more operational than philosophical. The author centers his attention on two differences. "The main difference grows out of the substantial difference in native ability, prior educational preparation, family background and personal motivation of their respective student bodies." This difference is based on more than processes of selectivity, according to Upton; some colleges serve well-defined constituencies based on "sex, geography, race, and/or socio-economic background" and may or may not emphasize academic selectivity within these groups. Upton adds that, because of these institutional differences, educational quality can only be determined on the basis of "value added," or "the actual growth that takes place among the students of a particular college consistent with its educational mission and as a direct consequence of its educational program." [154]

The second difference highlighted by the author is the manner in which the colleges blend liberal arts and career preparation. "All accept the liberal arts as the best preparation for the full dimension of life's demands" and have some concern for career preparation, but institutional initiative in terms of the latter varies greatly. Still, Upton reports that there is a growing awareness in all the institutions that there is a false dichotomy in too rigid attempts to separate liberal from vocational education.[155]

Giving high praise to the colleges, Upton, nevertheless, identifies three weaknesses for comment. First, attainment falls short of the design. Some faculty and administrators are not adequate to the task, and some—about 30 percent according to Upton—are unsympathetic to the mission of the colleges. Second, while making much of the virtues of the smallness of size, the colleges do not take full advantage of this potential. Upton notes some mimicry of structure and style of large, prestigious universities. Third, adequate instructional facilities and equipment are lacking in many, if not most, of the colleges related to the UCC.

Noting the irreplaceable importance of church-related colleges to the health of the whole of American higher education, as well as the enormous contribution of the churches in founding and sustaining them, Upton contends that the combined pressure of low-tuition state institutions and progressive inflation and the recent inattention of the churches are making the church-related colleges an endangered species. Elaborating on the inattention of the churches, Upton states that the church has turned the focus of its missionary outreach from formal education—and health care, welfare, care of the aged—towards social issues, which are also deserving of serious attention and corrective effort. However, in the long run, this is a misplaced emphasis, according to Upton.

> Uplifting human society is what formal education, particularly higher education, is all about. It is the only social service which is developmental in basic purpose rather than ameliorative, prophylactic rather than therapeutic. This is why the Church's mission is inevitably and intimately tied to the mission of formal education, particularly when that educational mission is given expression by way of institutions that are themselves committed to the dignity, worth and sovereignty of the individual citizen. In fact, it is difficult to comprehend how an enlightened ministry can be propagated except by an enlightened citizenry.[156]

Following the presentation of Upton's report, and with his assistance, the Council for Higher Education of the UCC prepared a statement entitled "The Case for Church-Related Higher Education." The document confesses that our society has not been faithful to the best in education. Among other failures, we have been more interested in providing instruction than in promoting learning; we have viewed all education "as equally supportive of human values and equally redemptive of human society"; and we have turned increasingly to the government to provide educational opportunity while more and more ascribing ultimate authority and meaning to that government.[157]

While the church-related college is as much a part of the society as public educational institutions, "it joins in a 'covenant' to include the transcendent as well as the secular in the educative process." And as an institution of liberal education, the church-related college is

> . . . obligated to keep the creative balance between the rational and the intuitive functioning redemptively. Therefore, the school and the church are linked, not in a proprietary sense but in a covenantal sense. Both institutions are in covenant with God to contribute to the redemption of society by being faithful to their respective authentic roles.[158]

The council document reiterates Upton's concern that the church has turned its attention from the nurturing of educational institutions to more direct involvement in social action as well as his belief that liberal education is the best means to the solution of social ills. In light of this concern and the argument above, the statement declares that it is time for the UCC to reaffirm its commitment to and support of church-related higher education. It concludes:

> The church and the church-related school share a common concern for the redemption of society—the church through faith in and knowledge of God, the school through learning and the quest for truth. Both institutions need each other to be faithful to this covenant. Moreover, the church needs the school as a tool for its continuing reformation; the school needs the church as a deterrent to intellectual idolatry.[159]

On the basis of its strong convictions about the church's responsibility for its related colleges, the council, with the concurrence of the United Church Board for Homeland Ministries, submitted a resolution to the Eleventh General Synod of the United Church of Christ, meeting in the spring of 1977. Calling attention to the history of the denomination's involvement in the founding and nurturing of colleges, the commitment of both church and college to the redemption of society, the council's understanding of the church-related colleges as an integral part of the church's contemporary mission, and the commitment of the schools to liberal education, the resolution calls upon the UCC to reaffirm its commitment to and support of denominationally related colleges.[160]

In general, the resolution calls upon the church to explore the renewed meaning of church-relatedness and to begin to devise additional strategies "for celebrating and affirming both historic and continuing cooperative relationships between the Church and the related educational institutions." More specifically, it calls upon conferences, associations, and local churches to affirm the importance of quality education for contemporary living, to affirm the covenant relationship between church and college, to affirm the diversity of the institutions "and the uniqueness of each institution within a common educational mission," to commend the colleges to the constituency, and to seek continued and increased support for the colleges.[161]

To facilitate support, the resolution suggests the recruitment of students in local churches, services of worship celebrating the church's mission in education, greater participation of professional church staff and lay persons in continuing education in the colleges, new options for deferred giving and unrestricted support, and denominational implementation of specific support programs for related colleges. The resolution was adopted by the Eleventh General Synod.

United Methodist Church

In the United Methodist Church (UMC), the Division of Higher Education of the Board of Higher Education and Ministry represents the denomination in its relationships with educational institutions and the campus ministry.

As outlined in *The Book of Discipline of the United Methodist Church, 1976,*[162] the division has as its primary objectives the determination of the nature of the church's mission in higher education; the development of policy to enable that mission; the encouragement of the church's involvement in and support of campus ministry and institutions of higher education; the promotion of Christian faith and service within the educational community; the interpretation of the church, university, and campus ministry to one another; the fostering of high educational and moral standards; and the preservation and protection of the church's resources which are devoted to higher education.

To accomplish its objectives, the division provides various consultative and support services to UMC educational institutions and campus ministry units, cooperates with denominational and judicatory committees and agencies concerned with the church's educational mission, and seeks to promote and provide for the financial support of institutions and campus ministry. Additionally, from time to time, the division establishes special committees and commissions to help fulfill its objectives. Two such commissions have been formed in recent years and are worthy of special attention.

In 1972, by action of the General Conference of the UMC, the Continuing Commission on the Black Colleges was created as the successor to an earlier study commission for a four-year period to study issues of finance, location, the possibility of merger, governance, and church relationship of the twelve black colleges historically related to the UMC.

The eighteen-member commission examined previous denominational studies and recommendations concerning the colleges, reviewed current studies of the black colleges and their role in American culture, and studied each of the twelve UMC-related institutions in considerable depth. On the basis of its work, the commission made its report to the 1976 General Conference of the church, "reaffirming its deepest conviction that what The United Methodist Church does in these colleges thrusts it further toward fulfillment of its call to reclaim, reconcile and release for their own mission and service every human being in the whole earth." [163]

In its report, the commission requests that the General Conference approve two pieces of legislation: one establishing a process for recommending the sum of money to be raised through the church's Black College Fund and the means for apportioning it to annual conferences "to provide financial support for current operating budgets and capital improvements of the black colleges related administratively to the church"; the other establishing a formula for the distribution of such funds to individual colleges. Further, the commission requests the adoption of a number of specific resolutions related to the new legislation, chief among them being a recommendation that the church raise six million dollars yearly through apportioned giving for the Black College Fund and that a Continuing Commission on the Black Colleges be established for the quadrennium 1977-1890 "to continue the work of this commission and other concerns related to the black colleges." [164]

In making its report, the commission also presented a list of "findings" which provide support for the recommendations. They include the observations "that relationship of these twelve colleges to The United Methodist Church is historic and real, mutually effective and openly desired"; that the colleges have never practiced segregation; that they have gone as far as is practicable in the processes of merger, relocation, or discontinuance; that "where they are located they provide essential educational ministries for the church" and an impressive record of "ministry in liberating higher education of black people"; and that projected enrollment statistics for these schools (through 1988) are good.[165]

The recommendations of the commission were adopted and the Continuing Commission on the Black Colleges continues to carry out the work assigned to it.

In January, 1975, the National Commission on United Methodist Higher Education was formed by the Board of Higher Education and Ministry of the UMC. The task of this commission was to analyze environmental factors and trends affecting higher education now and likely to influence it in the future, to analyze public policy and legal issues concerning church/state relations, to suggest alternative social goals for public policy, to analyze a variety of institutional factors relevant to present and future health and identity of the colleges, and to analyze the current system of UMC campus ministries. The commission was also charged with the responsibility of developing recommendations on the analysis which could be useful to public policymakers, institutions, campus ministers, and church members and officials.

"Committed to what is probably the most comprehensive study ever undertaken by any denomination of its interest and investment in higher education," the board named a diverse group of nationally prominent persons to the National Commission, hired an experienced staff, and brought together an Interdenominational Advisory Group.[166] The major research and recommendations of the commission, plus supporting papers by staff members and others, were contained in the publications issued in the name of the commission.

The first volume, *A College-Related Church: United Methodist Perspectives,* presents a statement of "The Mission of the United Methodist Church in Its Institutions of Higher Education" and supporting papers. In the opening paragraph of the document, the commission declares:

> . . . the most impelling reasons for The United Methodist Church to continue direct relationships with institutions of higher education are due to its:
> * Theological perspective;
> * Wesleyan tradition and heritage in higher education;
> * Concern for a liberally educated laity and clergy;
> * Concern for value-centered inquiry;
> * Concern for the empowerment of the individual through liberal arts education;
> * Commitment to cultural pluralism and educational diversity.[167]

The UMC is involved in higher education because "it is the nature of the church to express itself in the intellectual love of God," and because the "purpose" of the church-related college is closely related to reflection on the "purpose" of God. Stating a theological rationale for higher education is difficult, however, for, according to the commission, ways of thinking about God have changed so greatly that "even institutions with close historic ties with the church have been cut off from the theologies that sparked their origins."[168] So the commission rehearses the central theological assertions of the Christian faith.

The primary theological assertion of the Judeo-Christian tradition is that God created the earth and its inhabitants so that persons might live in harmony with the ecology and one another and worship and enjoy God forever. "Thus, fundamental to all theistic statements are the ideas of joy, responsibility, care for the world, love of neighbor, and a lively sense of wholeness (holiness) of all things." But, in the fall, the alienation of humanity from God occurs and God's purpose for the creation is obscured. "Joy is replaced by despair, responsibility by self-centeredness, care by distraction, love by hate, and wholeness by fragmentation." At the heart of the Christian revelation "is the assertion that creation is set in the direction of wholeness by the person of Jesus of Nazareth." Through his death and resurrection the creation, though flawed, is restored.[169]

In this theological tradition, the commission states

. . . learning becomes ideally an act of worship and joy. It becomes a gesture of human response to a knowable and good world. Persistent in the scriptural tradition are themes such as "knowing," "seeing," and "learning" in the context of which "believing," "acting," and "loving" are counterpoint.[170]

It is a major problem in higher education today, according to the commission, that we have lost the tradition of learning which leads to "wisdom" in the theological sense of the word and have inherited the utilitarian tradition of learning. As a result, higher education is a joyless matter for most people today; but for the Christian, "education ought to be the highest joy because it is an act of the acknowledgement of the freedom for us to be what God intends us to be." The commission concludes on this major point:

If we argue only on utilitarian lines, then the argument for continued and expanded church interest in higher education is weak. But if we argue on faithful theological premises, from the biblical story, the New Testament sense of liberation in the Gospel, and the uses of the intellect as an act of thanksgiving and praise, then profound necessities for the church's life in higher education are evident.[171]

Rooted in this theological tradition and understanding are other reasons for the involvement of the UMC in higher education. Its grounding in the Wesleyan tradition which sought the uniting of "knowledge and vital piety" and eschewed a narrow sectarianism has led to the founding of myriad colleges, many of them for persons not traditionally served by higher education. Its concern to provide a liberally educated clergy and laity capable of serving both church and society has continued to fuel its interest in higher education. Its commitment to "value-centered inquiry and to action based on belief" has sustained its interest in supporting colleges where this dimension of learning could enjoy full parity with other modes of thinking and discourse. Its commitment to liberal arts education which is concerned with the whole person and the full development of the individual has led it to maintain this form of educational institution. And its belief that cultural pluralism and educational diversity are essential to maintaining freedom of choice and a prophetic witness to the larger society has encouraged it to work for the maintenance of the independent sector of higher education.

For all these reasons, says the commission, "The United Methodist Church should continue and strengthen its commitment to its mission in institutional higher education." [172]

To Give the Key of Knowledge: United Methodists and Education, 1784-1976 represents a staff attempt to achieve an understanding of the historical origins of the present United Methodist higher education system.

In the first section, which traces the development of the tradition and the evolution of the United Methodist system of schools, colleges, and seminaries, it is shown that education has been an inseparable part of the almost 200-year history of the UMC in America. Throughout its history, 839 distinct seminaries, schools of theology, colleges and universities, secondary schools, and elementary schools have been affiliated with the UMC. Twenty-four percent, or 198, of these 839 institutions have survived to the present, either as distinct institutions or through merger—the pattern for UMC schools.

The report indicates that the increase of state-controlled institutions has been a factor in the decline of United Methodist institutions almost since their founding. With the development of public institutions, state funds for support of church-related colleges began to dry up; and since the public institutions "were founded on many of the same democratic ideals which characterized the United Methodist tradition," they represented special competition. The report also suggests that the continual merging of institutions and assets and official attempts to insure that there be "fewer and stronger institutions strategically located" and better supported give evidence of long concern for the development of a system of education in the UMC. One hundred and thirty-four educational institutions are currently affiliated with the UMC. [173]

Among the major concerns that have characterized the UMC tradition in higher education are the following ones. Through the founding and continuing relatedness to institutions serving differing purposes and constituencies, the UMC has sought to provide educational opportunity to persons "regardless of sex or ethnic, economic, or social background." Needful of a more learned clergy to attract the increasingly affluent and educated Americans to the church and in response to members concerned with the education of their children, the UMC founded both colleges and seminaries. The UMC also became involved in higher education because of its conviction that education was incomplete without a religious dimension and that the end of knowledge is the enhancement of the individual as well as the service of church and society. Indeed, "the empowerment of the individual's spiritual, intellectual, aesthetic, emotional, and physical resources is of paramount concern, and this concern underlies all United Methodist support for education, especially liberal arts education."[174]

The second and more extensive part of this volume presents the chronological histories of UMC-related colleges and schools—including information about their founding, mergers, disaffiliations and closings, and continuation.

The staff discovered some important lessons of history in this study. First, and above all else, Methodists have an impressive history of support of higher education. The report notes that the church-related colleges have been supported primarily for their educational value, rather than for the purpose of religious indoctrination. Second, it is evident that United Methodist higher education institutions have been responsive to the growth of the nation.

> They moved west with the frontier. They arose and closed in response to the moving population, and as they developed, they reflected the American ideals of democracy by emphasizing the provision of educational opportunity for all.
> . . . the system was dynamic, never being frozen in an artificial equilibrium, but always responding to the changing society it served.[175]

In this light, the changes within the Methodist higher education system need not be seen as catastrophic but as natural, evolutionary events in the development of a viable system.

Toward 2000: Perspectives on the Environment for United Methodist and Independent Higher Education is a third report prepared by the staff of the National Commission. The report reviews four major environmental elements which will help shape the future of independent and church-related institutions of higher education—

United Methodist institutions in particular. These elements are population trends and related social factors, the economy, government regulations and requirements, and the policies and practices of the UMC.

Based on population trends, the 1990s and the year 2000 will see a decline in the traditional college-age population of 18-24-year-olds. Evidence suggests that the percentage of those from this age group who enroll in institutions of higher education is declining. The report shows that enrollment in United Methodist institutions has not kept pace with enrollment in the independent sector generally. The report states that the future stability of United Methodist institutions will be determined largely by how they deal with a variety of other social factors, including the declining importance of education among social priorities, the limitations of parental expectations and resources, the nature of supply and demand of college graduates in the job market, the developing nature and extent of technological influences on the culture, and the changing character of credentialing requirements for employment.

The authors state that the information and accountability requirements and regulations of federal and state governments sometimes conflict with an institution's autonomy and mission, especially the mission of a religious nature. These requirements place a financial burden on independent institutions in their challenges or obligatory responses. The costs colleges and universities incur in their obligations to government regulations are nonproductive from the point of view of the primary purpose of these institutions—education. Whereas state institutions tend to have the resources for implementing or challenging government regulations and for engaging in litigation in other areas, independent institutions—particularly small colleges—do not. State institutions, according to the report, may be expected to compete against independent institutions as they lobby against public policies and funding programs which would remove their competitive advantage over independent institutions. Further, as a labor-intensive enterprise ("typically 80% of the educational and general expenditures of colleges and universities are personnel costs"), higher education is particularly vulnerable to inflation, and its rate of inflation will likely continue to run ahead of general economic inflation. Thus, higher education. to maintain itself, will have to increase its productivity or obtain funding growth at a rate which exceeds the general economic growth.[176]

> At the national level, the present mood of The United Methodist Church with respect to its colleges and universities can perhaps best be described as one of continuing concern for the institutions, careful inquiry concerning their status, and reaffirmation of the importance of the church's role in education.[177]

The report points to recent church actions, such as the establishment of the Black College Fund, the calling of the National Commission, and the adoption of the Commission's mission statement, as evidence of this concern. The report also calls attention to other actions of the 1976 General Conference which promise to strengthen the church's understanding of and support for church-related higher education. The report suggests that there are a number of services which the boards of the church might develop as a way of aiding their institutions of higher education. While the formal affiliation of colleges and universities occurs at the national level (through the University Senate and the Board of Higher Education and Ministry), annual conferences and local churches provide the greatest financial support and have the closest ties with these institutions. These facts and past experience suggest that "a major variable in determining future levels of church support will simply be the level of commitment the church feels towards its colleges and universities."[178]

The report concludes with the enumeration of several characteristics of future "successful" institutions. Successful institutions will have clearly defined purposes and goals shared by constituents; will search for new opportunities for service not being met and align these with purposes and expectations; will review operations to select those which are the most effective, focusing on quality and efficiency; will have developed institutional slack which will both allow them to absorb some considerable measure of short-term revenue shortfall and also permit flexibility to respond positively to new opportunities. According to the report:

> Those institutions which can make a unique claim for their institutional purpose will likely find a market. Those institutions which can abandon traditional views of institutional autonomy and join together with others to share resources in creative ways may cope with their economic and demographic environment. New models are possible.[179]

Recommendations from the commission on public policy and a discussion of issues and strategies related to these are presented in a fourth volume, entitled *Endangered Service: Independent Colleges, Public Policy and the First Amendment.*

Believing that the problems of independent higher education cannot be solved at the institutional level alone, the National Commission urges public policies which will preserve independent higher education, now endangered by the growing tuition gap between state and independent sectors. This tuition gap, according to the report, is created by state subsidies to state institutions. As its rationale for a public policy designed to preserve independent higher education, the commission points out that independent institutions provide such public services as minimizing state expenditures for higher education; serving a cross section of constituencies, including low-income and minority students; conferring a substantial proportion of professional degrees; contributing to the economic and cultural well-being of the communities in which they are located; and maintaining diversity and preserving autonomy in American higher education. Institutions independent of the state promote pluralism by serving a particular constituency and by protecting academic freedom from political interference.

The commission sets out three principles which it believes are basic to the formulation of an adequate higher education public policy in the United States. First, because independent higher education performs an "essential public service function," public policies at the state and federal level should reflect an understanding of that service "and seek to preserve its benefits for society." Second, state and federal governments should preserve the diversity that now exists in higher education "by assuring the autonomy and viability of individual institutions." Third, public policies which directly or indirectly prevent attendance at independent institutions should be changed.[180]

To facilitate these principles, the commission recommends the expansion of federal and state programs of student financial aid aimed toward facilitating student choice among a diversity of institutions; the restructuring of Social Security and veterans' benefit programs which discriminate against students attending independent institutions; the continuance of federal and state tax policies which provide incentives for voluntary support of educational institutions;

the maintenance of tax-exempt status of education properties if used for educational purposes; the nonduplication of unique programs offered by the independent sector within the coordination of state systems of higher education; and the revision of federal and state regulations which require excessive administrative burdens and costs for both state and independent higher educational institutions, including the abolition or amendment of regulations inimical to institutional autonomy.

In addition to discussing specific ways in which the recommendations above can be accomplished, the document presents an analysis of the First Amendment and other legal issues—the context in which the public debate must be conducted. Concluding that "public funding is constitutional and challenges can be won in the courts," the report suggests the nature of the challenges likely to be made and the steps that colleges can take to be prepared for and safe from those challenges. The report urges independent institutions to work together in devising effective litigation strategy. "What happens to one, affects all." [181]

The fifth volume to emerge from the deliberations of the National Commission is entitled *Ministry on Campus: A United Methodist Mission Statement and Survey Report.*

In the fall of 1976, the staff of the commission conducted a survey of UMC campus ministers. The purpose of the survey was "to obtain information about the current purposes, activities, and organization of the campus ministries in which United Methodist ministers work; and to learn the views of those ministers concerning both their current operations and their aspirations for campus ministry." [182]

The survey discovered wide differences in the backgrounds, career patterns, and institutional settings of campus ministers. Campus ministers in ecumenical settings most often cite a sense of mission or calling as their reason for entering campus ministry and are desirous of remaining in campus ministry for the rest of their careers; Wesley Foundation directors less often cite that reason and wish to remain in campus ministry for only a brief time. According to the survey, "the first priority of nearly all campus ministers was providing pastoral care." Generally, campus ministers take as their second priority the prophetic task of ministry—"study and action intended to bring about a more just society." At the same time, they report a greater interest among their constituents "in more traditional church functions of religious witness and nurture" and much less interest in the prophetic task.[183] In terms of financing and staff, the data "suggest that many campus ministries may be best equipped to function in the pastoral mode" while the greater resources and multiple staff in many ecumenical ministries probably facilitate "the greater involvement in non-pastoral activities reported by the ecumenical ministers." [184] In the area of governance, the survey found that campus ministers generally express the view that they should be accountable to that church authority or that agency which controls their employment and provides their basic funding. Finally, the survey found that an overwhelming percentage of campus ministers believes that "provision of special professional education for campus ministers" could be useful and that there is a need for in-service training after entering into campus ministry.[185]

With the survey results as background, the commission prepared a statement on the mission of the United Methodist Church in its campus ministry and offered a recommendation to the 1976 General Conference of the UMC for churchwide support for campus ministries. The recommendation was adopted by the General Conference.

In the mission statement, the commission traces the development of campus ministry from Wesley's "Holy Clubs," the student work of the Student Christian Movement, the development of the Wesley Foundations, and the often ecumenical programs of the Evangelical United Brethren tradition. In the present day:

> This limited concept of campus ministry has expanded to include a lively concern for the whole campus. Campus ministry has sought involvement with the entire university to enhance the quality of life in the whole institution. This sense of mission led to United Methodist cooperation with other denominations in order to broaden and enrich its ministry.[186]

The commission notes that ministry needs continuous evaluation. And given the UMC's investment in campus ministry, the dispersion of its campus ministers in nonchurch institutions of higher education, and the current questioning of established denominational and ecumenical patterns of campus ministry, there is a particularly urgent need for an evaluation of campus ministry.

Acknowledging that the ministry of all in the church is one of "witness and nurture, outreach and service," the statement claims that "the distinctiveness of campus ministry is that it is Christ's ministry present in a university community." It is the function of a ministry to higher education to gather a community of faith to search after and witness to the will of God; to provide pastoral care that challenges inhumane structures and demonstrates the wholeness of life; to champion freedom of inquiry; to engage in an examination of operative values in light of the Christian tradition and to enable persons to make judgments and to act on the basis of their faith; and to provide "leadership that is representative of the best traditions of the church: truly ecumenical, interracial, intercultural, and integrative of varied groups and traditions."[187]

The statement goes on to set out criteria for evaluating the effectiveness of campus ministry; suggests new strategies for ministry that seek to be responsive to the needs of a learning society, a pluralistic culture, community colleges; calls on campus ministry to explore the possibilities of partnership with local congregations and laity; and invites consideration of new forms and means of staffing and financing campus ministry.

The resolution calling for churchwide support for campus ministries—noting the historic role of the UMC in campus ministry, the obligation of the church to provide ministry to young people, the enrollment of most UMC students on non-Methodist campuses, the role of campus ministry in enabling faithful and ethical action within the university, and its role in stimulating the care and concern of the church for higher education—calls on the church to reaffirm its support of higher education and campus ministry.

Though the commission was terminated in June, 1977, two monographs resulting from its work are yet to be published. The sixth volume will summarize data collected by the commission; the seventh will constitute "the final report and recommendations as they have emerged from a continuing evaluation, adoption, and implementation by the Division of Higher Education and the Board of Higher Education and Ministry." Awaiting the publication of the final volume, the board has issued an interim report and recommendations of the commission, noting that the board has already adopted the recommendations in principle and with some modification.[188]

According to the interim report, there are four principles which are fundamental and form the basis for the recommendations. First, "The United Methodist Church should continue and strengthen its commitment to its mission and witness in institutional higher education and campus ministry"; second, the resources of the UMC should be used to provide a level of support for these institutions which demonstrates that the church "cares for the question of the knowledge of God and for its responsibility to model communities of humane and objective learning and vital piety"; third, a sense of mutual responsibility and "mutual understanding of shared values" should provide the basis for the church-college relationship; and fourth, a strong independent sector is essential to the vitality of the national system of higher education, just as a congenial public policy is essential to the survival of the independent sector.[189]

In light of these principles, it is recommended that a design and comprehensive program for making higher education a quadrennial emphasis of the UMC be presented to the 1980 General Conference. Further, a series of recommendations is set forth concerning public policy. The division is directed to continue working collaboratively with other church and higher education agencies to insure the continued existence, autonomy, fiscal integrity, and vitality of independent and state sectors of higher education, to continue to provide consultation to annual conferences on public policy issues affecting higher education; and to "initiate continuing consultations with all agencies of the general church to reach accord in matters related to public policy issues bearing upon the church's mission in higher education."[190]

Numerous recommendations are made regarding the role of the Division of Higher Education. The interim report states that the primary task of the division "is to promote and to implement General Conference higher education policies in the annual conferences, the institutions, and the campus ministry units" through "planning, policy development, and advocacy at both the general church and annual conference levels." To accomplish these tasks, the division should continue to utilize and develop further the systems established by the National Commission for collecting and analyzing data on funding and the assessment of the academic and financial strength of institutions; continue to provide strategic services to institutions and the campus ministry—at the same time encouraging interinstitutional cooperation in the development of and contracting for additional consultative services; initiate consultations with the annual conferences to clarify and/or strengthen fiscal and legal relationships to institutions and campus ministry units; and determine that all colleges and universities which are recommended for the church's funding "meet appropriate standards of academic strength and service to the church's mission in higher education. . . ."[191]

Finally, recommendations are made to a number of church agencies which have education-related responsibilities. "Each annual conference and its related institution(s) should develop an explicit written agreement defining their relationship and the mutual expectations." The University Senate—primarily responsible for accrediting UMC-related colleges and universities—will advise the division in determining the academic and financial strength of institutions and the eligibility of colleges for continuing church funding. The denomination's Office of Loans and Scholarships should rename its undergraduate scholarship program "The United Methodist Tuition Equalization Grant Program," and it should "be designed to facilitate access of United Methodist students to United Methodist institutions." Conferences and local churches should be encouraged to promote the observance of Student Day more vigorously and to contribute to the scholarship and loan fund. The division should encourage annual conference committees on higher education and campus ministry to formulate goals and objectives and "explicit written agreements defining the relationship and mutual expectations for each campus ministry unit," and should provide increased opportunity for continuing education and mobility within campus ministry.[192] As the document notes, a great number of the recommendations are already in the process of being implemented.

The United Presbyterian Church U.S.A.

In 1973 the Program Agency of the United Presbyterian Church U.S.A. (UPCUSA) and the Presbyterian College Union—a voluntary association composed of synod representation and the presidents of related colleges—joined in developing agreements which "describe the essential basis of what can and should be a dynamic relationship between the church and its related colleges and universities."[193]

This statement, although a nationally drawn document, is seen as pointing the direction for a variety of covenants which in recent years have related the colleges more and more to state and regional synods. It is also used as the basis for the recognition of colleges and universities by the national body, the General Assembly of the United Presbyterian Church, as well as by its judicatories, and it constitutes a prerequisite for membership in the Presbyterian College Union.

The document, *The Church and Related Colleges and Universities: A Statement of Mutual Responsibilities*, affirms the value of the historic relationship between the church and its colleges:

These institutions of higher education generally were founded by men and women committed to Jesus Christ as Lord. As participants in the Reformed tradition, their faith called them to establish these colleges and universities that successive generations might discover and appropriate the knowledge found in the many disciplines. We value our common heritage and we pledge our continuing commitment to be involved together in service to God and society through higher education.[194]

The statement goes on to note that, at the time of the founding of the various colleges, differing relationships were established between the colleges and the judicatories of the church. It notes further that the relationships have undergone "substantial and appropriate change" over time. It is not desirable, according to the statement, that "a uniform code of relationships" be agreed to; nor is it advantageous that the relationships be firmly fixed. But it is judged agreeable by the two parties that "we here declare these responsibilities which we believe to be basic as guidelines for maintaining our mutual association."[195] The statement then sets forth several responsibilities of the church, the colleges and universities, and joint responsibilities.

According to the document, it is the responsibility of the church to regard the colleges and universities as independent corporate institutions not under the control of the church which "aid in extending the outreach of the church to each new generation and which also contribute to the continuing mission of the church throughout the world"; to encourage each institution "to serve as a center of learning committed to providing maximal opportunities for the responsible exercise of academic freedom"; and to provide leadership, services, and financial support—"to the extent permitted by its resources and priorities and as determined by the judicatories"—to strengthen the related colleges and universities.[196]

For their part, the colleges and universities will provide opportunities for both students and teachers "to attain their highest possible level of achievement and by instruction in and by emphasis on human values will encourage each person to seek and reach a significant commitment of the self in service to individuals and society." Further, the colleges will offer instruction in religious studies "with emphasis on the Judeo-Christian tradition as important to liberal education"; will make their educational resources available to the churches in order to assist them in meeting current needs and addressing social problems; will state their relationship to the church in catalogues and other appropriate publications; and will maintain accreditation—which "shall be regarded as a minimal indication of the quality sought by the college or university."[197]

Lastly, the church and the related colleges and universities "commit themselves to share with one another results of research, insights, and experiences that inform and reinforce the capacities of each to serve society with sensitivity and skill," and together to "support the struggle for full recognition of all persons as children of God." It is noted also that both the church and the colleges and universities understand that the responsibilities they affirm are central "to their declared and continuing relationship."[198]

In 1975, two years after the statement of mutual responsibility was adopted, the Presbyterian College Union commissioned J. Garber Drushal, then president of the union and the College of Wooster, to prepare a review of the national church-college scene. A personal reflection of the author not formally endorsed by the church or colleges, the statement was printed by the Program Agency and distributed widely under the title *The Church and Its Colleges: A Status Report for The United Presbyterian Church in the U.S.A.*

In the preface to his review, Drushal states that, contrary to the general conclusion conveyed by the media, the day of the "church college with its Christian influence" is not over. "We can point to a strong group of colleges affiliated in one way or another with the United Presbyterian Church as a striking exception."[199]

Drushal explains that reorganization of the denomination's administrative structures and synodical boundaries has made it necessary to redefine relationships; therefore, each synod has had to develop guidelines for the church-college relationship within its area. Having examined the synodical statements, Drushal reports that no two are identical. He writes:

> They all start from the common assumption that as a denomination there should be a relationship with the colleges but from there on they develop in widely divergent ways. The statements vary on such things as the rationale for the relationship, methods of fund raising and types of financial support, and suggested interaction between presbyteries and the colleges within their boundaries.[200]

However, underlying the diversity of relationships and understandings represented in the synodical statements—and the diversity among the colleges which "in many ways are a reflection of intradenominational diversity"—Drushal finds significant mutual resolves. There is a general agreement, he finds, that "each synod headquarters will be in some way an agency of support for the colleges" and that "the colleges will seek to be an expression of ministry within the synod," each college finding its own identity and working out its particular mission and structural relationship as a church-related college.[201]

He also finds two important basic principles or common denominators "accepted as the reasons for being which give encouragement for a workable common commitment." Drushal describes these as follows:

> First, there is an impact on the student of a place where things of importance to the church matter to real people. Often it is a silent impact of the environment of the campus. It may lie in the concern with the spirit, whether in familiar words of worship or in the everyday interaction of students and faculty. . . . In any case, it is the influence of intangible informal ties with a campus whose personality is built of people whose actions demonstrate goodwill and concern and an understanding of the Christian life. . . .

> Second, if the ministry of the church as a concern for the immediate situation where love is relevant to justice and justice to love is even partially achieved on campuses in forms flexible enough to meet the demands of the day, the life goals acceptable to students will not be at the lowest level of casual purposeless living, but rather a high commitment to responsible Christian freedom.[202]

Given this basis for a continuing, vital relationship between church and college, the author suggests that there are immediate, tangible ways the church can help to strengthen these institutions. First, it can interpret the colleges to prospective students within its own membership; second, the church can respond to the financial plight of its own institutions.

In keeping with both suggestions, the Vocation Agency of the church and the colleges yearly provide approximately 75 National Presbyterian College Scholarships. The scholarships to UPCUSA-related colleges are awarded, on a competitive basis, to church members who have not previously been enrolled as full-time students. Further, as a part of its 1977–1980 Major Mission Fund, the church is committed to raising $12.6 million in the three-year period to strengthen the denomination's mission to seminaries, overseas missions, and higher education. One million dollars of that money is designated for United Presbyterian college scholarships; more than $2.6 million will be devoted to the support of six UPCUSA minority educational institutions.

Finally, at its February, 1978, meeting, the Nexus—or executive—Committee of the Presbyterian College Union requested "authorization of the PCU to work with the Program Agency for the creation of a National Task Force to study and recommend ways by which the mutual responsibilities of the UPCUSA and the colleges related to it can be more fully implemented and the visibility and support of the colleges augmented." [203] Subsequently, the request has been approved and the appointment of the task force, to be broadly representative of church and college constituencies, is proceeding.

Conclusions

The preceding review of recent denominational studies, policies, and statements regarding the church's mission in higher education does not by any means tell the whole story of Christian interest and involvement in post-secondary education. Indeed, some seasoned observers have cautioned that a discussion of official, national denominational documents does not get to the heart of the matter. Nevertheless, the review is sufficiently inclusive of religious traditions and deals with such a range of documents—many of them having received input, discussion, or confirmation at many levels of denominational life—that it is warranted to attempt to draw generalizations from the documents, make some observations about their significance, and venture some opinions about what they portend for the future.

Following are some generalizations about the materials which have been reviewed above.

1. On the basis of the material reviewed, it is evident that there is widespread interest among the churches in maintaining and strengthening relationships with their colleges and universities. Though the loci of responsibility for higher education and the authority over institutions vary among the denominations, there is increasing acknowledgment at the national and judicatory levels of the churches of interest in and responsibility for church-related higher education. This is seen most clearly in recently adopted resolutions of interest and concern and actions empowering review, study, support, and advocacy of church-related higher education in many denominations.

2. Though the specific understanding of the purpose or mission of the church-related college differs significantly among denominations, most of the college-related churches hold the following general purposes in common:

- The church-related college is concerned with the development of the individual's mental, physical, and spiritual resources.
- The church-related college will provide opportunities for exposure to Christian faith and teachings.
- The church-related college is committed to value-centered inquiry.
- The church-related college affirms the importance of the liberal arts in the total education of its students.
- The church-related college is committed to the upgrading or the transformation of society.

3. Though the rationale for maintaining church-related higher education differs among the denominations, most of the college-related churches hold the following reasons in common:

- Biblical and theological understandings of the nature and purpose of human life impel the church to take responsibility for the intellectual and spiritual development of persons. The church-related college is one vehicle.
- The church-related college provides a forum within higher education for relating faith and reason.

- The church-related college provides leaders for church and society who have been educated in the liberal arts and exposed to value-centered inquiry.
- The church-related college provides the church with a means for expressing its prophetic concern and making its prophetic witness in society and a way for the church to be confronted and challenged directly by the academy.
- The church-related college provides an arena for experimentation in higher education that is relatively free of public control.
- The church-related college preserves pluralism and a dual system of education in United States society.
- The church-related college serves society and provides a means for the church to serve particular constituencies.

4. There is significant agreement among the college-related churches about what constitutes the external threat to the survival of church-related higher education.

- Rising education costs, inflation, costs of government compliance, the tuition gap, or the competition of low-cost public institutions are a threat to the survival of church-related higher education.
- The declining number of 18-24-year-olds in the population and the declining percentage of persons in that age group going on to college are a threat to the survival of church-related higher education.
- The increasing accountability of church-related higher education to the government in return for financial assistance is a threat to the survival of the religious identity and distinctiveness of church-related higher education.

5. There is less agreement—and in light of their differing experience, less basis for agreement—among the denominations on what items constitute internal threats to church-related higher education. While churches identify the lack of church support, the lack of church commitment, conflicting expectations among various constituencies, inadequate communication between church and college, the increasing secularization of colleges, and more, these and other problems seem to be rooted in a larger identity crisis: what is the present and future mission of the church-related college, and what is or ought to be its relationship to the church?

In the attempt to address the external and internal threats to the survival of church-related higher education and in order to strengthen the church-college relationship, the college-related churches are engaged in the planning and implementation of an impressive array of strategies. They represent the blessed diversity of church-related higher education. They provide a basis for commenting on trends and differences in denominational approaches. They also invite some questions and observations.

6. A number of denominations are engaged in formulating, revising, or reaffirming their theological rationales for involvement in higher education. In most instances this appears to be mainly the work of people professionally identified with the church or the collaborative efforts of people in church and college. In a few instances, however, it appears to have been initiated by people professionally identified with the colleges.

While the former represents the traditional pattern in church-college relations, the latter breaks with what has come to be the normative trend. More than simply a break with the traditional pattern, however, it suggests that the colleges of some denominations, in their search for a *raison d'etre* or in their desire to assert some genuine claim of distinctiveness over against their competitors, have rediscovered their religious heritage and purpose and feel compelled to call this to the attention of—even to make a religiously based claim upon—the parent church which has grown indifferent to the relationship or become timid about claiming any theological kinship with its colleges.

Such evidence is neither extensive nor decisive enough to suggest that the long-term trend from "claim" to "no claim" as outlined by Merrimon Cuninggim is about to be reversed. However, this evidence and the evidence of wider rethinking about the theological basis for church-related higher education do mean that the process is being slowed down for the moment, thus affording a genuine opportunity for even more intensive reflection, discussion, and decision making about the nature and purpose of the church-related college and the obligation of church and college to one another.

7. Interested in having their colleges maintain, recover, or achieve a distinctiveness of mission and purpose which will contribute to the viability and vitality of the institutions, some denominations are

encouraging their colleges to reaffirm the religious, cultural, and social roots from which they spring. Thus, one denomination calls for the recovery of the Wesleyan heritage of knowledge and vital piety; another seeks the recovery of the prophetic character of the church-related college; a third advances an historically rooted philosophy of peoplehood education. At the same time, other denominations—including some of those referred to above—are encouraging their colleges to broaden their mission to become more responsive to the rapidly changing issues and needs of a dynamic and volatile world. In one tradition, the colleges are asked to be particularly responsive to the needs of the poor and oppressed; in another, the colleges are invited to develop the human and material resources needed to lead in the battle against world hunger; in a third, curricular revision is urged so that the learning process may reflect the realities of a globally interdependent world.

As the review suggests, the proposals for renewal advanced by some denominations result from an earnest wrestling with the basic purposes of church-related higher education. But in some instances, the discussion of renewal appears to beg the central question: that is, why is the church involved in higher education in the first place? Unless this question is earnestly probed again and again within the churches and between them and their colleges, there is likely to be no shared and mutually informed basis on which to judge the centrality of one tradition over another or the importance of one task in contrast to another task.

8. Aware that they can no longer provide substantial funding for the general operations of their colleges, eager to have their colleges participate in and be viewed as supportive of the mission priorities of the denomination, and concerned that denominational funding of higher education have higher visibility, a number of denominations are moving to strategic funding. In some cases, colleges now compete for funds that must be used to advance a denomination's specific, current mission priorities (i.e., research related to the problem of world hunger; peace and justice studies). In other cases, financial assistance is made available primarily to particular categories of persons (preministerial students, racial minorities) or to special-purpose institutions (those serving primarily racial minorities; those designated as national or churchwide institutions). In still other

cases, special programs (the chaplaincy, voluntary service projects) or departments (religion; teacher education) are funded.

Certainly, strategic funding promises to fulfill these expectations; yet it presents at least two dangers which must be kept in mind when it is applied. First, if mission priorities change frequently and grants are made for short periods of time or if priorities are imposed on the colleges without their advice and consent, colleges may not be willing or able to make the investment in planning, supplementary resources, and staffing necessary to use the special funds. Second, if a denomination funds specific programs and projects only, it may inadvertently appear to identify that one priority as *the* concern of the church in higher education and vitiate its claim of interest and support for the whole educational enterprise.

Strategic funding provides a way of using limited funds for maximum benefit to the church-college relationship. But even more than the block grants it generally replaces, it will demand continuous evaluation and interpretation if it is to continue to be a creative and useful tool.

9. A number of denominations, convinced that they must work at the formulation and advocacy of public policy more favorable to the church related college, are engaged today in identifying the issues, strategies, and technical capabilities needed for the task. Further, a growing number of denominations are beginning to find common cause with one another (for example, through the informal organization of Executives for Church-Related Higher Education) and with secular higher educational agencies (such as the National Association of Independent Colleges and Universities) in the formation of wider public policy-oriented networks.

Because a public policy favorable to the maintenance of a dual system of higher education, committed to equitable funding for all of higher education and protective of religious and academic freedom is essential to the survival of church-related higher education, the development and advocacy of favorable public policy positions must be accelerated. Because of their stake in higher education, the churches must participate in and help to develop the broader coalitions interested in strengthening and winning support for public and independent higher education. But as has been noted in more than one document reviewed earlier, public policy effectiveness will depend in large measure on the development of a concept of desirable public policy which is relatively consistent, generally accepted, and widely supported within a denomination or among a group of cooperating denominations.

While denominations are making great strides in developing appropriate public policy positions in relationship to church-related higher education, it is evident that a good deal of groundwork needs to be done with denominational constituencies to be sure that their views are known and guide the formulation of policy; that their unfavorable attitudes or misconceptions about desirable policy are discussed and, if possible, changed; and that their active interest and strategic support are being sought and encouraged. The most important focus at this moment in the long-range development of public policy favorable to church-related higher education is among the constituents of the denominations, for their collective understanding, commitment, and advocacy are necessary to carry the day.

10. Many denominations—particularly those in which a significant measure of responsibility and authority for higher education has recently shifted from national agencies or traditionally resides at the middle judicatory and institutional level—are reviewing or beginning afresh to make individual covenants between the middle judicatories and the colleges. At the same time, some denominations—including a few of those described above and those with more centralized governance and authority—are expressing the need for system-wide planning among their colleges and are beginning to develop or attempting to strengthen such strategies for higher education.

The former group of churches and colleges is discovering that covenantal agreements have the advantage of making explicit the expectations and responsibilities of one for the other, make possible a differentiation of relationships and functions among institutions, and provide the opportunity for greater mutual accountability at the local and regional level. The latter group suggests that system-wide planning and strategy are essential if costly duplication of effort among the denomination's colleges is to be overcome, if equitable funding of the church's institutions is to occur, if a public policy position congenial to the survival of independent higher education is to be formulated and widely supported within the denomination, if there is to be a sense of common purpose and identity among the colleges of a denomination, and if there is to be some standard for determining which colleges deserve the continuing support of the church.

While there are ample historical and contemporary reasons to understand why one or the other pattern of relationship would appeal to the several denominations, the cumulative message of the foregoing review would seem to be that some combination of the two—individual covenantal arrangements and system-wide planning and strategy will best serve most denominations and their institutions of higher education in the future.

Undoubtedly some denominations will have to give up a measure of central authority in moving toward covenantal agreements— though others have already shown that broad agreement on basic guidelines for covenant-making can protect common form, structure, and purpose. Likewise, institutions and middle judicatories within some denominations may find that participation in system-wide planning will entail giving up a measure of local autonomy though others are demonstrating that such planning can be focused on issues which institutions agree need to be dealt with jointly. But the change that is demanded can be increasingly justified on the basis of the fact that all capabilities mentioned above are essential to each denomination if its colleges are to survive and thrive in a rapidly changing cultural context.

11. To fulfill their Christian mandate and to meet the changing educational situation, denominations are working at the creation of comprehensive strategies to give form and substance to their role in higher education. Some are advancing plans for greater inter-institutional cooperation and for the refinement and expansion of services to their colleges. Some are beginning to approach their colleges as a possible integrated system without unnecessary duplication in program, staff, and facilities. Some are addressing the issues of curriculum using new global models as their base. Some are attempting to redefine their mission in the whole of higher education and are including parish-based education, campus ministry, and church-related colleges in their planning. Some are reaching out to find new ecumenical bases for cooperation in the mission in higher education. Almost all confess the need for greater joint effort and

cooperative planning on behalf of this segment of higher education. But the fact remains that, while most denominations are pursuing at least one of these or similar strategies and some denominations are engaged in a few of them, few if any are working on most or all of these strategies—either alone or cooperatively.

The organization of Executives for Church-Related Higher Education now meets regularly and seeks to work together on issues of common interest. Members of various religious traditions were named to the National Commission on United Methodist Higher Education and to its informal ecumenical advisory committee. A number of denominational higher education associations come together for joint sessions in the context of national educational meetings. This study has involved a significant group of denominations in a common endeavor. But the review suggests that denominational higher education agenda continue to be determined largely in isolation from one another and with little coordination of efforts or systematic use of one another's findings and observations.

While it would appear that the denominations are at the time and place in their history when they have a sufficient sense of the urgency of common problems to want to be able to work together on their resolutions, they have not yet achieved a strong enough sense of common identity and purpose nor had a productive enough experience working together that they are ready to labor ecumenically on the creation and implementation of comprehensive higher education strategies.

If ecumenical cooperation is to proceed on more than a piecemeal basis, a common understanding of what identifies this subsystem of higher education as a whole and what distinguishes it from the rest of independent and public higher education will have to be forged by those who understand it from within. The essentials of church-relatedness formulated by Merrimon Cuninggim provide a solid basis for a systematic discussion of mission and purpose within and between denominations. Further, agreement will have to be reached on what issues are so important to the whole group of institutions that they demand cooperative planning and strategy, even if one or another denomination or agency provides the primary leadership in addressing particular problems. A useful model may well emerge from the cooperative action around constitutional and legal issues which has recently begun as these have become a common concern.

Finally, however, the creation and implementation of comprehensive higher education strategies on an ecumenical basis will not likely proceed much further unless and until the churches determine that there is a critical need in higher education and the society and that a critical contribution can be made through ecumenical effort. While the churches and their colleges have made great strides in the past decade toward understanding and affirming one another's history, tradition, and distinctiveness, and have made an impressive beginning at identifying and addressing common issues and problems, they have not discovered the common mission and contribution they can make together. Such a compelling conviction is essential if the energy and patience are to be found to work through those things which impede cooperation. Such an organizing principle is necessary if the churches' resources and energies in higher education are to be brought into common focus.

The quest for an understanding of that critical contribution deserves to be at the heart of the churches' higher education agenda in the next decade.

CHURCH-RELATED COLLEGES

These listings come from denominational reports, for the most part as of 1975–1976, and include both junior and senior colleges.

Protestant

African Methodist Episcopal Church	7
American Baptist Churches in the U.S.A.	24
American Lutheran Church	12
Christian Church (Disciples of Christ)	19
Christian Methodist Episcopal Church	5
Church of the Brethren	6
Church of the Nazarene	8
Episcopal Church	9
Lutheran Church in America	18
Lutheran Church—Missouri Synod	13
Mennonite Church	6
Presbyterian Church, U.S.	22
Seventh-day Adventists	10
Southern Baptist Convention	53
United Church of Christ	30
United Methodist Church	107
United Presbyterian Church U.S.A.	53

Less overlap (joint sponsorship)	(13)	
Total		389
Roman Catholic	250 (approx.)	
Total		639
Evangelical and Other Denominations	100 (?)	
Total		739

NOTES—Chapter 6

[1] *A College-Related Church: United Methodist Perspectives* (Nashville: National Commission on United Methodist Higher Education, 1976).

[2] *The Book of Discipline of the African Methodist Episcopal Church*, 40th rev. ed. (Nashville: The A.M.E. Sunday School Union, 1972), pp. 280-281.

[3] *Ibid.*, p. 282.

[4] "Fund of Renewal," mimeographed, Jan. 20, 1976, p. 1.

[5] "Educational Projects," mimeographed, undated, pp. 1-3.

[6] "Collegiate Education. 1976 Grants," Board of Educational Ministries, ABC, U.S.A.

[7] Calvert N. Ellis, *The Colleges and the Church of the Brethren*, Committee on Higher Education, Nov. 1, 1972.

[8] James H. Lehman, *Beyond Anything Foreseen: A Study of the History of Higher Education in the Church of the Brethren*, prepared for the Conference on Higher Education and the Church of the Brethren, June 24-27, 1976, at Earlham College, Richmond, Indiana.

[9] "Recommendation of the Conference on Higher Education and the Church of the Brethren," Earlham College, Richmond, Indiana, June 27, 1976, mimeographed, July, 1976, p. 1.

[10] *Ibid.*, pp. 2-3.

[11] *Ibid.*, pp. 5-6.

[12] "Constitution of the General Board of Christian Education," *The Book of Discipline of the Christian Methodist Episcopal Church* (Memphis: Christian Methodist Episcopal Church, 1974), pp. 227-229.

[13] *Ibid.*, pp. 235-236.

[14] Morris P. Fair, Alandus C. Johnson, and William R. Johnson, Jr., Editorial Committee, "A Compiled Report Describing the Christian Methodist Episcopal Church's Investments in Higher Education," presented at the Twenty-Seventh General Conference, May 12, 1974, Philadelphia, Pennsylvania, mimeographed.

[15] *Ibid.*, Quadrennial Income and Table VIII.

[16] *Ibid.*, Table II.

[17] *Ibid.*, Tables IX and X.

[18] "Higher Education Evaluation Task Force Report to the General Board of The Christian Church (Disciples of Christ)," June 12-15, 1976, mimeographed, p. 1.

[19] *Ibid.*, pp. 5-7.

[20] *Ibid.*, p. 10.

[21] *Ibid.*, p. 11.

[22] *Ibid.*, pp. 12-13.

[23] Booze, Allan, and Hamilton, "Summary of Existing College-Church Relationships" and "Considerations for Future College-Church Relationships," a study of the Association of Episcopal Colleges, mimeographed, 1969, p. 7.

[24] *Ibid.*, pp. 10-11.

[25] *Ibid.*, p. 15.

[26] John Paul Carter, "White Paper," in "Colloquium 20-20," mimeographed, March, 1974.

[27] *Ibid.*, p. 7.

[28] Francis C. Gamelin, *Church-Related Identity of Lutheran Colleges,* a report to the Commission on the Future, Lutheran Educational Conference of North America (Washington, D.C.: LECNA, June, 1975), pp. 21-22.

[29] *Ibid.*, p. 57.

[30] Allan O. Pfnister, *Trends in Higher Education in the United States: A Review of Recent Literature,* a report to the Commission on the Future, Lutheran Educational Conference of North America (Washington, D.C: LECNA, May, 1975).

[31] Arthur L. Olsen, ed., *Cooperation for the Future,* a report of the Commission on the Future to the Lutheran Educational Conference of North America (Washington, D.C.: LECNA, January, 1976), p. 13.

[32] *Ibid.*, p. 17.

[33] *Ibid.*, p. 22.

[34] *Ibid.*, pp. 22-23. See also Appendix B, pp. 54-58 in Olsen, *op. cit.*

[35] *"Toward 1985—": Report of the ALC Workshop on the Church College,* Luther College, Decorah, Iowa, June 28–July 2, 1975 (Minneapolis: Division for College and University Services of the American Lutheran Church), p. 99.

[36] The Council on the Mission of LCA Colleges and Universities, *The Mission of LCA Colleges and Universities,* adopted by the Board of College Education and Church Vocations, Lutheran Church in America, October 23, 1969, pp. 8-9.

[37] *Ibid.*, p. 11.

[38] *Ibid.*, pp. 14-15.

[39] Charles R. Bruning, *Relationships Between Church-Related Colleges and Their Constituencies: A Review of the Literature* (New York: Division for Mission in North America, Department for Higher Education, Lutheran Church in America, February, 1975).

[40] Merton P. Strommen, *A Survey of Images and Expectations of LCA Colleges,* research report to the Joint Committee of the Division for Mission in North America and the Council of LCA Colleges (New York: Division for Mission in North America, Department for Higher Education, Lutheran Church in America, June, 1976).

[41] *Ibid.*, p. 226.

[42] *Ibid.*, p. 227.

[43] *The Basis for Partnership Between Church and College: A Statement of the Lutheran Church in America,* adopted by the Eighth Biennial Convention, Boston, Massachusetts, July 21-28, 1976, p. 2.

[44] *Ibid.*, p. 3.

[45] *Ibid.*

[46] *Handbook of the Lutheran Church—Missouri Synod,* 1975 edition, p. 143.

[47] *Ibid.*, p. 144.

[48] *Ibid.*, p. 141.

[49] "Mennonite Board of Education. Roles and Relationships," mimeographed, April 28, 1977, pp. 1 and 3.

[50] *Ibid.*, pp. 1 and 4.

[51] *Ibid.*, p. 5.

[52] Albert J. Meyer, "Two Models—Some Theological and Policy Perspectives," Princeton Consultation, National Council of Churches, Department of Higher Education, mimeographed, September, 1972, p. 6.

[53] "Mennonite Board of Education: Roles and Relationships," p. 5.

[54] *Manual/1976, Church of the Nazarene* (Kansas City: Nazarene Publishing House, 1976), pp. 165-167.

[55] "Report of the Ad Interim Committee on the Church in Higher Education," *Minutes of the 117th General Assembly of the Presbyterian Church in the United States,* June, 1977, p. 232.

[56] *Ibid.*, p. 236.

[57] *Ibid.*, p. 233.

[58] *Ibid.*

[59] *Ibid.*, p. 234.

[60] *Ibid.*

[61] *Ibid.*

[62] *Ibid.*, p. 235.

[63] *Ibid.*, p. 236.

[64] *Ibid.*, p. 237.

[65] *Ibid.*, p. 238.

[66] *The History and Scope of the Friends Council on Education,* Philadelphia, Friends Council on Education, 1978.

67 *What Does a Friends School Have to Offer?*, Philadelphia, Friends Council on Education, 1970.

68 *Ibid.*

69 *Ibid.*

70 *Ibid.*

71 "The Catholic University in the Modern World," statement of the Second International Congress of Delegates of the Catholic Universities of the World, Rome, Italy, November, 1972, reprinted in *College Newsletter*, vol. 35, no. 3 (March, 1973), p. 2.

72 *Ibid.*, p. 5.

73 *Ibid.*, p. 9.

74 National Conference of Catholic Bishops, *To Teach as Jesus Did: A Pastoral Message on Catholic Education* (Washington, D.C.: United States Catholic Conference, 1973), pp. 1 and 2.

75 *Ibid.*, p. 3.

76 *Ibid.*, pp. 4 and 7.

77 *Ibid.*

78 *Ibid.*, p. 18.

79 *Ibid.*, p. 20.

80 *Ibid.*, pp. 20-21.

81 *Ibid.*, p. 21.

82 *Ibid.*

83 Recent lectures have included the following: Ladislas M. Orsy, "Interaction Between University and Church," *Delta Epsilon Sigma Bulletin*, vol. 19, no. 2 (May, 1974); James F. Hitchcock, "How Is a College or University Catholic in Practice?," and Frederick J. Crosson, "How Is a College Catholic in Practice?," *Delta Epsilon Sigma Bulletin*, vol. 20 no. 2 (May, 1975); and John Tracy Ellis, "To Lead, To Follow, or To Drift? American Catholic Higher Education in 1976; A Personal View," *Delta Epsilon Sigma Bulletin*, vol. 21, no. 2 (May, 1976).

84 "Relations of American Catholic Colleges and Universities with the Church," Position Paper of the College and University Department, National Catholic Educational Association, *Occasional Papers on Catholic Higher Education*, vol. 2, no. 1 (April, 1976), p. 3.

85 *Ibid.*, p. 5.

86 *Ibid.*, pp. 6-7.

87 *Ibid.*, pp. 7, 8.

88 *Project 1: The Jesuit Apostolate of Education in the United States, An Introduction* (Washington, D.C.: Jesuit Conference), No. 1, March, 1974, p. 4. For a more detailed description of the Jesuit Conference, see pages 4-7.

[89] *Ibid.*, pp. 18-25.

[90] *Project 1: The Jesuit Apostolate of Education in the United States, An Overview* (Washington, D.C.: Jesuit Conference), No. 2, April, 1974, p. 33.

[91] *Ibid.*, pp. 53-55.

[92] *Project 1: The Jesuit Apostolate of Education in the United States, The Issues,* (Washington, D.C.: Jesuit Conference), No. 3, April, 1974, p. v.

[93] *Ibid.*, p. 2.

[94] *Ibid.*, pp. 13-14.

[95] *Ibid.*, p. 15.

[96] *Ibid.*, pp. 15-16.

[97] *Ibid.*, p. 16.

[98] *Ibid.*, p. 18.

[99] *Project 1: The Jesuit Apostolate of Education in the United States, Some Options* (Washington, D.C.; Jesuit Conference), No. 4, August, 1974, Introduction.

[100] *Ibid.*, p. 33.

[101] *Ibid.*, p. 34.

[102] *Ibid.*

[103] *Ibid.*, p. 37.

[104] *Project 1: The Jesuit Apostolate of Education in the United States, National Consultation* (Washington, D.C.: Jesuit Conference), No. 5, February, 1975, p. 35.

[105] *Ibid.*, p. 39.

[106] *Project 1: The Jesuit Apostolate of Education in the United States, Agreements and Decisions* (Washington, D.C.: Jesuit Conference), No. 6, October, 1975, pp. 11-12.

[107] *Ibid.*, p. 12.

[108] *Ibid.*

[109] *The Jesuit Mission in Higher Education: Letter from the American Provincials,"* (Washington, D.C.: Jesuit Conference), April, 1978, p. 2.

[110] *Ibid.*, pp. 2-3.

[111] *Ibid.*, p. 3.

[112] *Ibid.*, pp. 4-5.

[113] *Ibid.*, pp. 6-7.

[114] *Ibid.*, p. 8.

[115] *Ibid.*, p. 9.

[116] *Ibid.*, p. 10.

[117] *Ibid.*

[118] "Working Policy, Board of Higher Education," General Conference of Seventh-day Adventists, North American Division, January 17, 1973.

[119] *Seventh-day Adventist Philosophy of Higher Education,* 1972, pp. C-D.

[120] *Ibid.*, pp. D-E.

[121] *Ibid.*, pp. E-F.

[122] *Ibid.*, p. G.

[123] *Ibid.*

[124] *Ibid.*, p. H.

[125] *Ibid.*

[126] *Ibid.*

[127] *Ibid.*, pp. I-J.

[128] *Ibid.*, p. J.

[129] *Ibid.*, p. K.

[130] *Ibid.*, p. L.

[131] *Ibid.*, pp. L-M.

[132] "Working Policy, Board of Higher Education," pp. 1-2.

[133] *Reaffirmations,* adopted by the Association of Southern Baptist Colleges and Schools, Williamsburg, Virginia, June, 1976.

[134] *Ibid.*

[135] *Ibid.*

[136] *Ibid.*

[137] *Ibid.*

[138] Earl J. McGrath, *Study of Southern Baptist Colleges and Universities, 1976-77* (Nashville: Education Commission of the Southern Baptist Convention, 1977).

[139] "Baptist Colleges Get Good Report Card," *Southern Baptist Educator*, vol. 41, no. 6 (July–August, 1977), p. 3.

[140] *Ibid.*

[141] McGrath, *op. cit.*, p. 99.

[142] *Ibid.*

[142a] *Ibid.*, p. 96.

[143] "Baptist Colleges Get Good Report Card," *op. cit.*, p. 4.

144 *Ibid.*, pp. 4 and 13.

145 "A Statement of Relationship," approved by the Seventh General Synod of the United Church of Christ, June, 1969, *Educational Institutions Related to the United Church of Christ,* p. 1.

146 *Ibid.*, pp. 1-2.

147 *Ibid.*, p. 2.

148 *Ibid.*, p. 3.

149 *Ibid.*, pp. 4-5.

150 *Ibid.*, p. 5.

151 Miller Upton, "Report to the Members of the Council for Higher Education of the United Church of Christ," mimeographed, June 2, 1976.

152 *Ibid.*, p. 3.

153 *Ibid.*, pp. 3-4.

154 *Ibid.*, pp. 4-5.

155 *Ibid.*, pp. 5-6.

156 *Ibid.*, p. 10.

157 "The Case for Church-Related Higher Education," a statement of the Council for Higher Education of the UCC, *Journal of Current Social Issues,* vol. 14, no. 2 (Spring, 1977), p. 88.

158 *Ibid.*

159 *Ibid.*, p. 89.

160 "Resolution to the Eleventh General Synod of the United Church of Christ," *Journal of Current Social Issues,* vol. 14, no. 2 (Spring, 1977), p. 90.

161 *Ibid.*

162 *The Book of Discipline of the United Methodist Church, 1976* (Nashville: The United Methodist Publishing House, 1976), pp. 470-476.

163 *The Continuing Commission on the Black Colleges,* report to the General Conference of 1976 (Nashville: Division of Higher Education, Board of Higher Education and Ministry. The United Methodist Church, 1976), pp. 5-6.

164 *Ibid.*, pp. 7-9.

165 *Ibid.*, pp. 9-10.

166 *A College-Related Church: United Methodist Perspectives* (Nashville: National Commission on United Methodist Higher Education, 1976), pp. 4-5. Used with permission of the United Methodist Board of Higher Education for the National Commission on United Methodist Higher Education.

167 *Ibid.*, p. 11.

[168] *Ibid.*, pp. 11-12.

[169] *Ibid.*, p. 12.

[170] *Ibid.*, p. 13.

[171] *Ibid.*

[172] *Ibid.*, p. 23.

[173] *To Give the Key of Knowledge: United Methodists and Education, 1784–1976* (Nashville: National Commission on United Methodist Higher Education, 1976), pp. 20-21.

[174] *Ibid.*, pp. 14 and 17.

[175] *Ibid.*, p. 30.

[176] *Toward 2000: Perspectives on the Environment for United Methodist and Independent Higher Education* (Nashville: National Commission on United Methodist Higher Education, 1976), pp. 37-44.

[177] *Ibid.*, p. 45.

[178] *Ibid.*, p. 53.

[179] *Ibid.*, p. 56.

[180] *Endangered Service: Independent Colleges, Public Policy and the First Amendment* (Nashville: National Commission on United Methodist Higher Education, 1976), pp. 87-89.

[181] *Ibid.*, pp. 126-127.

[182] *Ministry on Campus: A United Methodist Mission Statement and Survey Report* (Nashville: National Commission on United Methodist Higher Education, 1977), p. 13. Used with permission of the United Methodist Board of Higher Education for the National Commission on United Methodist Higher Education.

[183] *Ibid.*, p. 53.

[184] *Ibid.*, p. 58.

[185] *Ibid.*, p. 64.

[186] *Ibid.*, p. 17.

[187] *Ibid.*, pp. 19-20.

[188] *Trustee*, vol. 2, no. 5 (October, 1977).

[189] *Ibid.*, p. 2.

[190] *Ibid.*, p. 3.

[191] *Ibid.*, pp. 3-5.

[192] *Ibid.*, pp. 5-7.

[193] *The Church and Related Colleges and Universities: A Statement of Mutual Responsibilities,* adopted by The Presbyterian College Union and The Program Agency, The United Presbyterian Church U.S.A., 1973.

[194] *Ibid.*

[195] *Ibid.*

[196] *Ibid.*

[197] *Ibid.*

[198] *Ibid.*

[199] J. Garber Drushal, *The Church and Its Colleges: A Status Report for The United Presbyterian Church in the U.S.A.,* Mission in Education, The Program Agency, The United Presbyterian Church U.S.A., 1975, p. ii.

[200] *Ibid.,* p. iii.

[201] *Ibid.,* pp. v and iii.

[202] *Ibid.,* p. v.

[203] Robert C. Lodwick, correspondence, February 13, 1978.

CHAPTER 7

Future Church-Culture Relations and Their Impact on Church-Related Higher Education—The Student Nexus

Martin E. Marty

Assumptions

We begin with five assumptions about the future:

A. *Efforts to envision the cultural context of higher education beyond one generation are futile.*

One generation may mean fifteen years, a figure that José Ortega y Gasset advocated with good warrant,[1] or it may mean eighteen years, to match the demographic charts depicting the cohort of already-born, future college student prospects. Beyond that period, cultural shifts are too dramatic to project.

Even eighteen years allows for awesome surprises. Explore the literature of 1959 and you will find that almost no one envisioned, among other possibilities, the following events or trends, each of which deeply affected the culture of church-related colleges:[2]

— The Second Vatican Council, Roman Catholicism's seismic internal shifts and changes related to other forces.

— The international challenges to American preeminence and the war and defeat in Vietnam.

— The opening up of Communist China and the many kinds of accommodation to the Communist world.

— The New Frontier and the Great Society.

— The boom in higher education occasioned in part by the Russian launching of Sputnik the year before and the American desire to remain the technological peer of Russia.

— "The space age," on the scale and at the pace in which it arrived.

— The change in race relations from models of integration to minority self-assertion.

— The revived "women's movement."

— The end of the postwar religious revival insofar as this meant a boom in mainline American religion.

— The cultural awareness of revived Fundamentalism, Evangelicalism, Pentecostalism, and the appearance of Eastern and occult faiths.

— The end of the "baby boom" and the suddenly changed expectations directed toward higher education.

— Student dissent with its accompanying backlash and a subsequent renewed student passivity.

These surprises, chosen out of scores of possibilities, all had dramatic impact on church-related higher education; yet they must have been somehow containable or comprehensible, because there still survive churches and colleges and church-related colleges and college-related churches about which to confer after all the changes.

For the longer future possibilities, even more drastic changes would lead to "all bets are off" circumstances. Of course, these could occur within eighteen years, but they more likely belong to the next century. Let me illustrate:

—Economic breakdown and the "end of business civilization" followed by some sort of controlled economy that demands ideological conformity.[3]

— A societal weariness with terrorism expressed in consequent new and efficient forms of repression.

— Thermonuclear war, lest we forget.

— "Changes in human nature," thanks to cloning and other laboratory devices and efforts.

— Societal need for an encompassing ideology, whether "Christian Democracy" or a systematic secularism.

The illustrations here again may bore readers who deal regularly with future scripting or even average citizens who do their own projections on the basis of the morning papers. They merely illustrate how sufficient unto the eighteen years are the evils or possibilities thereof and suggest that short-range envisionings are of more use than long-range speculation. Pierre Teilhard de Chardin may have worried about how to get us through the next two million years, but we have first the next two decades to think about. Or two years.

B. *Church-culture relations will not remain what they are.*

Most critics of educational or ecclesiastical adaptation to the spirit of the times are unaware of how adapted they are to the spirit of even newer times. Most successful movements play amanuensis to the *zeitgeist* and then act as if *it* will not change. They forget that in a viscous and volatile pluralist culture like that of the United States— especially because of the role of mass media—one law of history has to be remembered above others: nothing lasts. To illustrate from the religious realm—which is certainly appropriate for our topic— halfway through the past generation a number of widely perceived shifts occurred in the culture. These include:

— A premium on personal experience. Religion in higher education has been unforeseeably affected by a turn to spiritual expressions that accent what Pascal called "the passions" and Jonathan Edwards called "the affections." Eastern, occult, charismatic, pentecostal, therapeutic, mystical, "born again," and much evangelical faith, whether Protestant or Catholic, correspond to the widespread secular obsessions with personal experience—even if they have a hedonistic or narcissistic tinge. With R. D. Laing, people seek not theories of experience but the experience that might give rise to theory.[4] This trend has long historic roots in America and further exaggerated the breach between knowledge and piety that has been an intense problem in American religion for over two centuries.[5] During an "experiential" period, church-related higher education need not die, but its accent on knowledge is jeopardized or recast.

— A trend toward authoritarian religion. If "authoritarian" sounds too ideological, let it read merely that people who are religious seek religions that are clear and definite about the sources and contexts of authority and that they tend to reject inquiry, tentativeness, relativity, skepticism, criticism, and ambivalence—all of them normal features of the learning process. The culture imposes this tendency to some extent. Serious social analysts like Robert Nisbet can bewail *The Twilight of Authority*[6] in general human relations; little wonder that religious people, who must chronically wrestle with the problem, feel it acutely at such a time. The erosion of papal authority in Catholicism and biblical authority in Protestantism are two indicators of zones for struggle. Many young people, after having been part of a soft or greened America, later chose repressive "families" or cults as contexts for their living and believing; they wanted decisions made for them. However readily professional sociologists criticized the "impressionism" of Dean Kelley's *Why Conservative Churches Are Growing,*[7] they knew in their bones and from their charts that overall the more authoritarian churches prospered at the expense of those whose boundaries were more ill-defined. The current search for personal identity and social location contributes further to the prosperity of well-defined, clearly bounded, and highly focused religious groups. This has a bearing on the higher educational enterprise for obvious reasons.

— A low premium on theology and religious thought. Whether or not theology has gone into eclipse or died or merely been relocated, there is no question but that the theological enterprise in the formal sense has less impact on church-related colleges and college-related churches than it did some years ago. This is not the place to speculate concerning all the reasons for the change; to what extent has the passing of a generation of geniuses—Tillich, Maritain, Niebuhr, Buber, Berdyaev—been responsible? To what extent has a "brain drain" of theological talent from churchly contexts to the American Academy of Religion orbit deprived the faithful of interpreters? Has the religion of experience simply exhausted the curiosities of people? The point here is that now it is more difficult than twenty or even ten years ago for collegians and church people in general to meet on the grounds of shared theological endeavor.

— A lower valuation on common Christian activity. We must be very careful about this theme: individual believers and local congregations may be enacting the works of love and uttering words of judgment as always. We are here discussing cultural perceptions; it is clear that the society in the recent past was not so regularly hearing pronouncements from church bodies, seeing clerics demonstrating for social causes, or paying attention to a bureaucratic address on the part of the churches. It is possible that the disputes over abortion, the Equal Rights Amendment, and homosexuality are seeing new expressions based on new alignments over new issues; but for some years the societal obsession with or media interest in activism has declined. All this has a bearing on churches' perceptions of the student world, since students and often, in particular, religiously inspired students were at the center of protest, dissent, and social reconstruction in the 1960s.

— An underestimation of the secular. The "cultured despiser" has been giving a free ride to religion for some years. When so many societal norms fell apart in the 1960s, when scientists and humanists called into question the values of science and humanism,[8] public tolerance for new paradigms of spirituality grew. The recent religious revival has led many theologians, anthropologists, and social thinkers to alter drastically their visions of a mono-dimensional or mono-directional trend toward a fully secularized world. In the process they have overemphasized the cultural impact of religious renewals and underestimated the degree to which "operatively," if not "passionally," our culture remains modern, differentiated, pluralistic, and secular. Attacks on the secular tend to come from religious groups who have done the most adapting to the norms of a secular society—capitalist, competitive, consumerist, commercial, and hedonistic as it is. Expect reaction soon to grow against pervasive and highly advertised religiosity and, in the academy at least—but also perhaps in the society of resentful taxpayers and impatient doers— anticipate a renewal of more secular assertion. The spiritual revivals have hardly changed the essential tone of the whole society and have not provided it with new coherence but instead have remained relegated largely to clearly defined spheres, including the private, the familial, the leisured portions of life.

These five accents are characteristic of life in the recent past. They all became culturally current about halfway through the last generation; whoever pictures trying to peddle astrology or the charismatic movement or films about finding Noah's ark on a state university campus in 1962 will recognize that cultural distinctives and norms change constantly. There is no reason to believe that the current ones will remain dominant, and, as here indicated, some are already changing and slipping.

Why may we reasonably expect change? We have already referred to the viscosity of the culture and the principle that "nothing lasts."

To this, one may add various historical theories about the swings of pendulums, the movements of cycles, the lessons from the dynamics of the past. One Hegelian who was asked why, after thesis and antithesis, synthesis did not last, answered: "Because it itches and needs to be scratched." Let it also be said that Christian church-related college leadership well knows that, however legitimate the present accents may be, they do not express the plenitude of the Christian ethos and outlook. Sooner or later thoughtful people try to recover elements of tradition that are overlooked during a particular societal stress.

If prosperous religious movements are in many ways wedded to the *zeitgeist,* what replaces them will also be, to some extent. Far from seeing nothing but wrong in it, it is possible to say that such bonding represents legitimate attempts to meet the changing needs of people. We argue only that such adaptation in any epoch—or half-generation—dare not exhaust the range of responsibilities for religiously informed people. The distinction Alfred Schutz makes between "imposed relevance" and "intrinsic relevance" is here worth adapting to the collegiate and cultural scene.[9] Imposed relevance calls for a response occasioned by the events and ethos of the day. Intrinsic relevance is born of a commitment to a certain truth or value which somehow sooner or later finds expression. Curricularly, it would mean that a college determine what is worth studying and embodying and then find ways to stay with it whether the culture finds this fashionable or not. Often people who know the value of the intrinsic are able to ride out many kinds of competing cultural changes. Anyone who wants to be religious is looking at least for meaning and belonging, but in different decades *how* these are expressed will differ.

C. *Nothing on the present cultural or ecclesiastical scene and nothing portended will make life easier for church-related colleges.*

There may be spotty and temporary exceptions. The recent McGrath report of the Southern Baptist Convention, for example, finds its collegiate complex to be a pocket of prosperity and health, although no presidents of Convention institutions are sitting back and relaxing. Demography is against them; population trends dim the prospect of ever-rising enrollment graphs. The economy cannot be of help; no one pictures helpful declines in the inflation that haunts every private college or a new tax-support that could come on a sufficiently massive scale without jeopardizing the values of the independent college. The valuation citizens place on higher education shows no prospect of increasing sufficiently to enlarge significantly the percentage of eighteen-year-olds who are to be college bound. Churches are not in a position to apportion their budgets in new ways to assure the future of colleges or even to show sudden and profound appreciation of their work.

This third assumption appears here simply to test the threshold of boredom of readers and hearers. These lines serve only to remind everyone that we are aware of the world in which we live and will move, but they do not represent the direct assignment for this paper.

D. *Church-related colleges are among the few bridges between communities of learning and communities of faith.*

What else is available? The theological seminary has been pressed into action beyond the call of duty, but its interests are ordinarily first of all professional; and Christian humanism, or the liberal arts and sciences impulse, has to be screened through nets representing other concerns. Campus ministries and student work as ecclesial expressions have made major contributions, whether on tax-supported or private college campuses. There are lay training centers, movements, and emphasis groups to fill in many gaps. People of expertise in religion departments on secular campuses now and then show interest in the church. Private-enterprising authors can state their cases in books. But with rare exceptions, these contacts are not sustained or sustainable. Neither party takes responsibility for the other, and the agenda tends to be restricted to theological themes as opposed to religious and humane-learning motifs.

The church-related college and the college-related church are not always highly aware of each other; but ties represented by even meager financial bonds, the bearing of a common name, the reminiscence of a covenant ("It's nice to have Old Trinity to remind us of divinity") at least suggest a potential bridge in the future. There are not going to be many new colleges and there are going to be fewer old ones, thanks to demise, collapse, merger, attrition, attenuation, and altered charters. So those that remain cannot hope to be much more than little lights in our new Dark Ages, dug in as monasteries chose to be when they bore responsibility for Christian culture and artifact without concern for augmentation of their numbers or power.

E. *The repertoire of basic styles for church-college relationships is limited, but the variations are infinitely rich.*

A quarter of a century has passed since H. Richard Niebuhr took the fun out of the relational game for others by preempting most of the choices with his prepositions: Christ *against, of,* and *above* culture, or Christ and culture *in* paradox, or Christ the transformer *of* culture.[10] It is hard to go further than to the edges of his spectrum (*against, of*) or to find gaps between the other points—though there may be room for overlapping between "paradox" and "transformation." This is a way of saying that the basic substantive range has been staked out, but that does not mean an exhaustion of practical variations in the church-college arena.

All these five main options may be present within our religious cultures, within a denomination, a specific college, and even, no doubt, within a department. (Yes, there are people who run Christian colleges of liberal arts with the "Christ against culture" culture approach, however paradoxical and in need of transformation that may seem!) Today there are signs that theologians and humanists are working on a range of problems that are corollaries to those raised by Niebuhr. *How* is Christ active in the world *beyond* the church? What is the role of, say, natural law, common grace, or civil righteousness in the Christian scheme for understanding the world and its arts and sciences today? These are all questions for the millennium, but this paper best serves if it seeks not to be reductionist about the options or to seek a personal theological theme for relating church to culture on the collegiate scene. Instead, we shall concentrate on *mechanisms* for relating church and college, allowing for a rich pluralism of understandings as to what is to be related.

Church—College Relations

Needed for tomorrow are people who can envision the relations between church and culture to help make the life of colleges more vivid in the churches, to build bridges between the two differing sets and styles of institutions, and to work out variations on the repertoire of theological options dealing with Christian humanism or liberal arts learning. That cohorts of such people are to be cherished becomes clear from every reading of denominational inquiries into the conditions of church-related colleges and college-related churches, and to their development we shall shortly turn after setting the context.

While church bodies and their bureaus and task forces monitor church-college relations regularly and reflectively and then issue reports as if by spontaneous combustion or in dutiful response to assignment, it is obvious that some crisis or other has occasioned the spate of extensive and impressive surveys and projects just now completed. The laicization of much of Catholic higher education has led to numerous inquiries in the early 1970s, but the McGrath report of the Southern Baptist Convention and the even more broadly based United Methodist Church studies are most indicative of the trend. Hardly less ambitious are the Bruning review for the Lutheran Church in America from 1975 or, typical of efforts by smaller denominations, the study by James H. Lehman for the Church of the Brethren in 1976. A mild request to the sponsor of this study by those of us who were preparing papers produced in a first mailing alone twenty-two official-looking documents from twelve denominations, and the flow of such materials has continued. Many of these make some reference to earlier studies in their denominations, but these date from several decades past, while the current crop comes entirely from the past six years. "Relationships" are clearly on the minds of responsible leaders.

Certainly these studies issue in part from economic concerns, since it would be unrealistic to picture colleges not taking a careful look at expenditures—even in a field where only very, very small percentages of college incomes and church budgets connect in any way. More generously, let us observe that the rebuilding and rethinking of ties results from efforts by colleges to rediscover or reassert their roots and their identity or genius. In the study of any institution, the intentions of the founders and long-term stewards are revelatory through countless transformations. In the current tribalization or balkanization of American cultural and religious life, it is important to know who we are in particular, to whom we belong, what we have come from, what we hope for together. One of the most consistent themes—and it is a good one—in all the studies is that higher educational institutions should discern and build on their particular genius.

Two opposing trends appear or at least are reported on in almost all reports. On one hand, colleges today for the most part do seek better articulated and more self-conscious church relations than they did a few years ago. Of course, it is impossible for schools whose ties were purely vestigial to scramble back and say to Mother Church, "Well, all along, we really have been proud to be your children. Remember us." But where there are living ties or retrievable bonds, the colleges advocate working with them; church leadership, within constraint of budget, seems ready to respond.

The countertrend, also born in part of economic necessity, is often apparent though seldom advocated. That is a further progression of laicization (often the Catholic term) or secularization. The celebrated case of Western Maryland College, where the court went beyond the normal call of duty in asking for removal of symbolic, reminiscent, and valuational ties between the shadow of the church and the reality of the college, is a harbinger. Sometimes these moves, as in Western Maryland, are made with the prospect of gaining tax support of some sort or other; just as often officials hope to change the image of a college—especially in the case of church-related urban universities— to make it attractive to a wider range of potential clienteles. Add to this a frequently reported-on theme that sees some faculty members and students feeling that the cutting of all church ties will enhance freedom of inquiry and improve the quality of education. Without doubt, wide liberation has often happened in the course of the past century, though some of the romanticism about the unfettered secular college may be waning among people who have found some churches more malleable to change and who saw there better defenders of freedom than in an isolated academy. A Roman Catholic university president probably spoke for many when he once told me of his envy of Pope John, who had an easier time reforming a five-hundred-million-member church than this administrator had in changing his five-person sociology department.

Whether we follow the "identity-seeking" or "snuggling up to the churches" trend or the secularizing countertrend, it is clear that the whole subject is easier to bring up and debate in 1978 than it was ten years ago. A reader of the literature from the colleges and the churches finds there great care, some daring, a passion for inclusiveness—and then comes away feeling that everything has been tried. In my case, after studying three or four major discussions of college-church relationships and religion-culture discourses, it seemed most worthwhile to ask whether any niches or crannies in the college ecology were consistently overlooked in charters for the future. One stood out, and after some appropriate introduction and qualification we shall enlarge on it.

Almost every study remembers that relationships have to be somehow borne by persons. The reports will not effect new ties, nor will more attractive brochures. *People* have to commute, make the transit, and form bonds between the vastly differing communities and intentions implied by the word "college" and "church." Almost all the authors keep referring to the term "critical mass" to designate these people until they start saying things like "the oft referred-to critical mass" or "the critical mass, if I may report to what is becoming a cliché." There must be some critical mass—the mathematical weight in each circumstance is up for debate—or no persons will care and there will be no relations. It is as simple as that. If there is no churchly or communally religious "presence" or if it is too small, the school will lose its identity and the church will not care. The question next is, who must make up this critical mass?

The answers are quite consistent. First, caring people in churches are needed, a minority of people who can be awakened to take the responsibility of being college-related churches. Second, trustees, it goes without saying, are crucial. If no one on the board cares, relationships will wither. So with administrations. Most attention is paid to faculties, which one study calls the "witnesses" to the church for colleges. Everything that follows in this paper implies involvement of faculties, but we have nothing new to say on this much-explored topic. It is best to recommend the existing literature which includes all the debates about percentages, expressions of "critical mass," attitudes of those faculty who do not share interest in church relations, the substance of what their caring might mean, and the like. The searcher for ecological niches and crannies still to fill has to move on because the faculty slot is the most crowded.

The great overlooked potential embodiments of "relationship" are the *students* (and alumni, though limits of time and space impel us to keep overlooking them). Treatment of the student potential in most studies is quite consistently perfunctory. It usually shows up in a paragraph or two, but almost never does it receive systematic treatment. An exception is the outline of "Questions for Institutional and Denominational Self-Study," which is background for this colloquy (see Section I of this book). It includes sixty-two questions; a generous twelve of these do explicitly mention students and more imply them. Thus one of them asks whether the college's relationship to the church is defined and represented only by the president or also by trustees, faculty, and students. Another asks to what extent do four constituencies—faculty, students, administration, and trustees—perceive that their expectations regarding the meaning of church relationship are being achieved. Again, do student-led organizations understand their responsibility in fostering a student culture or atmosphere which supports the denomination's concerns? Does the college's practice and culture foster lay initiative by students and faculty or a hierarchical trickling down of values and tradition? These four are basic, and the others are corollaries of or supports for them. The concerns for students are *not* anticipated in much of the recent denominational literature and may have appeared in our agenda because the planners sensed a void.

Why overlook the numerically largest constituent of the colleges? Depending upon one's view of original sin, there are any number of possible answers. Students are overlookable because student bodies tend to be more amorphous and evanescent than trustees, administration, and faculty. Paternalists tend to shun them; veterans of the 1960s, some still bruised from contacts with misguided students or wised-up from seeing many student misdiagnoses of power in the governance of colleges, have not yet rebuilt trust. The almost proverbial student apathy today, or an engrossment with vocational-ism in the 1970s, may cause elders to bypass students at the moment when perhaps they most need to be challenged. Experts in the history of tradition or religion further well know that older adolescents, while probing their own identity and values, are one of the less stable elements for perpetuating a culture or system. And some people may have tried everything on the student front and failed, only to dismiss students from consideration.

At this point the historian in me wants to attempt to gain some confidence from skeptics by pointing to the record. Well aware as we are that historical circumstances and contingencies do not line up the same way twice, it is still possible to be informed by paths taken before, by choices people have taken. Thesis: in the matter of church movements,* at least in the past two centuries of American Protestantism, the two most ambitious and even intoxicating movements had their roots and early spread among students on campuses.

The first of these was the worldwide expansion of Protestantism through a missionary movement before the nation itself was filled up or churched. Think what one will of such missions, they have world-historical significance in the modernization process. The British Marxist historian E. J. Hobsbawm lists Anglo-American Protestant expansionism as the most startling religious response to *The Age of Revolution.*[11] He may account for it on capitalist-imperial grounds. John A. Andrew III has recently suggested convincingly that in America missionary effort represented first of all a New England attempt to recoup status and losses in the competition of churches and the attempt to build a certain style of Protestant empire.[12] Others attribute the outbreak to the work of the Holy Spirit. No matter, the combustion came in the 1810s from collegians and then seminarians, from Samuel J. Mills and his circle at Williams College and Andover Seminary, from Amherst, eventually from Princeton, and elsewhere. The movement soon "trickled up" into a voluntary network in which students shared space with voluntary associations, bureaucracies, clerical promoters, and the like. But they both responded to new initiatives and helped create a fresh climate. The movement had impressive intellectual underpinnings in the thought of Jonathan Edwards and Samuel Hopkins; it paid attention to technological change in transportation and communication and to issues in many practical policies, all of which have relations to collegiate life.

Near the end of the century, coming to a first fruition almost exactly a century after the missionary outbreak, was the first ecumenical stirring in North America, one that connected the United States with much of the rest of the world. Here the dominating figure was John R. Mott, who worked with the decade-old missionary network on campus, with the YMCA and the Student Volunteer Movement, and the World Student Christian Federation that he helped found to stimulate interchurch activity first on campus and

*In this paper we do *not* restrict the meaning of "church" to "supporting denominations." The contexts usually make the usages clear.

then on the postgraduate level. This activity went far beyond Protestantism into contact with Catholics, the Orthodox, and, in the subsequent decades of his long life, other world religions. From bases at Upper Iowa University and then Cornell University, Mott found other students who shared his vision and they soon transmitted it to congregations and denominations.[13] The student impetus in ecumenism lasted well beyond the formative years of the conciliar and federative stages of ecumenism.

Both of these accents, though they seem so remote in context that they look medieval, live on in the conservative evangelical colleges and may account for some of the more visible ties there to supporting churches. The missionary and evangelizing accent is obvious, but there has also been increasing support for "Lausanne-type" ecumenical endeavor and some social activism in the network of evangelical students.

For this new need among evangelical students and to work out the bases of a new Christian humanism or to bridge church-related colleges with college-related churches, there will have to be stimulants for students to do much of the theorizing and acting. Mills and Mott and their kind did not generate their activity without encouragement or without tutelage, though they soon seized initiative. Have the new needs for relationship been spelled out for any "critical mass" or core of students?

On the contemporary scene, we are aware of some kinds of activities already present, particularly in the Southern Baptist Convention colleges and among the smaller peace churches like the Mennonites and the Church of the Brethren, who have systems of study and work projects that make the larger church body aware of the campuses. Among the larger main-line churches, very little activity of this sort on an intercollegiate and interdenominational basis is apparent. The campus student movements tend to be demoralized, the churches unaware of their activity.

Every report we have read stresses the need for "more and better communication." First, there must be something to communicate and then there must be communicators. For this the concept of the "critical mass" is helpful but not quite accurate, since it stresses numbers more than perspective. For some years I have been impressed by proposals of José Ortega y Gasset in the *Mission of the*

University.[14] His university and its contexts differ so vastly from our colleges and their settings that at first it seems a strain to connect them. His program has been misread by people as well read as Clark Kerr, who thought Ortega was interested mainly in turning universities over to students. Ortega also slighted the role of inquiry and research in the life of the university. He is easy to misunderstand, and at this point we need only snatch an aspect of one scheme.

Ortega thought that to fulfill the mission of the university as a bearer of culture there must be what he called a "culture faculty," a core of people who were ready to risk interdisciplinary conversation and take responsibility for the main themes and intentions of the culture. Such faculty elements exist almost everywhere already in our skein of college and university. They are not and need not be—shall one say *dare* not be?—segregated or endowed with badges and honors and club names. All that is necessary is some consciousness-raising, some increase of awareness that a certain number of people have to look beyond routine and pay check and discipline to the care not only of the college but also of its relation to church.

To go one step further with Ortega, there has to be a kind of external relational "culture student body." Here again, let me argue that nuclei of these already exist. Any of us who have toured the campus circuit for a couple of decades could visit most church-related colleges for two or three days and, after even such superficial contact, put the names of a number of students in an envelope, knowing that an astonishing number of these some years later will turn up as transmitters of that college's vision in a variety of callings and disciplines. This list would include a melange of sacred and secular, orthodox and heretical, curricularly bounded and extracurricularly driven editors, musicians, theologues, nettlers of faculties, bull sessionists, and scholars, who somehow have caught what their common venture is all about. Such a collection provides much of the cohort for being the "Christian culture" or "church-related" or "humanist" student body that, with all its varieties and ambiguities, can do much for church relations. Not all administrations, faculties, and hierarchs would trust these students to serve as commuters between the two spheres, but no one else more responsible or potentially effective seems to be in sight.

(It is obvious from the past two paragraphs that I would not be welcome at a gathering of the task forces that are following upon the mandates of the Nairobi World Council of Churches Assembly on church-related educational institutions. That council asked for help for "member churches to reappraise the role of church-sponsored schools in order to liberate them from elitism and from the heritage which hinders their real participation in human development and nation building." Though we are mindful of Third World necessities, it is still not clear that "nation-building" is always the best way to carry out divine mandates and to serve human purpose. It is certainly not proven that educational elites must *a priori* hinder human development—most of the creative and revolutionary leadership has come from educational elites! It may be possible to distinguish between elitism, which is bad, and the need for elites, which is not, but there seems to be a more romantic note in this WCC paragraph.[15] In any case, the approach we advocate here frankly calls for an elite. Non-elite or anti-elite education is a contradiction in terms. A ghetto child who goes to nursery school has joined an elite.)

The historical illustrations provided so far have probably suggested that the emphasis upon students has to do with voluntary associations and extracurricular activity, but more than that is necessary. The development of these "relators" is a curricular responsibility as well. Here is a splendid field for field workers in anthropology and researchers in sociology, a case study for historians and psychologists. Such an approach builds in an extension of "sociology of knowledge." The philosophical problems, the issues of freedom, the realities of everyday life embodied by all that is meant by "church" are often now more neglected at church-related colleges than at their wholly secular counterparts. It is not difficult to get a discussion of church power, tax exemption, church and state, or religious behavior on secular campuses. Church-related colleges must take special responsibility for making provisions for such topics.

The denominational reports we read show that the authors are aware of this sociology of knowledge, of the circumstantiality or perspectivalism that goes into the very conception of schools in different traditions. The United Church of Christ authors speak of their covenantal tradition; the Mennonites say they are concerned with "peoplehood education." Some of the Lutherans urge that they are extending Luther's concept of the calling. Do students, even in the fields that study such ideas, have a chance to explore what these mean in their traditions and schools and churches?

Of course, beyond the classroom, this "critical core" will inevitably find extracurricular expressions, and some of these should lead to formal contact with the church at large. Just as "church" has not meant only "denomination" on these pages, so it does not here mean only "congregations." If collegians are engaged with the culture on ecumenical and nonparochial bases, they will also better understand and be visible to or in contact with congregations or denominations that connect with their schools. Certainly the makeup of this set of "relators" on campuses would not be restricted to members of the related denomination. Such a conformity would be even less necessary here than in the faculty instance, where most proposals suggest that a certain number at least must be from the sponsoring group. The Church of the Brethren campuses, for example, include only 14.5 percent of students from Brethren churches, yet the churchly ethos spreads far beyond the card-carrying members in student bodies.

These proposals that call for trust toward students for transmission in both directions, college and church, may sound foolish and utopian. I have suggested, however, that there is historical warrant for some faith in their potential, and I have no doubt that were one to chart where churches have comprehended and supported colleges, they have been in most contact with students. If the students catch the idea, faculties will be freer to be better "witnesses," and administrations and trustees will not bear so much of the weight of connection nor feel so isolated in their bridging work.

From the mainline churches, one can expect to hear suggestions that rebuilding church ties through students, because of the pluralism of student bodies and the broad range of ideas tolerated among them, will lead to a new repressiveness on the part of these sponsors. Curiously, the churches where there is almost no danger of such outside interference—the United Church of Christ, the American Baptist Churches, the Episcopal Church, and the like—include the most reports of worriers about potential limitations on freedom. One can lie awake quite a number of hours wracking brains trying to picture just how those churches as churches would act to enforce any orthodoxy at this date in history. The clienteles, to be sure, might not like everything they see upon contact; neither now do alumni/ae associations of secular schools, or state legislatures, parents, faculties, or fellow students. But to keep from view the actual character of a school seems to be either disingenuous or a sign of bad faith. Our proposal may not mean that church-related colleges whose churches do insist on rather severe boundaries to intellectual freedom would loosen up tomorrow, but the students would inevitably begin some task of education, if not by design then simply by the fact of their own varieties.

The point of all these relations is not simply public relations. The intention behind the stimulation of relators and even a network of students engaged in developing church ties is not simply a growth in awareness on the part of financial supporters. Church bodies as such generally provide a very small percentage of college budgets and will continue to do so. Instead, our interest is substantive, in the character and content of the transmission from both sides. Students—certainly then followed by faculty members—who are somehow engaged with religious movements, voluntary associations, congregations, judicatories, task forces, conventions, and other expressions would have a sort of pedagogical role toward the churches and churches in turn would make their impact on the student and faculty worlds. At present, where there are no such ties, it must be said that the college-related church acts out of habit or with a sense of responsibility but gets nothing directly in return. And similarly at present, students now can spend four years at a church-related college and not only have no direct awareness but might even have total ignorance that such a tie exists at all. Neither side gets much return on an investment if only a president and board of trustees are conscious of a tie.

The United Methodist Church study speaks of the church-related college as being one of Edmund Burke's "little platoons" that stands between the individual and the encompassing state.[16] At the moment the churches are not feeling the effects of that "little platoon." If a little student "platoonlette" were to form on each campus and each became part of an informal nexus between campuses, without doubt people on both sides of the hyphens in the words "church-related-college" would become increasingly aware of the other. Last of all, but not least of all, such an approach would have great educational value because it would demonstrate to another generation of students the ways in which traditions, like Jewish and Christian, possess them even where students do not possess the traditions and that to negate the traditions is not to be rid of them. Fresh grappling with the traditions on the part of students would without question trickle up beyond faculty to administrations and boards and clienteles who also are both possessors and possessed by the lineages.

This approach toward reactivating student involvement in church relations may seem foolish to some and inordinately modest to others. When in crisis—and every report agrees that we are in crisis—it seems wise to work on the least developed fronts. If no gains can be made on this one, it is not likely that all the reports and study guides, all the public relations efforts and brochures will have the slightest impact at all on the future of church-culture relations.

NOTES—Chapter 7

[1] For an elaboration of the generational motif in Ortega and others, see Julian Marias, *Generations* (University, Ala.: University of Alabama Press, 1970).

[2] For comparison, see Geoffrey Barraclough in *An Introduction to Contemporary History* (New York: Basic Books, Inc., Publishers, 1965). On p. 29, the author argues that around 1960 "contemporary history" began. He summarized many features of the kind of world that now looks obsolete.

[3] Robert Heilbroner, in *Business Civilization in Decline* (New York: W. W. Norton & Co., Inc., 1976), is among many who picture vast ideological consequences along with basic economic shifts.

[4] R. D. Laing is quoted by Theodore M. Roszak, *The Making of a Counter Culture* (New York: Doubleday & Co., Inc., 1969), p. 49.

[5] The familiar statement of this case in the field of education appears in Richard Hofstadter, *Anti-Intellectualism in American Life* (New York: Alfred A. Knopf, Inc., 1963), part 2, pp. 55 ff.

[6] See Robert Nisbet, *Twilight of Authority* (New York: Oxford University Press, 1975).

[7] Dean M. Kelley, *Why Conservative Churches Are Growing* (New York: Harper & Row, Publishers, Inc., 1972).

[8] Typical of this literature is Theodore Roszak, *Where the Wasteland Ends* (New York: Doubleday & Co., Inc., 1973).

[9] See Alfred Schutz and Thomas Luckmann, *Structures of the Life-World* (Evanston: Northwestern University Press, 1973), pp. 152 ff.

¹⁰ H. Richard Niebuhr, *Christ and Culture* (New York: Harper & Row, Publishers, Inc., 1951).

¹¹ E. J. Hobsbawm, *The Age of Revolution: 1789-1848* (Cleveland: World Publishing Co., 1962), pp. 217 ff.

¹² John A. Andrew III, *Rebuilding the Christian Commonwealth* (Lexington: The University Press of Kentucky, 1976); see also Clifton J. Phillips, *Protestant America and the Pagan World: The First Half Century of the American Board of Commissioners for Foreign Missions, 1810–1860* (Cambridge: Harvard University Press, 1969).

¹³ See Basil Mathews, *John R. Mott, World Citizen* (New York: Harper & Row, Publishers, Inc., 1934).

¹⁴ José Ortega y Gasset, *Mission of the University* (New York: W. W. Norton & Co., Inc., 1944), pp. 36 ff., 75.

¹⁵ "Programme for Church-Sponsored or Church-Related Educational Institutions," mimeographed report, appendix I.

¹⁶ John W. Donahue, "A Church-Related College," *America* (September 10, 1977), p. 124.

RESPONSE

Mary C. Kraetzer

No one knows who will live in this cage in the future, or whether at the end of this tremendous development entirely new prophets will arise, or there will be a great rebirth of old ideas and ideals, or, if neither, mechanized petrification. . . .[1]

We are indebted to Professor Martin E. Marty for expanding the horizons of our discussion. Clearly the subject of the future of church-related higher education requires consideration within a holistic perspective.

Floyd Matson noted that "the historic reliance of the social sciences upon metaphors and routine methods appropriated from classical mechanics has eclipsed the ancestral liberal vision of 'the whole man, man in person' (to use Lewis Mumford's phrase)—and has given us instead a radically broken self-image."[2] The fragmented mechanistic-rationalistic paradigm of the "established" social sciences produced the peculiar conditions observed by Errol Harris:

> The salient characteristic of our time is the conspicuous contrast between the achievements of the human intellect in science and technics and its abysmal failures in the spheres of morals and politics.[3]

Both scholars make some rather unfounded assumptions. The social sciences were and are still not monolithic, as Matson claims. Not all social scientists agree with Harris that the successes of science and technology are primarily the products of reason. The scholars who question the supremacy of reason in human events can be loosely aggregated as the "philosophers of life" as against the "philosophers of the machine." "The philosophers of life" insist that human events grounded in emotion, in charisma,[4] are as important as the ones governed primarily by rationality. In general, they envision history as a current of potentially creative human experiences, sometimes giving birth to creative forms of social structures.

Confrontation between the mechanists-rationalists and the philosophers of life is deeply rooted in the American experience and became especially vivid in the historical conflict between Jonathan Edwards and Charles Chauncey. Edwards insisted that "religious affections" were as important as evidence of election for admission to the Lord's Supper and, therefore, admission to the membership in the congregation, as were the rational briefs and material signs of "visible sainthood." The American pragmatists, especially Dewey,[5] are heirs of Jonathan Edwards.

The philosophers of life strongly believe that affections must be taken seriously and that emotion rather than reason may be the source of human creativity. No one can argue the case of the philosophers of life better than they themselves can.

Life, according to Georg Simmel, in its entirety wells up the contents of human experience as feelings. Eventually, the surfaced feelings may surge into a receptive social form. "Piety," according to him, "is an emotion of the soul, which turns into religion whenever it projects itself into specific form." It often crystallizes into the "group life we call peaceableness." Religion, in Simmel's image of reality ranks as the highest of human expressions of sociality. "Religion welds human society together and comes to the fore in social conduct, in customs, and social interplay."[6]

In the *Elementary Forms of Religious Life*, Emile Durkheim also perceived religion as the epitome of social life, of collective sentiments, but he also explored other feeling-generated human events.

When individual minds are not isolated but enter into close relation with and work upon each other, from their synthesis arises a new kind of psychic life. It is clearly distinguished by its peculiar intensity from that led by the solitary individual. *Sentiments born and developed in the group have a greater energy than purely individual sentiments.* This is a world not only more intense but also qualitatively different.

It is . . . at such moment of collective ferment that are born the great ideals upon which civilizations rest. The periods of creation or renewal occur when men for various reasons are led into a closer relationship with each other, when reunions and assemblies are most frequent, relationships better maintained and the exchange of ideas most active. Such was the great crisis of Christendom, the movement of collective enthusiasm which, in the twelfth and thirteenth centuries, bringing together in Paris the scholars of Europe gave birth to Scholasticism. Such were the Reformation and Renaissance, the revolutionary epoch and the Socialist upheavals of the nineteenth century. At such moments this higher form of life is lived with such intensity and exclusiveness that it monopolizes all minds to the more or less complete exclusion of egoism and the commonplace. At such times the ideal tends to become one with the real, and for this reason men have the impression that the time is close when the ideal will in fact be realized and the Kingdom of God established on earth.[7]

An important investigation in modern times of what we, after Max Weber, called charismatic events was conducted by the historian and philosopher of science, Thomas S. Kuhn. In his book *The Structure of Scientific Revolution,* Kuhn suggested that advancement in the natural sciences proceeds not in a gradual, rational, cumulative, evolutionary fashion but surges forth in almost Kierkegaardian leaps of faith. When a given scientific paradigm fails to serve as an efficient guide to the solution of scientific puzzles, the ensuing crisis brings about the conditions for an abrupt changeover to a new perspective, new general rules of scientific conduct. The transition from one paradigm to another is not a rational event but, as Kuhn suggests, resembles conversions or Gestalt switches.[8]

Humans in general seem to be endowed with an ability to develop the capacity for transcendental experience during which either individuals or social aggregates can revitalize, renew, or create motivating authority structures—the blueprints for human conduct. Such motivating structures are extremely important in all aspects of human advancement because they enable humans to act against overwhelming odds. If indeed the transcendental experiences or the capacity for them were removed or totally inhibited, then quite likely human development would cease.

The fragmentation and expropriation of authentic and relatively free human experiences have provided for us a broken image of social reality. Power-geared societies tend to suppress and expropriate not only the "religious affections" but also the "creative affections" in all aspects of social life and consequently destroy transcendental authority which rests on transcendental experience. In a power-geared society, a person refrains from theft out of fear of apprehension. The motivational structure of authority-geared societies, on the other hand, relies on interiorization and commitment to principles/ideals—values. In an authority-geared society, a person will not steal because he or she sincerely believes that stealing is wrong for some transcendental reason—e.g., religious or political.

In authority-geared societies, transcendental experience of all kinds is institutionally maintained. Consequently, religious life and its expression play a vital, creative role in the social history and individual biography. Traditionally, the authority-generating institutions were religion, education, and often the family. Yet the power-generating institutions, such as the economy, polity (including military), technology and, in modern times, mass media, as C. Wright Mills suggested, have come to dominate the authority-generating institutions.

In power-geared societies, authentic transcendental experiences, if any, are channeled into artificially created forms. The function of such devices is to preserve the status quo by providing safety valves. One of the most vivid indicants of power-geared societies is the resurgence of retreatist religious movements in which the personal, rather than the social, religious experience predominates. The rapid growth of cults modeled after Eastern religions is but an import of religious forms from societies in which change was once hopeless.

In general, societal dynamics can be perceived as a dialectic between power and authority, between social control and social self-regulation. The foundation of power is force; the basis of authority is charisma. Max Weber suggested that the first changes humankind from without, through external manipulation, whereas the other changes from within, through conversions in charismatic events. The first can be accomplished with scientific, technological, economic, political, or legal means. The other occurs through changes in images of reality, values, identities, and the like.

When the institutions facilitating transcendental capacity and experiences are impaired, the entire social fabric begins to disintegrate. The liberating human events which pave the way for creativity and for authority-generating institutions are authentic openness to the human phenomena described by Weber, Simmel, Durkheim, and Kuhn and acknowledged by the philosophers of life in general.

NOTES

[1] Max Weber, *The Protestant Ethic and the Spirit of Capitalism* (New York: Charles Scribner's Sons, 1930), p. 182.

[2] Floyd W. Matson, *The Broken Image: Man, Science and Society* (New York: George Braziller, Inc., 1964), pp. vii-viii.

[3] Errol Harris, "Reason in Science and Conduct," *Human Values and Natural Science,* Ervin Laszlo, ed. (New York: Gordon and Breach, Science Publishers, Inc., 1970), p. 95.

[4] Drawing on the insights of Max Weber, Robert Nisbet provides a workable definition of charisma. "Charisma may be found in every sphere and at every level of society. Its essence is simply possession of—or belief in possession of—supra-rational qualities by an individual that are variously deemed prophetic, sacred, and transcendental." Robert A. Nisbet, *The Sociological Tradition* (New York: Basic Books, Inc., Publishers, 1967), p. 253.

[5] John Dewey, *Art as Experience* (New York: Minton Books, 1934). See especially pages 67-81.

[6] Georg Simmel, *Sociology of Religion* (New York: Philosophical Library, Inc., 1959), p. 27.

[7] Emile Durkheim, *Sociology and Philosophy* (London: Cohen and West, Ltd., 1953), pp. 91-92.

[8] Thomas S. Kuhn, *The Structure of Scientific Revolution,* 2nd ed. (Chicago: University of Chicago Press, 1970).

RESPONSE

Wesley A. Hotchkiss

I am very appreciative of Martin Marty's focus on the students because I have a feeling that this is the key to the issue. I don't have much argument with him about his proposition that the future is difficult to predict. I'll accept that. I think I see in our colleges, in a few places, a great regression in the whole matter of students and the attitude of the academy toward the students. I was involved in the redrafting of the governance mechanism for one of our colleges just recently. And I was appalled with the new form of governance that the faculty and campus community came out with; it put the students back in the sandbox. It looked like something in the pre-1960s. This may be more widespread than we think.

The use of Alfred Shutz's observations on "imposed relevance" and "intrinsic relevance" in Mr. Marty's paper were very helpful, and I tried in my mind to relate those to his marks of church-culture relations of our time, to the five qualities or descriptions that characterized present church-culture relations—the emphasis on personal experience, the authoritarianism, the low estimate of theology and religious thought, the low estimate of Christian activity in the customary sense, and the underestimation of the power of the secular. I was wondering if those together, taken as a body, could characterize the religious situation of the present student generation. Do they represent an "imposed relevance" and should we accept it or should we rail against it and try to establish some "intrinsic relevance" concepts and try to change the situation? Or should there be a tyrannic kind of balance between them? These are a few of the questions I had as I went through the paper. There is a sense in which we ought to respond to the market. I think that is not just opportunism. I think that's being relevant. And whether or not it's imposed or intrinsic I'm not too sure. But it may be smart.

I found the concepts about the bridges a very informing one. Many traditional things can be said about learning and faith bridges. But as I thought about this, it occurred to me that what we are seeing here perhaps is a very strange paradox that may be unique to our generation. And this paradox is vaguely hinted at in Dr. Marty's paper. It is a paradox particularly for us who are in the liberal-rationalist part of the contemporary Christian community and it has to do with the confusion of the role of the academy for us. The concept of the prophetic academy, which we hold, is based on the biblical concept of the role of the prophets as those persons who brought the rational, ethical judgments of God to bear on the mystical, irrational, and unethical practices of the religious community. That is where the schools of the prophets came down. And so in this sense they were the secularists of their day. Now in the social-activist end of the liberal-rationalist movement, the prophetic always had to do with social action; but in this context the church college, the prophetic academy, has to do with the balance between rational judgment and an irrational excess of ecstasy that ends up as being unethical or having some kind of idolatrous sin connected with it. So the prophets are the rationalists of the period.

The paradox is this: In liberal rationalism the religious community is subverted by the rational empirical outlook, and in a sense, Mr. Marty is implying that the new religious movements in the academy are expected to help liberal rationalism overcome this seduction. It is almost a reversal of roles. There may be here something of a confusion between the church and the academy for us liberal, rational Protestants. And one reason why I am so pleased that we have been able to get along with each other in this pluralism is that I look over at the left end of Merrimon Cuninggim's continuum and I see the Mennonites out there, and they don't seem to be in the dilemma we are in over on this end. Maybe the next conference should be on the theological implications of the confusion of roles in this continuum. If we did the proper preparation for that discussion from a purely theological point of view, even Christologically, it might be a very interesting experience.

So what we are saying is that the church—or at least one significant part of it—is already excessively rational. Its great need is for ecstasy or at least, to put it a little less pejoratively for some of us, a rebirth of the nonrational, intuitive apprehension of symbolic reality. And if we are looking to the academy to help us do that, it is almost a paradoxical reversal of roles. So when Mr. Marty points, rather nostalgically, one senses, to the intoxicating student movements of the past, he is really asking for a departure from the traditional role of the prophetic academy and in fact for almost a reversal of roles between church and academy. Now I appreciate the fact that he is not a romantic or a sentimentalist and he understands the dangers and the limitations of romanticizing the student movements which we, in our dull kind of rationalism, look so longingly at.

So—and here I agree with him—the students are the key to these new relationships, and the confusion of the roles of church and academy, I think, points up the central question underlying this confusion, which is the way in which these purposes are expressed in both method and curriculum. It is the question of the sociology of knowledge or the definition of knowledge—the epistemological question. The fact is that both the church and the academy have been seduced by the dead hand of empirical rationalism. Now this is a bias of mine, and I will be glad to move away from it—if I have to. We need the help of this generation of students in order to define the new synthesis of these two modes of operation. And the cry for help comes from both the church and the academy. For those of us who are working primarily in church bureaucracies, particularly in our brand of liberal rational Protestantism, we know too well how desperately we need this help, because our survival, too, is really at stake. And unless we can find these purposes, we may not survive. But I would agree with Martin Marty in taking care that we not romanticize these demonstrations, these evidences of new religious forms, for I am not sure that the new emergent form of the church is there on the campus yet. It may be, however, and we should stand by and discern as well as we can to see if it might possibly be emerging.

But I have some skepticism at that point. I think there may be more possibility in the arts than in these newer forms of emergent religion. Perhaps it is just because we in the liberal-rationalist part of the Christian community can deal with the arts more safely than we can with these charismatics. We cannot build a sawdust trail to the new religion. Maybe there are others who can, but we cannot. The arts can do this for us, even with the emergence of the new charismatic camp. It may be that in both church and college the arts have a chance to build the bridges between those two modes of thought, and that is Mr. Marty's whole point. And then we—school, church, and academy—may be able to walk over those bridges to some rebirth of imaginative vision.

In reading Professor Marty's paper, I was particularly struck with the broadening of the context of the discussion which his paper provided, and it seemed to me a necessary correction of some of the earlier discussions of religion and church-relatedness. So I saw this positively in terms of the movement of the total society. I was particularly struck with Marty's assessment of what seemed to be two critical trends as described in the following:

> The recent religious revival has led many theologians, anthropologists, and social thinkers to alter drastically their visions of a mono-dimensional or mono-directional trend toward a fully secularized world. In the process they have overemphasized the cultural impact of religious renewals and underestimated the degree to which "operatively," if not "passionally," our culture remains modern, differentiated, pluralistic, and secular.

This is really a subject of considerable concern to me. In looking over the literature in the field, it seems to me that there are two somewhat, or at least apparently, contradictory trends being described. The first, which I would call the "persistence of religion hypothesis," recognizes the renewed interest in religion and vitalization in some of the religious denominations; and the second, the decreasing influence of religion over social affairs, or what is glibly referred to in the social sciences as the "secularization process." And I find it useful in trying to reconcile the contradictory sets of data to go back to the ordering of institutions proposed by C. Wright Mills—that on the one hand, the economic, political, and military institutions are pivotal in shaping the cultural matrix, whereas on the other hand, the family, religion, and education are basically institutions that are influenced by and shaped within the matrix formed by the others. If you work on this assumption, it is somewhat discouraging both in terms of religion and the educational institution. However, I think it is realistic. It seems to make sense out of the two areas of data. If you look, on the one hand, to the role of multinationalism in society, then the role of education and religion is somewhat lessened. However, if we have made this distinction, then the areas of revitalization can be identified, and they are particularly within the family or the sphere of leisure. This is where, it seems to me, most of the religious revitalization of late seems to have taken place.

My other area of concern has been the question of what seems to me to be a kind of detachment in our discussion from what is the foundation of sects, denominations, churches, and the like, and that is the question of religiosity. Drawing on Simmel, who said that religiosity begets religion, not vice versa, and upon Jonathan Edwards who said the religious effects of a rational, altered state of consciousness were manifestations of human creativity, I would relate these areas to what Gronowsky tried to do in his work in linking high levels of scientific creativity with artistic creativity and what Thomas Hume did for the scientific revolution in trying to explain the development of new paradigms and new visions which periodically enfuse the scientific realm. It seems to me that we have to look into any area within sociological literature that might be helpful in this regard—these that I've mentioned plus the classics. Weber's discussion of charisma—the ability of some individuals to enthuse people—is relatively well known. But even more striking is the work of Durkheim, in an area that is not particularly well known: his concept of angelic idealism, or those periods of collective ferment from which new ideals or new visions are born that seem to support or provide an integrating experience.

It is in this area of attempting to provide a collective integrating experience—the kind of thing Douglas Sloan is talking about in relation to epistemology, or what I would see in terms of a collective spirit—that we have relatively few experiences. It is in this area that we are in danger. We do not really have, by virtue of the main thrust of the society, experiences which strengthen creativity, regardless of the form it takes, whether in religion, in art, or in science.

RESPONSE

Edward B. Lindaman

Future Tense: Someone has said, "The future is mutually shared time and space." It is good to begin in a "future tense." Dr. Marty's first assumption is that the future cultural context of higher education is essentially futile to predict. Predicting, which has unfortunately become a cliché connected with futurism, is not really futurism. Higher education, as well as many other societal institutions, needs to *shift from predicting to envisioning the preferred future.* If church-relatedness in higher education means anything, it ought to mean the liberal arts tradition assisting the church to vision the preferred future set forth in the Christian myth and to do this within the paradigm of a global technological society.

Dynamism: Dr. Marty's second assumption that church-culture relations will not stay as they now are provides us with an important setting, a context which says that there *is* more to come. The nature of any future horizon is that as you move toward it, it changes. Even after you pass it by and it becomes the past, it is subject to change. We need constant reminders that our interaction with the past, present, and future is dynamic. Again this is an argument for church-relatedness. In the midst of such dynamism, not all of which is positive, there is need for the stabilizing aspect, the roots, the story of our Christian heritage.

Difficulties: Assumption three, that life will not be easier for church-related colleges, is more of a prediction than an assumption, perhaps. It sounds logical, but again one could argue that, as the population of college students grows (after a temporary decline in the middle eighties) and large universities become even larger, the smaller church-related institutions will become far more attractive by virtue of their ability to deal with students in a human, personal way.

Bridges: That church-related colleges are among the few bridges that integrate faith with learning is perhaps the most powerful assumption in support of the whole concept of church-relatedness! This is the "why" of church-relatedness. It is the basis of our very existence. Father William Lynch, in *Images of Faith,* says that "faith patterns facts, it recomposes them in accordance with its terms," which means, of course, that faith does not *add* to knowledge; it precedes knowledge.[1] The future of society will depend upon the images that faith provides to facts.

Styles: Assumption number five reminds us that, though basic styles of church-college relationships are limited, the variations are infinitely rich. There is an open-endedness about how the Christian message can be made relevant to society. Theology may be the queen of sciences, but in our scientifically oriented world we are hearing the voice of God through physics, biology, and astronautics, as well as music, art, and literature. The richness of the future expressions of the faith, as the universe continues to open up to us, is staggeringly profound. It ranges from the possibility of extraterrestrial life to the non-Newtonian concept of relationships in the nucleus of the atom in quantum physics.

Students: It is easy to fall into the trap of assuming that faculty, administration, and trustees are the real key to church-relatedness, but Marty is right; history says differently. Students are the key. Yet an administration openly committed to the Christian stance, a faculty holding diverse faith perspectives, and trustees drawn from the ranks of the organized church are the minimum requirements. Students catch a glimpse of their future mission, are best supported in their endeavors, and move out as "little platoons" in the context of a college that has clear and open overtones of the Christian faith.

Careers: The strong career orientation of today's student does provide a unique possibility when this basic motivation is linked up with a "vision of the Christian mission in the world." The student is asking, "What should I do and what should I be, as I look at the needy world?" The Christian faith speaks very clearly to this question, and when combined with, integrated with, the academic disciplines, a powerful synergy results.

Bible Study—Church Attendance(?): Often the college campus provides society with an advance version of what ultimately takes place in society. There is a new and important question presently coming out of campus life. How can we explain the large numbers of students studying the Bible on college campuses (apparently more than ever before), *yet* there is lower attendance at traditional worship services in churches? Has not the Bible always led to a church relationship?

The following "categories" of church-relatedness may give us an opportunity to deal with our subject, especially when viewed in the student context:

Christian Identity. Identity, as perceived by the world, has to do with the "up-frontness" of the college's "PR" relative to its stance as an institution that takes the Christian faith seriously. There has been a problem with this in that such a stance in past years may have indicated a narrowness rather than an openness to the future. There needs now always to be a "bold" statement that enables moving far away from previous narrow confines (fundamentalism and its remains) and gives Christ free reign to deal with the imponderables of future "space age" culture, and to do this within and through the academic disciplines.

Human Development: Students, faculty, and administrators alike need continual assistance in their personal development as whole human beings. Competencies, special understanding, emotional maturity, ability to cope, decision making, interpersonal skills, etc., all must be an integral part of the academic experience. Only in this way can students "go out into the world and change it for good." And human development can never be restricted to students; it has to be the goal for all who work together in the institution.

Mission: Why do we learn at all? Is civilization worthwhile? What are we here for? Until and unless the college can *begin* the *process* of articulating answers to such questions, it will merely be feeding the present system, which may not be leading to desirable ends. Through all college experiences and through other-culture experiences, students need to sense the "mission" of which we are all a part to change the world. Words like peace, cooperation, human rights, quality of life, ecological responsibility, stewardship need to be translated into the fabric of all that the institution does. This would be in contrast to narrow specialization for specialization's sake or training merely to fill a slot in the sociological network of society. The college is always on the lookout for the creative minority who can focus upon the issues that really do change the world.

Liberal Arts: The best of culture resides in the liberal arts approach to education. Care needs to be taken not to fall into the trap of vocationalism. We ought to find new ways to bring the liberal tradition into a supporting dialogue with career education. Careers have a chance to change the world; jobs are subheadings under careers and are only tools being used by those with a much wider vision of the future. Both are needed, true, but holistic visions of the future are needed more now than "supplying spare parts for wornout sections of obsolete social machinery."

Church-Relatedness: Church-related colleges can, and should, without exclusiveness, draw upon a church constituency. Such a constituency is diverse with respect to geography, background, and economics and therefore can be a source of broadly based support.

Academic Excellence: Quality and excellence in the academic program must have the very highest priority. To sacrifice academic quality is to cut at the very roots of responsible education.

In his book *Religion, Revolution and the Future,* Moltmann says that the great task before us is not one of revolution, which focuses on the return, but rather one of *provolution,* which focuses upon the new, forward movement—*on the creation of that which has not yet ever been present in history,* a dream turned forward.[2] This is what will be demanded of church-related higher education. Not prediction, not a mere recitation of the past, not supplying spare parts for social machinery, but envisioning that which will be demanded of us in the coming decades of transition out of the industrial era.

NOTES

[1] William E. Lynch, *Images of Faith: An Exploration of the Ironic Imagination* (Notre Dame: University of Notre Dame Press, 1973), p. 12.

[2] Jürgen Moltmann, *Religion, Revolution and the Future,* M. Douglas Meeks, trans. (New York: Charles Scribner's Sons, 1969).

Study/Action Committee
Postscript

In his introduction to this study, Harry E. Smith briefly outlines the development of the project and states those questions which the committee has come to believe are deserving of the attention of people who care about church-related higher education. Those questions were discussed at length with all who have undertaken research and writing for this project, and what is presented in this volume are the substantive answers of the writers to one or more of these queries. It would be redundant for the committee to attempt to summarize the findings of the various writers and inappropriate to attempt to pass judgment on their conclusions. The value of what appears here should and will be ascertained by those in church and college who attempt to test the insights and conclusions of the writers in specific contexts.

It may be useful, however, to rehearse those ideas to be investigated which the committee developed early in the study; summarize those general findings which it believes have emerged with some clarity in the process of research, writing, and consultation; and suggest those areas which, in the mind of the committee, the study did not address or answer sufficiently and which still need further attention from persons concerned about the future of church-related higher education.

As a result of its early deliberations, the Study/Action Committee concluded that investigation of the following ideas or notions about the present state of church-related higher education might help to answer the particular questions posed in the study.

- An institution's understanding of its church-relatedness must be assessed, in part, in relation to the denomination's understanding of its own role in society, because what may be authentic church-relatedness in one denomination may not be accepted in another.
- The self-understandings of church-related colleges are shaped by external factors as much as by self-conscious collegiate and denominational decisions to be certain kinds of institutions.
- When colleagues try to define their church-relatedness in terms of service, they often tend unknowingly to take the meaning of service from society itself, thus losing the religious intentionality with which they may have begun.
- In "viable" colleges which are church-related, the indices and perceptions of church-relatedness change through time, but the commitment to relatedness remains.
- The attitude of the chief executive is directly related to the church-relatedness of the institution, *or* the chief administrative officer is the one mainly responsible for defining the church-relatedness of the institution.
- The financial dependency of the college on the church is but one measure of church-relatedness.
- The greater the theological sophistication of the religion and philosophy department(s), the more questions there are about church-relatedness, *or* the seriousness of theological interest is inversely proportional to the degree of church-relatedness.
- The push for academic excellence is in tension with a demand for piety and leads toward the diminution of church-relatedness.
- The rising age of the college population, as students beyond the traditional age become more numerous, and the increase in the number of commuting students both weaken denominational ties, since these student populations tend to choose colleges on the basis of academic quality, location, and/or programs rather than on the grounds of denominational affiliation.

In light of the investigation—research, writing, and consultation—undertaken as a part of this study, the committee is in general agreement that at least the following findings of some importance have emerged. These are, in effect, the committee's final conclusions and comprise its own report.

1. The diversity of church-related colleges is now abundantly clear. It shows itself both in the character of the institutions and in the nature of their church relationships.

2. Among the constituencies of church-related higher education, there is a growing understanding of and appreciation for the pluralism represented within this segment of higher education.

3. The theoretical construct developed by Merrimon Cuninggim, which allows placing all church-related colleges along a single continuum, provides a constructive alternative to ranking church-related colleges according to an ideal type and contributes to the possibility of a growing understanding and cooperation within this segment of higher education.

4. The theoretical construct which allows church-relatedness to be measured on the basis of intentionality and congruence between a college and its church provides a valuable alternative to the traditional measures based on an ideal type of relationship.

5. While the long-term trend toward secularization within church-related higher education is increasingly evident, there is a good deal of experimentation and innovation within and between the colleges and the churches which suggests that in many instances the future is being approached positively.

6. In many cases, implementation continues to lag behind the commitment of the churches and the colleges related to them for full participation of women and minorities in staff positions and student enrollments.

7. While churches are increasingly interested in their role and responsibility in higher education and more and more in agreement about the external threats to the survival of church-related higher education, they are not equally involved in exploring with their colleges the nature of

church-relatedness for the present and future.

8. One of the findings of the study is that the church-relatedness of a college can be measured, in part, by the congruence of its intentions and practices with its own denomination and not according to an ideal type. But if the denomination's sense of its mission in higher education is unclear or inadequate for the times, the vitality of the college-church relationship can hardly be compelling.

9. Another finding is that the initiative in revitalizing the college-church relationship sometimes comes from the college. For this initiative to be most significant, the colleges need to address issues of deepest importance both to church and society, some of particular importance to their denomination, but such others also as the dominance in contemporary culture of instrumental reason over all other ways of knowing—such as the emotions, ethical insight, and intuitive imagination—and the societal issues of human justice and a globally interdependent world.

While the committee has sought through this study to address some problems of church-related higher education, it has consciously abandoned some others which it believes still need to be addressed and, in the process of investigation, has discovered still other questions which, with 20-20 hindsight, it wishes it could have addressed. Following, then, are several questions which the committee hopes may be addressed in another forum by other persons concerned with church-related higher education.

• If the diversity within church-related higher education is to be understood with even greater clarity and if further judgments about the congruence between churches and their colleges are to be made, there needs to be further investigation of the history of church-related higher education in America which probes the particular understandings of mission and purpose which motivated the founding and sustaining of colleges by the several denominations.

• While this study has documented the immense diversity within church-related higher education and has advanced the general understanding of the distinctiveness of this segment of higher education, it has not sufficiently examined the question: Does the system of church-related higher education provide or introduce a significant diversity into the whole of American higher education? Further, if it does provide such diversity, how much is needed?

- By design, this study has dealt only with institutions which currently consider themselves to be church related. The committee feels, however, that it is important for a study to be made of those church-related colleges that have ceased to exist (Has their death been postponed by their church-relatedness? Hastened by it? Or neither?) and of those colleges which have disaffiliated (What has happened to them in terms of financial support, student enrollments, and general health?).
- While this study has made a useful start at investigating those church-related colleges that have succeeded in or are making an effort toward strengthening and renewing their ties with their churches, a more extensive and systematic study of that development could profitably be made.
- While this study has acknowledged the enormous importance of external pressures which impinge on church-related higher education, even at the point of defining and maintaining its own church-relatedness, it has not been able to give proper attention to either the problem or creative solutions to it. Immediate attention needs to be given to the whole matter of formulation and support on an ecumenical basis of public policy congenial to church-related higher education and its purposes.

Contributors to the Project

Authors

Merrimon Cuninggim
President, Salem College
Winston-Salem, North Carolina

Martin E. Marty
Professor, The Divinity School
University of Chicago
Chicago, Illinois

Robert Rue Parsonage
Associate Executive, Education
   in the Society
National Council of Churches
New York, New York

James H. Smylie
Professor of Church History
Union Theological Seminary
Richmond, Virginia

Repondents

Ben C. Fisher
Executive Director-Treasurer
Education Commission
Southern Baptist Convention
Nashville, Tennessee

Wesley A. Hotchkiss
General Secretary
Board for Homeland Ministries
United Church of Christ
New York, New York

William R. Johnson, Jr.
General Secretary
Board of Christian Education
Christian Methodist Episcopal
   Church
Memphis, Tennessee

Shirley M. Jones
Executive Director
Division of Christian Higher
   Education
American Baptist Churches,
   U.S.A.
Valley Forge, Pennsylvania

William A. Kinnison
President, Wittenberg
   University
Springfield, Ohio

Mary C. Kraetzer
Associate Professor of Sociology
Mercy College
Dobbs Ferry, New York

Edward B. Lindaman
President, Whitworth College
Spokane, Washington

Albert J. Meyer
Executive Secretary and
   Director of Educational
   Development
Mennonite Board of Education
Elkhart, Indiana

342

John D. Moseley
President, Austin College
Sherman, Texas

John F. Murphy
Executive Director
Association of Catholic Colleges
and Universities
Washington, D.C.

Douglas Sloan
Associate Professor of History
and Education
Teachers College
Columbia University
New York, New York

William J. Sullivan
President, Seattle University
Seattle, Washington

Campus Visitors

George Allan
Dean, Dickinson College
Carlisle, Pennsylvania

Louis Brakeman
Provost, Denison University
Granville, Ohio

Donald Costello
Professor, Department of
English
Notre Dame University
Notre Dame, Indiana

Thomas Davis
Dean, University of Puget
Sound
Tacoma, Washington

Ralph Dunlop
Retired Chaplain
Northwestern University
Evanston, Illinois

Patricia P. Kendall
Lecturer, Department of
French
Rosemont College
Rosemont, Pennsylvania

Mary Metz
Professor of Sociology
Mount Mary College
Milwaukee, Wisconsin

Anne A. Murphy
Professor of Government
Eckerd College
St. Petersburg, Florida

William Nelson
Dean, St. Olaf College
Northfield, Minnesota

Edgar C. Reckard
Provost, Centre College
Danville, Kentucky

Glen Stassen
Professor of Ethics
Southern Baptist Theological
Seminary
Louisville, Kentucky

Haywood Strickland
Director, Academic
Administration Program
United Board for College
Development
Atlanta, Georgia

Herndon Wagers
Retired Professor of Theology
Perkins School of Theology
Dallas, Texas

Prince Wilson
Vice-President for Academic
  Affairs
Atlanta University
Atlanta, Georgia

Study/Action Committee

Mary C. Kraetzer
Associate Professor of Sociology
Mercy College
Dobbs Ferry, New York

Joseph T. McMillan, Jr.
Secretary for College
  Relationships
Board for Homeland Ministries
United Church of Christ
New York, New York

Dorothy M. Schneider
Academic Dean, Marymount
  College
Tarrytown, New York

Douglas Sloan
Associate Professor of History
  and Education
Teachers College
Columbia University
New York, New York

Harry E. Smith
Executive Director, Society for
  Values in Higher Education
New Haven, Connecticut
President-Elect, Austin College
Sherman, Texas

Staff

William N. Lovell
Executive, Education in the
  Society
National Council of Churches
New York, New York

Robert Rue Parsonage
Associate Executive, Education
  in the Society
National Council of Churches
New York, New York